Delivering Policy Reform

Anchoring Significant Reforms in Turbulent Times

Delivering Policy Reform

Anchoring Significant Reforms in Turbulent Times

Edited by Evert A. Lindquist, Sam Vincent & John Wanna

ANU
THE AUSTRALIAN NATIONAL UNIVERSITY

E PRESS

ANU
E PRESS

the Australia and New Zealand
School of Government

Published by ANU E Press
The Australian National University
Canberra ACT 0200, Australia
Email: anuepress@anu.edu.au
This title is also available online at: http://epress.anu.edu.au

National Library of Australia Cataloguing-in-Publication entry

Author: Lindquist, Evert A.

Title: Delivering policy reform [electronic resource] : anchoring significant
                reforms in turbulent times / Evert A. Lindquist, Sam Vincent, John
                Wanna.

ISBN: 9781921862182 (pbk.) 9781921862199 (eBook)

Series: ANZSOG series.

Notes: Includes bibliographical references.

Subjects: Policy sciences.
                Public administration.

Other Authors/Contributors:
                Vincent, Sam.
                Wanna, John.

Dewey Number: 320.6

Cover design by ANU E Press

Funding for this monograph series has been provided by the Australia and New
Zealand School of Government Research Program.

John Wanna, *Series Editor*

Professor John Wanna holds the Sir John Bunting Chair of Public Administration at the Research School of Social Sciences at The Australian National University and is director of research for the Australia and New Zealand School of Government (ANZSOG). He is also Professor of Politics and Public Policy at Griffith University, and formerly principal researcher with the Centre for Australian Public Sector Management and the Key Centre for Ethics, Law, Justice and Governance at Griffith University. Professor Wanna has produced about 40 books including two national textbooks on policy and public management. He has produced a number of research-based studies on public management including: *The Reality of Budget Reform in the OECD* (2010); *Comparing Westminster* (2009); *Westminster Legacies: Democracy and responsible government in Asia and the Pacific* (2005); *Yes Premier* (2005); *Controlling Public Expenditure* (2003); *From Accounting to Accountability* (2001); and *Managing Public Expenditure* (2000). In 2009 Professor Wanna completed a study of service delivery in the Australian Government entitled *Policy in Action: The challenge of service delivery*. His most recent book, produced with Tracey Arklay, is *The Ayes Have It: The history of the Queensland Parliament 1957–89* (2010), a major legislative study of historical significance. Professor Wanna has held many Australian Research Council grants over the years, but also conducts research independently and through ANZSOG. His research interests include Australian and comparative politics, public expenditure and budgeting, and government–business relations. His political commentary has appeared in *The Australian*, *The Courier-Mail* and *The Canberra Times* and on Sky News as well as ABC Radio and TV. The ANZSOG ANU E Press, which he edits, is now approaching 30 titles. See <http://epress.anu.edu.au/titles/anzsog.html>

Contents

Part I. The reform challenge

Part II. National reform initiatives

Part III. Tackling and anchoring reform initiatives

Foreword

This volume of essays had its origins in our thinking about the global financial crisis—when, in 2008, the major economic shock emerging out of the mortgage and financial sector in the United States swept around the world with disastrous consequences. High-risk sub-prime lending in the United States might have precipitated the crisis, but its full impacts affected almost every nation and every industry sector as banks collapsed, credit dried up, share markets and property markets fell spectacularly and government budgets took a big hit in deficit and debt levels. The crisis suddenly and unexpectedly posed a major threat to international and domestic policy settings.

In Australia, we tended to see the crisis as a consequence of poorly regulated and badly managed markets that went spectacularly out of control. Professor Joseph Stiglitz, while recently in Australia, said that the phrase the 'global financial crisis' was a peculiarly Australian term invented to label the credit crunch as an exogenous shock. Indeed, we all know that the term was very carefully chosen by the Rudd Government as a way of describing the impact of the economic crisis on Australia, hinting at the fact that its origins, in their view, had nothing to do with anything happening in Australia. It is almost a unique label that we use in this part of the world to convey the impression we caught the infection from elsewhere.

The global financial crisis, of course, gave rise to immediate policy challenges about how we anticipated the looming problems, how we chose to react to them, and what we actually did to alleviate the worst aspects of the crisis and in what order we did them. Now, as we start to come out of that global crisis, and with fairly good performance in this part of the world, we ask ourselves how appropriate the interventions were, how well they appear to have worked, and when we can expect to be 'through the crisis'. But once the impact of the present crisis fades—if it does, as we hope—governments have to again think about their policy futures. How do we conceive of longer-term policy resilience; how can we enhance our capacities; how should we protect and reinvigorate our regulatory and assurance systems; how should we pursue strategically informed interventions; and which proactive programs are necessary to deal with future social, economic and environmental challenges?

Thus, this volume concerns the conception and development of new policy regimes, including the creation of new policy responses to longstanding or emergent dilemmas. We are interested in exploring future needs and challenges and how we might better address them, asking what are the right policies to adopt to address current and future challenges? But in rising to meet these challenges, it is very important that we take a complete view—a 'whole-of-policy' approach;

a longitudinal analysis of an entire policy trajectory or entire policy life cycle. This in turn involves working out not only how to bring about a particular reform, but also how to make it work, how to make it stick and how to anticipate its adaptation. Reform must be durable, dependable and defendable.

Contributors to this collection assess policy from various vantage points: the processes of formulation and development, the administrative dimensions of implementation and delivery, the issues associated with evaluation and feedback. They also explore the types of problems that emerge within policy fields and program activities. These include not only some of the political obstacles that arise after reforms have been adopted, but also the obstacles that can actually stop policy from working, or sometimes, to be more positive, the political forces that build up and support that reform and its continuation, and perhaps trigger further reforms. They are generally asking what is happening with (and to) various policy reform scenarios and their specific program components? How do we assess what works effectively, what should be preserved or enhanced, what should be reversed or redesigned? The dimensions they explore are crucially concerned with the relationship between the current contours of the policy choices (the objective or intent, the design, the instruments and implementation and outcomes) and the problems they are meant to address.

So, in this volume, we are analysing not just how to get a reform through Parliament or through the Government (the enactment phase), but also the whole life of the reform and the challenges that arise during its existence. We are asking how do the challenges facing our communities translate to government as demands for strategic policy reforms that propel policy settings in new directions? How does good policy come about? How do governments and especially public servants design and broker reform proposals and packages that are smart and feasible and able to actually address contemporary challenges? How do we incorporate good features and practices of implementation that are sustainable in the longer term? If a particular policy is going wrong during its lifetime, how do we bring about improvements without at the same time resurrecting all the opposition to the reforms and opposition that might bring them unstuck?

These are the questions this collection of essays seeks to address and answer. Our contributors have exceptional expertise and qualities to enable them to reflect and comment on these issues with authority. They each emanate from different backgrounds and address different policy sectors. But the themes they explore are consistent. We have included contributions from leaders in political life and the Public Service, from investigative journalists, national and international scholars, and representatives from national and international non-governmental bodies including the Organisation for Economic Cooperation and Development. While Australia and New Zealand have in the past been noteworthy as 'policy laboratories' and 'social experiments' in pioneering new policy settings, they still have much scope for policy improvement and to learn from and contribute to the rest of the world in policy development.

Allan Fels

Dean of ANZSOG

Melbourne

September 2010

Contributors

Jonathan Boston
Jonathan Boston is Professor of Public Policy and Director of the Institute of Policy Studies at the School of Government, Victoria University, New Zealand. Professor Boston has published over 25 books and 180 journal articles and book chapters in the fields of public management, tertiary education, research funding, social policy, comparative government, New Zealand politics and climate change policy.

The Hon. Aart de Geus
As Deputy Secretary-General of the OECD, Aart de Geus is responsible for the organisation's agenda in the areas of employment, labour, social affairs, education, public governance and territorial development. He is a Dutch citizen and served as the Minister of Social Affairs and Employment in the Netherlands government from 2002 until 2007.

Janet Dore
Janet Dore is CEO of Victoria's Transport Accident Commission (TAC). She is an entrepreneurial executive with extensive experience in local council governance, having been CEO of Newcastle City Council prior to joining the Transport Accident Commission in 2007.

The Hon. Sir Roger Douglas
Sir Roger Douglas MP served as New Zealand's Minister of Finance between 1984 and 1988, presiding over an era of market-led restructuring of the New Zealand economy, which would come to be known throughout the world as 'Rogernomics'. After an 18-year hiatus, Sir Roger re-entered New Zealand's Parliament in 2008 as a 'list MP' for the ACT Party.

The Hon. Bill English
Bill English MP is the Minister of Finance and Infrastructure and Deputy Prime Minister in the John Key-led National government in New Zealand. He was first elected to New Zealand's parliament in 1990 and has served as Minister of Health, Minister of Finance and Minister of Revenue in previous National governments, and held senior posts in opposition.

Allan Fels

Professor Allan Fels served as chairman of the Australian Competition and Consumer Commission (ACCC) from its inception in 1995 until 2003. Upon his retirement from the ACCC, Professor Fels became the inaugural Dean of the Australia and New Zealand School of Government (ANZSOG). He has been a much sought-after policy advisor to federal and state governments of different political persuasions.

Paul 't Hart

Paul 't Hart is Professor of Public Administration at Utrecht University in the Netherlands. From 2005 until 2010 he was Professor of Political Science at the ANU, convening ANZSOG's Towards Strategic Leadership program and a course on leading public sector change within the school's MPA program.

Paul Kelly

One of Australia's most accomplished political commentators, Paul Kelly is editor-at-large of *The Australian* newspaper. His best-selling titles on Australian politics include *The March of Patriots: The Struggle for Modern Australia*; *100 Years: The Australian Story; The End of Certainty*; and *The Hawke Ascendancy*. Paul Kelly is an active member of the Academy of the Social Sciences in Australia.

The Hon. Michael Kirby

When he retired from the High Court of Australia in 2009, Michael Kirby was Australia's longest serving judge, having been first appointed as a Deputy President of the Australian Conciliation and Arbitration Commission in 1975, and later serving in the Federal Court of Australia, the New South Wales Court of Appeal and the High Court of Australia. Since his judicial retirement, Michael Kirby has been a member of the international Eminent Persons Group which is investigating the future of the Commonwealth of Nations.

William E. Kovacic

William E. Kovacic has served on the Federal Trade Commission of the United States since 2006, having previously worked for the Commission from 1979 until 1983. Before serving on the Commission, Professor Kovacic taught law at George Washington and George Mason universities.

Evert A. Lindquist

Evert A. Lindquist is Professor at the School of Public Administration at the University of Victoria, Canada, serving as its Director since 1998. In 2010 Professor Lindquist held the ANU/ANZSOG Chair in Applied Public Management at the Australian National University.

Ken Matthews

Ken Matthews served as the Chair, CEO and one of seven government-appointed commissioners of the National Water Commission from 2005 until his retirement in 2010. A career public servant, he was previously Secretary of the Department of Agriculture, Fisheries and Forestry and Secretary of the Department of Transport and Regional Services.

Andrew Metcalfe

Andrew Metcalfe is Secretary of the Department of Immigration and Citizenship, having been appointed to the position in 2005, and reappointed in 2009. Between 2002 and 2005 he served as Deputy Secretary of the Department of Prime Minister and Cabinet, having joined the Australian Public Service in 1980.

Rob Moodie

Professor Rob Moodie is Chair of the Nossal Institute for Global Health at the University of Melbourne, having previously been CEO of VicHealth between 1998 and 2007. Professor Moodie is Vice-President of the International Union of Health Promotion and Education, and a member of the Asia-Pacific Leadership Forum on HIV/AIDS.

Mary Ann O'Loughlin

Mary Ann O'Loughlin is Executive Councillor and Head of the Secretariat of the COAG Reform Council. Between 2000 and 2008 Ms O'Loughlin was Director of the economics and public policy consultancy firm, Allen Consulting Group. She has also previously been a senior advisor to Prime Minister Keating, and held a number of senior positions in the Australian Public Service.

Eric M. Patashnik

Eric M. Patashnik is Professor of Politics and Public Policy and Associate Dean of the Frank Batten School of Leadership and Public Policy at the University of Virginia. Professor Patashnik's research on US public policy has focused on the interaction of institutions, agendas and interest groups in the development of major legislation; his most recent book is *Reforms at Risk: What Happens After Major Policy Changes Are Enacted*, winner of the Brownlow Book Award for outstanding contributions to the literature of public administration.

Jeremy Pope

Jeremy Pope is a New Zealand Human Rights Commissioner, barrister and solicitor of the Supreme Court of New Zealand, and barrister-at-law with the English bar. Jeremy Pope co-founded Transparency International, and Tiri, a London-based NGO striving for sustainable development through increased integrity in government and business.

Stephen Sedgwick

Stephen Segwick became the Australian Public Service Commissioner in 2009 after a period as Professor and Director of the Melbourne Institute of Applied Economic and Social Research at the University of Melbourne. He has had a distinguished career in the public sector, having served as the Secretary of the Commonwealth Departments of Finance, Employment and Education between 1992 and 2002.

The Hon. Lindsay Tanner

Lindsay Tanner served as Minister of Finance and Deregulation from 2007 until 2010 in the Rudd and Gillard governments. Upon retirement from politics at the 2010 federal election, he was appointed a Vice Chancellor's Fellow and Adjunct Professor at Victoria University, Australia, and as a special adviser to financial firm Lazard Australia.

John Wanna

Professor John Wanna holds the Sir John Bunting Chair of Public Administration at the Australian National University, a research chair established by ANZSOG in partnership with the ANU. He is also Professor of Politics and Public Policy at Griffith University, and formerly principal researcher with the Centre for Australian Public Sector Management and the Key Centre in ethics, Law, Justice and Governance at Griffith University.

Part I
The reform challenge

1. Delivering policy reform: making it happen, making it stick

Evert A. Lindquist and John Wanna

The challenge

Cascading and often unpredictable challenges continually confront the policy settings and policy frameworks of governments. They provide a constantly changing dynamic within which policy making operates. Sometimes these challenges are born of crises, sometimes of more systematic forces such as climate change or environmental threats. Some are the result of social and demographic trends, such as ageing or social inclusion. Sometimes they emerge by stealth, travelling under the radar until they suddenly manifest themselves. Such transformative changes are occurring across many fields simultaneously: technological, economic, international, defence and security related, environmental, social and demographic. They force governments to rethink what they do, when they do it and how they do it. Governments need constantly to re-examine and readjust their policy responses to align to the new challenges. But often the opportunity to respond in policy terms happens in very compressed time frames with inchoate ideas and incomplete information. That is the policy conundrum we increasingly face today.

Governments at all levels are asking their public services to identify innovative and workable reforms to address these challenges. Public service leaders around the world are struggling not only to better anticipate emerging demands but also to address reform backlogs. Time and time again, however, major policy reforms prove tough to become adopted in turbulent environments, and even tougher to anchor over time. This leads to considerable uncertainty and inefficiency as governments and societies try to keep pace with change and thrive. Policies that unravel are wasted opportunities and costly. They lead to cynicism about the effectiveness of governments and public service advice more generally, making it more difficult to deal with other emerging challenges.

This volume of essays on delivering policy reform offers an intriguing blend of strategic policy advice and management insight. It brings together a diverse range of top-level contributors from overseas as well as from Australia and New Zealand, including political leaders, public service executives, heads of independent agencies, and leading scholars. The contributors cover all levels of government. The purpose of this chapter is to provide a high-level guide and point of departure for sharing insight about particular cases, and to introduce the following key questions to be explored within the volume.

- What are the challenges confronting governments and the societies they serve? How is this translating into demands on governments—often induced by crisis—for strategic policy reforms that move sectors in new directions and work in different ways?

- How can governments and public servants design and broker reform proposals and packages that are smart and feasible, with potential to address contemporary and emerging challenges in breakthrough and sustained (or durable) ways?

- How can governments and public servants configure and consolidate reforms so that, once adopted, they cannot be undermined by the forces that resist or corrode reform?

- How can policy makers perform adjustments in light of evidence and engagement during implementation without losing the integrity and momentum of the original reforms?

- How should public service leaders build the requisite capabilities to anticipate and analyse these challenges to provide useful policy advice and designs to governments? Indeed, how do they ensure that policy reforms are implemented reasonably intact?

These questions anchor our discussion.

The new demands: challenges and expectations for effective policy reform

The global financial crisis is only the latest challenge to confront governments around the world with a demand to respond quickly to stabilise a rapidly deteriorating situation and then follow up with new regulatory regimes and policy responses for the financial sector and to develop ways to regain control over public finances. We have only to think about the H1N1 flu epidemic, the 'mad cow' or BSE crisis, the equine flu outbreak, tropical cyclones, or the Asian financial crisis of the late 1990s—and many more that could be named—to see that these tipping-point challenges seem to be increasing. We tend to focus on dramatic crises, but we can also see similar slow-burning crises and demands for solutions emanating from challenges such as increases in national populations, significant demographic change in society, severe drought that lasts for years, and global climate change. This is not a passing spike in challenges on government radars, but increasingly should be seen as an ever-present reality that confronts governments at all levels, which creates significant demand for policy reform.

When we scratch below the surface of any of these challenges, we see that they are often a complex but disentangle-able mix of factors. They are not mono-causal.

Complex change is the order of the day; governments are expected to provide suitable answers promptly. There are several implications flowing from this. Governments and public service leaders need better analytical skills and policy capacities. They need to design effective and workable policy reforms that address these challenges and maintain momentum as solutions are implemented. They need to ensure that these reforms actually stick, while striking a balance between ensuring that reforms are durable and that they are open to adaptation based on experience.

Recent international and national crises have demonstrated that, notwithstanding the litany of anti-government rhetoric permeating much of the public debate over the past few decades, citizens still expect governments to deal with or avoid crisis, and to identify policy reforms. Governments remain the community's insurer of last resort. It is also clear that the media, citizens and other stakeholders have high expectations about how well governments should implement policy reforms. Community disappointments are treated as policy failure. An inability to meet stated time lines and stay to budgets leads to the rapid corrosion of government credibility. On the political front, those actors who lose out in the policy process are increasingly prepared to undermine or undo policy reforms in the deliberative or legislative process and even after enactment. The big 'P' and small 'p' political struggle never ceases. Poor design and administration leave the door open for policy reversal. The stakes remain high after enactment, suggesting that implementing policy reforms requires strategic political and administrative mobilisation every bit as sophisticated and concerted as securing enactment.

The stakes are, thus, high for designing and implementing policy reform. Yet most governments typically tend to these issues only belatedly or haphazardly as a result of crisis. Australian governments, for example, have been prepared to announce public policies hastily without much thought to the implementation issues or the likely risks associated with the design and delivery. This is true of major announcements on such items as investments in water reform, price-monitoring schemes, home-insulation programs, educational-performance standards and school ratings, and school facilities.

Another important part of their strategic arsenal is for public service institutions to improve their ability to anticipate and understand these challenges, and to envision a workable menu of policy options. Here public service leaders need to ensure that departments and agencies have good scanning capabilities, and that this information can be shared and considered across government and the community. Such information exchanges (and perspective contesting) are necessary to build the consensus for action and follow-through. The information gathered must be assessed for salience, risk, interconnectedness with other issues, and prioritising in terms of securing more data, and deeper analysis of trends, drivers, and outcomes. A critical issue concerns how public service leaders then test these assessments with political masters and with external experts and stakeholders, recognising that there might be sensitivities for governments' political agendas.

Engaging governments on the need for policy reform—let alone the merits of different kinds of interventions—is not simply a matter of sharing information. It is fundamentally about raising awareness, sharing dialogue and finding ways to persuade action. Busy, committed decision makers need compelling arguments and rigorous evidence, accompanied by feasible proposals for action and new policy frameworks. They need to develop their own narratives for reform and implementation that fit within broader narratives developed by the government. This engagement is a critical phase of policy reform, particularly when challenges are anticipatory as opposed to reactive in nature (for example, climate change and demographic change). How public service leaders engage governments will vary greatly according to ideological frames, time horizons, political and ministerial styles, the phase of the government's mandate (early, mid-stream, late), and by the nature of the issue. Governments must decide whether they have sufficient political capital and will to press forward with significant policy reform. What frames a government chooses to work with will greatly affect the options and strategies for securing enactment of the proposed reforms.

Designing and enacting policy reforms

Once a government commits to action—and regardless of the urgency of the challenge—there remains the detailed work of designing and securing approval of policy reform. While it has become commonplace to publicly characterise all of our contemporary challenges as 'wicked'—despite considerable variation in their character—the essence of the label is perhaps salient. Addressing most of the complex and demanding challenges we have in mind requires non-incremental reform (or comprehensive policy innovation, which can range from deep to shallow in terms of the extent of policy and institutional change envisioned), as well as tapping into expertise and authorities across public service institutions and often across levels of government and the non-government sectors.

There has emerged considerable research-based writing on how policy reforms come to be enacted by governments, particularly in fluid and often overly complex policy environments (Christensen and Laegreid 2001; Kingdon 1984). There has been a focus on serendipity and how 'policy entrepreneurs' position ideas and solutions to take advantage of 'policy windows' that might quickly open, allowing decisions to be taken, and then shut. For our purposes, the key takeaway from this perspective concerns the fact that advisors to governments must be ready with frames, evidence, and policy solutions; all of the players will have to work with what they have; there will not be time to undertake meaningful policy research on short notice. This perspective, however, understates the strategic and organisational capacity dimension of developing policy designs and ensuring enactment inside and outside government.

As noted above, policy reforms intended to address significant challenges necessarily involve working across the vertical boundaries of government and public service institutions. This requires identifying the implicated departments and agencies, assigning lead responsibility for assembling and coordinating the required technical and policy work, ensuring sufficient central oversight of this work, and linking it to political decision-making repertoires. Policy task forces or 'adhocracies' might need to be established for this purpose (Desveaux et al. 1994; Waterman 1992), requiring skilled leadership that can navigate the political, technical, policy, administrative, and external boundary-spanning aspects of policy development, and assemble a high-performing team in support.

An open question concerns the extent to which governments engaged in such coordinating capabilities will also engage key stakeholders and rely on broader public consultations (Huxham and Vangen 2008; Stewart 2009). The answer depends heavily on the nature of the issue, time pressures, the tactical posture of the government (does it seek to surprise?), the extent to which it has fleshed out its policy design and has developed an overarching narrative to support its intervention, and whether it is prepared to be flexible or negotiate. If governments have more time, or require the support and buy-in of other governments and non-governmental actors in order to proceed, external engagement on design issues becomes a relatively important feature of the process, requiring additional leadership and administrative capabilities. It is not merely about rushing policy into law.

Most of the above remarks point to considerations when designing any sort of significant policy reform or comprehensive intervention. But a critical focus of this volume concerns the extent to which designers—ministers and public service executives alike—thoroughly anticipate the political, policy and administrative challenges that await approved policies after enactment. Much like planning for transitions in government, do policy designers think carefully about who will take over once a policy has been formulated, approved and enacted? Have the ministers thought through who will take on custodial responsibility for overseeing the political aspects of implementation? How will the strategy of implementation (roll-out, phasing, stages) affect the integrity and durability of the reforms? Do new administrative capabilities have to be reconfigured? Are new leaders required in the Public Service to maintain momentum? Who will exercise stewardship for the policy reforms?

Finally, it must be noted that policy reforms—no matter how open the process— can proceed iteratively, in fits and starts, both internally and externally. Indeed, this dynamic will likely stand as the most intriguing aspect to reflect on. The iterative process forms the constantly changing context in which evidence, arguments, and narratives are tested, challenged, and reformulated at the political and administrative levels. This often leads to new perspectives and approaches, and sometimes a call by governments for new policy-advising capabilities.

Making reforms stick: design, durability, implementation

It is one thing for governments to design and enact policy reforms, and quite another to ensure that they are fully implemented, particularly when dealing with complex challenges. Indeed, the origins of modern policy literature— seeking to understand the daunting challenges of implementation—were stimulated by overwhelming evidence of policy failure (Goggin et al. 1990; Hill and Hupe 2002; O'Toole 2004; Pressman and Wildavsky 1973). Much has been written on policy implementation from the perspectives of administration, collaboration and project management, but here we focus more on the politics and strategies for ensuring that reforms are more likely to succeed, even if they might be modified over time.

The implementation literature has long recognised that the success of even the best-designed policies depends considerably on the motivations and capabilities of those assigned to deliver the envisioned programs, which might include other governments and non-governmental actors, and the incentives of front-line staff, and whether the grain of the policy fully anticipates on-the-ground realities of service delivery (Barrett 2004; Huxham and Vangen 2008). This, in turn, has led to considerable interest in the ability of agencies administering reforms to collaborate and problem solve with other entities, and to mutually adjust in order to achieve the best possible results. While bottom-up and top-down perspectives on implementation have been explored extensively, this volume seeks instead to explore the extent to which and how these dynamics— along with concerted efforts by affected stakeholders to roll back or undermine the policy during the implementation phase—are anticipated by governments as designers and overseers of reform.

Several questions arise here. One set of questions focuses on the robustness of the policy design. Did the policy design attempt to anticipate the political, administrative and inter-organisational challenges of implementation in a compelling way? Or was it, in fact, 'under-designed' and iterative, left open to reinterpretation and renegotiation? If the proposed implementation plan was under-funded because of resource constraints, have further risk assessments been made and the plan for implementation amended? If not, we invite failure or disappointments. If cabinets are prepared to cut the operational funds from programs, are they equally prepared to 'de-scale' the program and tailor policy to the resources they chose to allocate? Indeed, there are some who claim that up to 25 per cent of program funds should be left uncommitted to permit enhancement and adaptation in delivery. A narrow concern with prudence and parsimony of funds can significantly undermine the aspirations of even the best-designed policy—either at the outset or at some later date. Alternatively, under what conditions can 'under-design' at the outset end up being an advantage for subsequently anchoring reforms (as with careful piloting or the use of prototypes)?

There are related questions about the time frames or temporal character of different policy reforms. Do reforms have different gestation periods? How long does it take to anchor certain reforms, to get beyond critical points that might place their integrity at risk? Are we thinking in terms of a few months, a couple of years, or even across the mandate of different governments? What political and strategic protection and guidance are required during the implementation phase? Where are the immediate 'big risks', the short-term critical moments, and how are these to be managed?

In the United States, Eric Patashnik (2008) has previously emphasised that successful policy reforms are durable when they are supported by some new configuration of interests. He argues that in the United States new constituencies emerge or existing ones become strengthened to fight for various policies enacted by Congress. They coalesce to promote change and defend the new policy regime rather than seeking to undermine its very foundations. Consequently, former stakeholders favoured under the previous regime tend to decline in strength. An interesting question for contributors to this volume is whether the emergence of new configurations of interests around reforms is merely left to chance, or whether this is something that is assiduously cultivated during the implementation phase through information and communication strategies, proactive promotion, consultative and deliberative forums and access to decision makers, and whether compensating interests are negatively impacted by the reforms.

Finally, governments tend to be more interested in designing and announcing new policies, then moving on. Typically they have no shortage of other policy challenges to address, which in turn suggests that they have less time and incentive to oversee implementation adequately. To what extent, then, are governments and public-sector leaders prepared to implement reforms as concertedly as enacting them? Once the policy is adopted, does a new set of reformers (political and public service leaders) take over? Are new champions found or appointed in the knowledge that a different skill set will be required to ensure that the reforms are anchored? And again, are there critical moments and phases during implementation when the integrity of the reform is at risk?

Making reforms last: from consolidation to adaptation and learning

Ensuring that much-needed policy reforms are supported and durable is a laudable goal, but one that is often left to the political realm alone (to ministers, parties and government advisers). But it need not be consigned purely to this realm. Public services have a role in explaining policy publicly and to stakeholders—and possibly even assisting with the government's narrative. This is not an improper role. It provides a new governance platform to deal with continual change and emergent risk. We also know, however, that policy reforms cannot anticipate all factors and contingencies; there will inevitably be a great deal of learning and adjustment in order to meet these realities. The issues at stake here concern managing the tensions between seeking durability in policy reforms and making improvements or adjustments in light of feedback from those responsible for implementation and evidence on the performance of the policy and programs without losing the integrity and momentum of the original reforms.

One way to think about this might be to consider what the critical point for securing a policy reform might be, as well as the pace of change in the policy environment. Once a point of no return has been reached, it might be easier to debate and adapt the policy reform. The earlier such debate and adjustments might be required, the more there is a risk that such deliberations will provide an opportunity for interests resisting the reforms to undermine the policy regime. This risk increases to the extent that the announced policy reform was directional and meant to be elaborated through negotiation and implementation.

This raises the question of how governments and public service leaders can structure time-monitoring and feedback processes so as to usefully identify and inform needed adjustments, which might be significant, without creating a political opportunity to undermine the reform itself. There might also be a symbolic dimension to this, where governments declare that the first phase of implementation has been completed, thus opening up the opportunity to refresh the policy in operational terms. Examples of where this feedback has worked well include: income-contingent loans for higher education and perhaps vocational education (tax-deferred schemes for tuition), Landcare programs for environmental sustainability, and prudential regulation of the financial sector. Alternatively, examples of where it has not worked well include: urban sprawl and a lack of public housing provision, poor transport integration, and significant deficiencies in aged care. Finally, we have to recognise that, under some circumstances, announced reforms might have been misguided, unworkable, or no longer relevant, and deserve to be terminated or significantly rethought.

Delivering policy reform: implications for public service institutions

In assembling this volume of essays, we commenced with a generic approach, tapping into international literature about improving policy design and implementation. A review of diverse Organisation for Economic Cooperation and Development (OECD) countries together with some prescient OECD publications shows that the themes of keeping pace with change and developing effective policy reforms are a concern of governments around the world. With this context in mind, we invited contributors to consider the distinctive challenges and opportunities that Australian and New Zealand governments have faced when designing reforms and attempting to make them stick. While much of the attention is on how governments have selected, designed and implemented reforms, it is also important to remember that other actors are caught up in the change processes, becoming participants or collaborators in the reform endeavours—such as other levels of government, business and farmers, road users, the community and non-governmental delivery partners.

This volume of essays commences by thinking broadly about the demands on governments to recognise and address policy challenges, especially after the turbulence of the recent past and the after-effects of the global financial crisis. Part 2 then explores national reform initiatives in Australia and New Zealand. Here the emphasis is on learning from successful attempts to implement national strategies of reform, showing how policy makers and their advisers designed and delivered more durable policy reforms often in the face of opposition. In Part 3 the attention turns to specific sectoral reform initiatives where policy makers were concerned to change community or organisational behaviour to improve social outcomes. The ultimate goal in each of these cases is to explore how those of us today engaged with public service institutions can be better prepared to meet these advising and implementation challenges—a crucial point to which Paul 't Hart returns with his 'rules for reformers' in Chapter 17.

Given the premise that governments should anticipate key challenges and seek to put in place durable policy reforms, this might change how we view the sort of capabilities that public service institutions should develop. Many governments at the federal, state and local levels have been having precisely this conversation about building new sets of capabilities in recent years (see, for example, the recent Moran Review of the Australian Public Service: AGRAGA 2010; and Lindquist 2010). We suggest that one way to approach this enormous topic is to revisit the different phases of policy reform, and to recognise that invoking the term 'durability' should not mean simply adding a throwaway adjective to policy reform. Rather, it involves setting a new standard for quality in design and implementation, and thus that analytical traction can be gained by looking for associated trade-offs. Consequently, the following suggestions could be considered.

- To achieve policy durability in the longer term might require far more research and front-end analysis, and more political and public service executive involvement during the implementation phase. In turn this implies that we need to scan emerging challenges and ascertain how one aspect of policy reform might fit in with or be traded off against other government priorities. But scanning, scenario developing and the selection of preferred options can take time and be administratively precarious. Policy analysts have to secure ministerial, executive and stakeholder buy-in so that the fruits of their labours are not wasted. Alternatively, where policy is more iterative and emergent—or even 'garbage-can'-like in its initiation—there will still be a need to adapt policy parameters strategically to continually align with the changing environment and to anticipate future changes.

- Recognising the need to make policy reforms more durable often requires more thorough testing and strategising of proposed policy designs at the outset. This requires more resources, acknowledging that implementation is not simply project management, and recognising that if *ex ante* engagement of interests is not possible, alternative and credible ways must be found to anticipate the reactions and needs of affected interests and citizens. Many problems with policies are practically discovered in the processes of implementation rather than anticipated and averted beforehand. Where it is not possible to pre-test, we might be able to devise better monitoring of the consequences of the policy in operation and make iterative changes.

- Implementing durable policy reforms requires robust evaluation, both inside the executive and in public. Public service leaders should persuade governments to undertake effective policy and program evaluation internally as a way of monitoring progress and recalibrating performance. Both ministers and senior executives need to pay closer attention to the evaluation of results of proposed reforms. Parliaments and other scrutiny actors need to become more assertive in requiring and undertaking performance evaluations as part of their overview. Many reforms will require shared evaluations with other governments and non-governmental partners to gauge the effectiveness of the changes. These suggestions are applicable whether the policy in question is planned and rationalistic or opportunistic and contingent. They also suggest that the Public Service must be able to marshal good evidence and have sophisticated and credible data on tap. They will also need good prudential judgment and the capabilities to assess the meaning of evaluative data, and be able to productively engage with societal interests and citizens over the findings. Ideally, ministers and senior public servants should be able to develop credible narratives recognising what has been accomplished and the need for subsequent policy adjustments.

Undoubtedly, there are other ideas to improve policy reception that arise in the remainder of this volume. But, standing back and looking across the panoply of government responsibilities and the thorny and novel character of the many challenges that political leaders must address, we observe that creating durable policy reforms is invariably a creative and emergent process in all phases. It requires anticipation, contingency planning, considerable prudential judgment and strategic leadership. Put another way, for us to realise the ambition of creating durable policy reform requires vision, verve, no small amount of energy, some luck, and a degree of comfort with what Robert Quinn has described as 'building the bridge as you walk on it'. Going forward, the question that emerges now is how can the requisite mental frames for taking on these challenges be developed as we groom public service talent for the future; how will tomorrow's policy makers and administrators acquire the necessary capacities to be able to manage effectively in a more complex and changing environment?

References

Advisory Group on Reform of Australian Government Administration (AGRAGA) 2010, *Ahead of the Game: Blueprint for reform of Australian government administration*, March, Commonwealth of Australia, Canberra.

Barrett, S. 2004, 'Implementation studies: time for a revival?, *Public Administration*, vol. 82, no. 2.

Christensen, T. and Laegreid, P. 2001, 'Transforming governance in the new millennium', in T. Christensen and P. Laegreid (eds), *New Public Management: The transformation of ideas and practice*, Ashgate, Aldershot, UK.

Desveaux, J., Lindquist, E. A. and Toner, G. 1994, 'Organising for policy innovation', *Canadian Journal of Political Science*, vol. 28, no. 3 (September).

Goggin, M., Bowman, A., Lester, J. and O'Toole, L. 1990, *Implementation Theory and Practice*, Harper Collins, New York.

Hill, M. and Hupe, P. 2002, *Implementing Public Policy*, Sage, London.

Huxham, C. and Vangen, S. 2008, 'Doing things collaboratively: realising the advantage or succumbing to inertia?', in J. O'Flynn and J. Wanna (eds), *Collaborative Governance: A new era of public policy in Australia?*, ANU E Press, Canberra.

Kingdon, J. 1984, *Agendas, Alternatives and Public Policies*, Little-Brown, Boston.

Lindquist, E. A. 2010, 'From rhetoric to blueprint: the Moran Review as a concerted, comprehensive and emergent strategy for public sector reform', *Australian Journal of Public Administration*, vol. 69, no. 2 (June).

O'Toole, L. 2004, 'The theory–practice issue in policy implementation research', *Public Administration*, vol. 82, no. 2.

Patashnik, E. M. 2008, *Reforms at Risk: What happens after major policy changes are enacted*, Princeton University Press, Princeton, NJ.

Pressman, J. and Wildavsky, A. 1973, *Implementation: How great expectations in Washington are dashed in Oakland*, University of California Press, Berkeley.

Stewart, J. 2009, *The Dilemmas of Engagement: The role of consultation in governance*, ANU E Press, Canberra.

Waterman, R. H. 1992, *Adhocracy*, Norton, New York.

2. 'Don't waste the crisis': the agenda for public-policy reforms in a turbulent world

Aart de Geus

A number of Organisation for Economic Cooperation and Development (OECD) member governments told us during the early 2000s that effective policy making was not only about 'where to go', but also about 'how to get there'. We heard ministers ask 'how to reform and to be re-elected' and 'how to reform and perform'. Almost all OECD countries face medium and long-term structural challenges in the context of global imbalances, economic recalibration, climate change, population ageing, and so on. On the other hand, these governments have implemented policy reforms in a wide range of domains, with a view to enhancing living standards by raising labour utilisation and productivity, increasing the resilience of the economy to shocks and improving welfare by addressing social concerns such as equity and environmental quality. In 2007, the OECD started a horizontal project to look systematically at the political economy of reform across our committees and our Centres of Government working group, which resulted in our 300-page report *Making Reform Happen*.

In this chapter I will draw on and update some of the findings in our study, which will be released in 2011. We need to have an understanding of past reform experiences that might be of use to policy makers seeking to design, adopt and implement reforms in the years to come. The value of such reform lessons is all the greater in the post-global financial and economic crisis environment. As OECD governments confront the challenge of trying to restore public finances without undermining a recovery that in many areas might remain weak for some time, they will need to pursue a careful mix of fiscal policies and growth-enhancing structural reforms. Designing, adopting and implementing appropriate policy mixes will require the identification of effective reforms and strategies for implementing them. To put it bluntly, the present crisis is a terrible thing to waste.

This chapter will first provide an update about our current position in the global economic climate—a necessary prerequisite for understanding the case for structural reforms. It will next explore some areas of structural reform, and, in the process, discuss some of the challenges to successfully implementing public-policy reform. These will be based on my own personal experiences in the Netherlands, but also, principally, on the experience of the OECD in executing reforms in different areas. The chapter will conclude with some lessons for making policy reforms effective and durable.

The global economic climate

The OECD nations currently find themselves trying to reconcile economic recovery with the demands of fiscal consolidation and budgetary repair. The recovery of the global economy is fast gathering pace—a recovery led by the emerging Asian market economies. We observe that the Asian markets are the fastest-growing economies, and that they accelerate world trade. But we also observe that in many of the OECD countries fiscal consolidation is a serious issue, and consequently, these countries still grapple with huge unemployment.

Concerning the global recovery, as Figure 2.1 suggests, the United States has recovered from the recession in 2008–09 to an initial growth rate of 5 per cent, before dropping back to about 4 per cent. Clearly, the growth peak in the second half of 2009 was also due to the huge stimulus package in the United States. Japan saw an even deeper recession but is now relatively stable in its economic recovery. The euro area also experienced a recession and is now recording only a very modest recovery due to factors this chapter will discuss later. As for Australia—currently growing at about 3 per cent—it managed to avoid a recession thanks in part to being closely related to the economies of the emerging Asian markets.

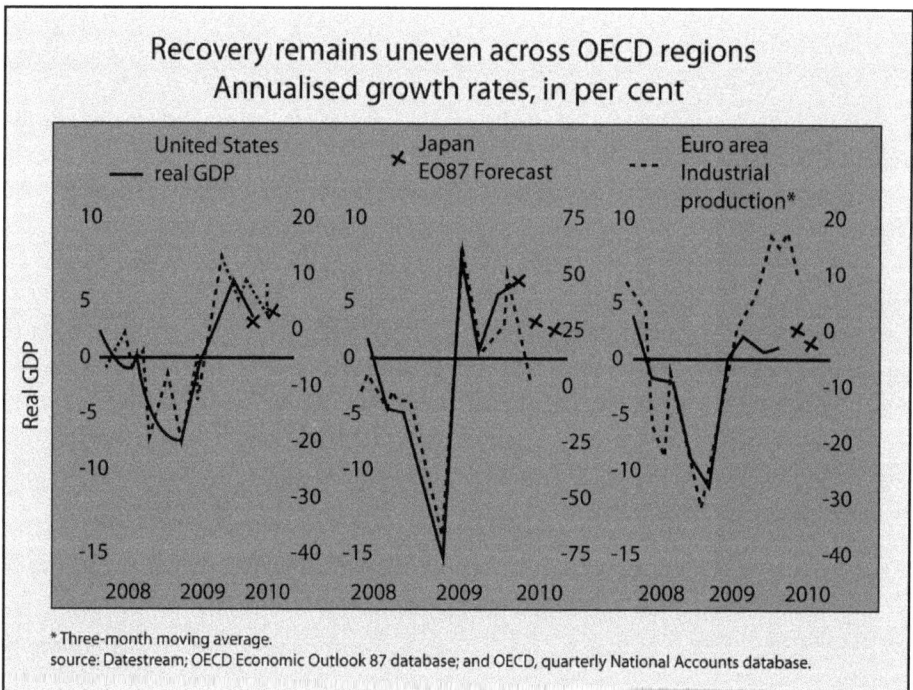

Figure 2.1

If we focus on the emerging economies in terms of their industrial production (their production rates as opposed to growth rates), it is interesting that countries such as China and India did not go below zero in terms of industrial production. Rather, their industrial production continued almost unabated—and this is one of the reasons Australia could continue to export to countries such as China, where demand did not fall too low. Even Brazil, which suffered significantly from the US economic downturn, has recovered to the point that, in industrial-production terms, it is one of the fastest-growing economies. Throughout the OECD, industrial production has recovered from its dip in 2008–09.

It is not surprising to learn (as shown in Figure 2.2) that while industrial production in the emerging economies at first increased in very buoyant terms, it is now starting to slow. This reflects the wearing off of the speed of recovery and whatever fiscal stimulus packages were injected into these economies. And yet, in spite of this small slowdown, the growth rate of these emerging economies remains strong. For example, in 2010 China was growing at 10 per cent, India at 8 per cent, Indonesia at 6 per cent, and Brazil at 5 per cent. Russia is an interesting case because its economy is heavily reliant on its energy sector, but as with the others it has recovered strongly—in its case, from a 2009 recession of −8 per cent to a current growth rate of +5 per cent.

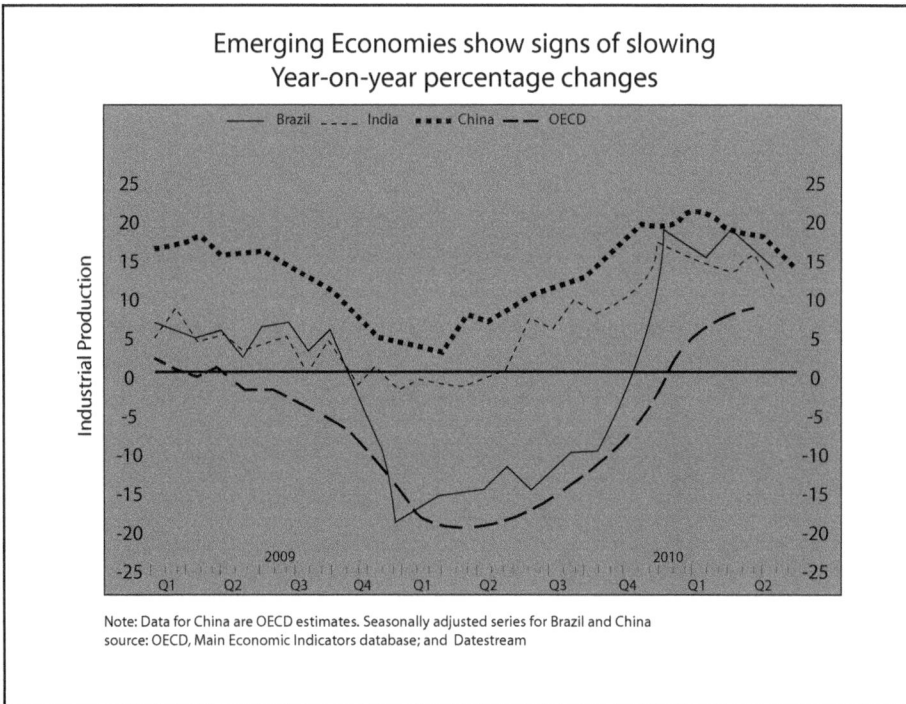

Figure 2.2

China and Brazil have already started to withdraw their policy stimuli, so naturally their growth will subsequently begin to slow. But they have been able to withdraw the stimulus only because their growth is sufficiently strong enough to support such a move. Other nations must follow their lead. Solid growth supports the expansion of global trade, and that is of course critical to the entire world. One need only consider that between the fourth quarter of 2009 and the first quarter of 2010, global trade grew at 5 per cent. According to the OECD's *Economic Outlook* of May 2010, future gross domestic product (GDP) growth in the United States, the European Union and Japan up to 2025 will be relatively modest, hovering between 1 and 3 per cent per annum. This stands in contrast with China, Indonesia and India, which are predicted to grow at a much faster pace—growth that Australia will benefit from over the next 10–15 years.

Now consider Europe. First, there is serious concern about Greece and its levels of indebtedness. The difference between Greek sovereign bonds and German ones—the latter essentially the standard in Europe—is currently growing at up to 8 per cent (as shown in Figure 2.3). In May, June and July, for example, we saw much higher figures for this than in 2007 and 2009. Portugal and Ireland are now also of some concern. Spain and Italy have been scrutinised in the media, but one cannot say a difference of 3 per cent to the German spreads is a reason to panic for these countries. There is, however, a need for fiscal consolidation, and this is related to the fact that all these countries have both a huge budget deficit and very high public (and private) debt. In Australia, the current deficit is about 5 per cent of GDP, but in the United States and the European Union the deficit is about 10 per cent of GDP—a very high figure indeed.

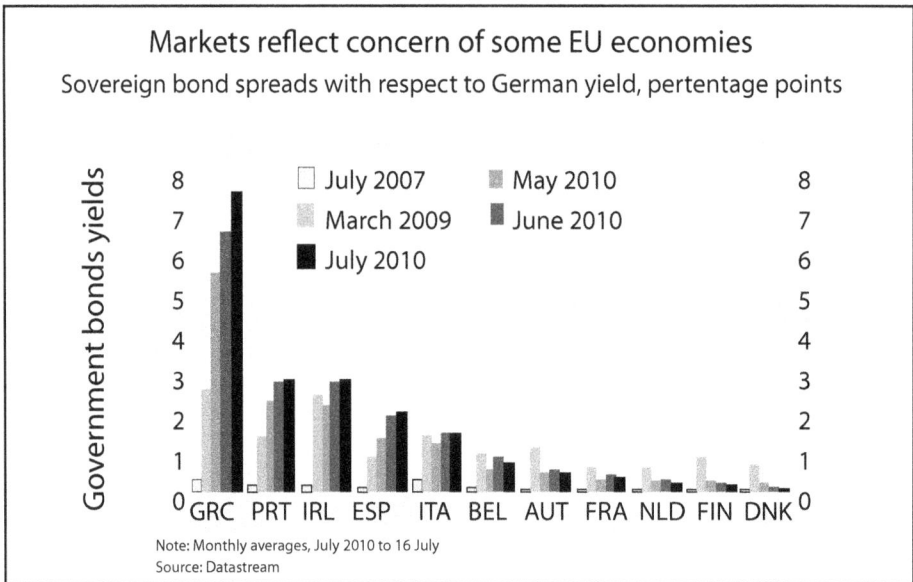

Markets reflect concern of some EU economies

Sovereign bond spreads with respect to German yield, pertentage points

Note: Monthly averages, July 2010 to 16 July
Source: Datastream

Figure 2.3

In terms of public debt, in Australia, the figure stands at about 6 per cent, whereas in the United States and the European Union it is pushing 100 per cent. Imagine what interest you have to pay if your public debt is 100 per cent of GDP? This is not about economies that do not work, but rather about governments that have spent too much in the past, and have failed to bring budgets back into balance. While on the one hand governments have to reconcile the fragile growth rates, on the other governments need to institute fiscal consolidation. This explains why the stimulus measures continue in some OECD countries, whereas in others their governments have announced severe fiscal-consolidation measures. These must be carefully designed in order not to break the balance. While it is probable that a country transferring its focus from policy stimulus to fiscal consolidation will experience smaller growth in the short term, it is fundamentally important to design a pathway to fiscal consolidation in order to gain the trust of the markets.

The opinion of the OECD is that such fiscal consolidation will not affect growth significantly in the long term, because most of the initiatives announced since the depth of the global financial crisis have been designed in terms of expenditure retrenchment and not in terms of increased taxation. The moment a government increases taxes it will damage growth or increase inflation. But when a government engages in fiscal consolidation through expenditure retrenchment, it can do so without significantly damaging economic growth. Additionally, with fiscal consolidation of this kind there will be an offset by lower private-sector savings and long-term interest rates.

The present global reform agenda

Let us now review which reforms are currently on the agenda. The first and most urgent area is the reform of financial markets. In the United States some reforms have already been announced and implemented. There is a new systemic risk council, for example, with the authority to break up American banks in the future if necessary. These US banks also face restrictions on trading with their own funds, and a limit of 3 per cent of their 'Tier 1' capital being invested in hedge and equity funds. In this regard, Europe has been slower to act, though it must be noted that the nature of the European Union—an aggregation of country sovereignties—means decision making is less coordinated than in the United States. On the other hand, the core European banks are doing relatively well. While some smaller banks in Spain, Greece and Ireland (and of course the German lenders) face current funding stresses, the core European banks remain solid. The *Basel III Agreement* on the financial markets for Europe will set new rules, and the region will also have some new institutions essentially in the same direction as the United States.

Nevertheless, the OECD has warned not to celebrate the fact that we are now able to control the financial markets with better regulatory reforms, because we can only 'control' present practices (what these institutions are currently doing). We cannot necessarily 'control' what they might get up to in the future (what does not yet exist). We need to recognise in financial markets there is always the drive to innovate and develop new 'products', and that is precisely how this global financial crisis began in the first place (the resort to high-risk instruments such as sub-prime mortgages and risky derivatives, for example). Part of the problem was poor supervision but it was also true that there were new products that had previously not existed. One cannot rule out in future that new innovation will bring new risks to financial markets.

In terms of the currently needed reforms, the policy agenda is not simply restricted to the financial markets. We also need reform regarding systemic integrity and the robustness of international tax administration—two fields closely related not just to financial markets but also to trade and foreign direct investment. Anti-bribery rules apply to all businesses, and this does not simply mean businesses in some of the more corrupt countries but also businesses with headquarters in the OECD nations. This explains the OECD Anti-Bribery Convention and subsequent UN efforts to clamp down on bribery. Businesses that have their headquarters in OECD and in UN member states are under scrutiny.

Concerning tax, we need consistency and better compliance regimes and a collective international effort to close tax havens. If not, we will still find that there are areas in the world where capital can hide without being taxed. There has been a tremendous effort in the past few years to tackle the problem of international tax evasion because, during the financial crisis, much was said about the fact that it was possible for some companies and people to store their money in locations where it was not taxed. This created a feeling of deep resentment among taxpayers towards tax-evading companies and individuals.

This spurred a chain of bilateral tax agreements. Indeed, we arguably saw more tax agreements in 2009–10 than in the entire previous decade. These tax agreements are not based on international rules but are founded mainly on the OECD Tax Convention. And here the difference between a convention and a rule becomes telling. A convention is something that is designed with government experts and is non-binding, serving rather to set an example that can be followed, implemented or applied voluntarily. Starting from this point, tax conventions can then set models for bilateral tax agreements and so on. It is clear that such examples of better international transparency—be they concerning bribery or taxes—can help to spur reforms in these areas. In this way, transparency can be a very powerful catalyst to make reforms happen.

A second area of concern in which reforms are necessary is the employment sector, particularly concerning participation. Across the OECD, we saw an enormous increase in unemployment in 2008–09. While in Australia unemployment now stands at 5 per cent, in other OECD countries it is up to 10 per cent. In the Netherlands it is about 4 per cent thanks to some reforms introduced before, rather than after, the crisis. But while both Australia and the Netherlands escaped relatively unscathed, in the OECD and in the euro area average unemployment is now about 10 per cent. Being an average, this reflects not just low figures such as that of the Netherlands, but also countries such as Spain, where 20 per cent of the population is unemployed. Spain's unemployment is of deep concern, but what is more concerning is that in all these countries youth unemployment is about double the overall level of unemployment. This causes real tensions. In Spain, France and other Mediterranean countries, almost half of all young people are without a job—a serious matter indeed.

This begs the question: should we adopt a policy of getting people first into work or into training programs to better equip them to work productively? This is a real dilemma. It is often asserted that unemployment is best combated according to the principle of 'find them work, whatever'. But we see now that the challenge is to prevent unemployment from becoming permanent, and therefore perhaps we have to shift to programs where we *train* first. If an unemployed person cannot find work despite their greatest efforts then perhaps we have to shift to a 'train first' form of intervention. Additionally, it is very important that we have directly targeted training programs for youth who find themselves unemployed because of the state of the economy. Some OECD countries, such as Denmark and France, already have such programs in place. We also have to consider that some of the employment-assistance measures adopted during the crisis to contain job losses should be phased out in order not to damage the growth of the economy. For instance, short-term work permits might have helped to cover up some unemployment, but if they continue to be subsidised by the government the situation will likely become unsustainable, resulting in companies relying on these permits defaulting. Such lessons from the past should now be implemented.

Another major problem today is not only the actual unemployed people, but also the so-called 'discouraged' and 'under-employed', who together represent as much as another 10 per cent of the population in some OECD nations. These are people who were once seeking work, but have ceased this endeavour because they consider their situation entirely hopeless. In other words, these people could enter the labour market but are not even trying, resulting in long-term damage to the supply of labour in the market. As with more orthodox cases of unemployment, in this area the focus should be on job-search and training programs, activation policies and well-designed employment subsidies. Arguably, this discouragement factor will not be solved or eradicated by a temporary response; it requires more fundamental reforms that go beyond the current crisis. This requires us to examine those aspects of society that needed fundamental reform well before the financial crisis existed, some of which I turn to below.

The long-overdue fundamental agendas for reform

The first fundamental issue we face is that babies and bosses are in competition for women, particularly in the thirty to forty age bracket. The recent OECD publication *Babies and Bosses* was produced to establish what can be done to reconcile these two sets of demands. The authors of *Babies and Bosses* consulted women on the subject, and realised that while governments are not entitled to proclaim fertility programs any more than they are to intervene in an employer's recruitment choices, what governments can do is facilitate the choices that mothers would like to make. This can be done by providing accessible, affordable and high-quality child care, by providing temporary-work rules, and by providing parental leave—a hot topic during the Australian Federal Election campaign of 2010. One conclusion of *Babies and Bosses* was for countries to look at the marginal revenues for those women who enter the labour market. If these are too low then the effect might be to further discourage workforce participation.

A second established need for reform concerns the ageing population across the OECD, and with it, an ageing workforce. Increased migration has been touted as one possible solution, but this is unwise, mainly because migrants themselves age over time. And if Australia were to address the problem of an ageing workforce simply by bringing in migrants to cover the labour shortages then it would need migration at more than double the current rate—an unrealistic solution. A more realistic solution would be to raise the minimum retirement age beyond sixty-five years. Luckily, for many professional and white-collar workers, this is not a problem—and is even logical, as experience and expertise in these positions often aid performance. There are, however, many manual or stressful jobs where it is not practical—or indeed possible—to continue working after age sixty-five. For these, generally more labour-intensive, positions, creative solutions must be sought. An agenda must be developed to build new competencies for certain workers once they hit the age of forty or forty-five. For example, a construction worker might gain teaching competencies to pass his experience to younger workers—to move, thus, to the vocational education sector. Similarly, the sixty-year-old professor who is losing enthusiasm in the classroom might benefit from a switch to more practical work such as assisting in the voluntary or non-governmental sector. Or a policeman who cannot do his work anymore might move into the administrative sector. This re-skilling agenda will be driven largely by the ageing of society.

As a footnote to these problems associated with employment, we must be wary not to make employment protection too rigid. When this is the case, people will not move, costs will go up, and employers will not hire all the workers they want. Thus, employment protection paradoxically does not always protect employees all the time.

Health is a third fundamental problem—made worse not just by the increasing cost of caring for an ageing population (as is the case in many OECD countries), but also by the increasing desire for ubiquitous health care. In the past there was a greater acceptance of the limitations of health care—helped by the greater prevalence of religion in Western societies. In contrast, there is now an ever-increasing demand for health care, anytime, anywhere. New technology will continue to bring new opportunities, but the reality is that the cost of health care will continue to grow. For this reason, bringing down the costs of health services is unrealistic and should not be on any reform agenda. Quite simply, it does not correspond with an ageing society.

And yet, we can institute some intelligent reforms in health care. The first is to determine and contain the so-called 'non-medical' costs of provision. For example, much of the cost in our health systems comes from transportation, administration and high costs of residence. If we rectify this—such as through collaboration and involving other parties—then as a society we can make gains. We can improve the administrative side (by streamlining bureaucracies and reducing gate-keeping) and thereby increase efficiency. We can, for example, use new technologies not only for better health care but also for more transparent administration (including some self-administration by users). In these ways, we can perhaps control the growth of the healthcare costs rather than simply avoiding it.

Another area for serious reform is migration. From the OECD's perspective, migration is overwhelmingly positive, contributing both to economic growth and to a balanced society. In addition to these benefits are the positive effects of regular remittances to the countries from where these migrants came. It is largely unknown that remittances are more important for these countries than official development aid. And yet, often governments try to reform what they see as problems with the system. This might mean deliberately not making provisions for what they consider 'temporary' migrants, or focusing only on highly skilled migrants. Both approaches are wrong. First, all new economic activities for the highly skilled are accompanied by activities for the low skilled. Further, 'temporary' workers tend to stay, socially investing in a country and enriching its culture. For this to happen smoothly, there must be a so-called 'integration agenda'—a policy in which migrants can retain their identity while successfully adjusting to the general characteristics of their new society.

Investment in human capital is another area where reform has long been needed. Governments must realise that social and educational spending is not a cost, but rather an investment with healthy returns. To do this (and to prompt governments to increase such spending), a mechanism must be in place to measure the outcomes—in educational and technical terms, but also in economic terms. Three such OECD-backed mechanisms include the Program for International Student Assessment (PISA), the Program for the International Assessment of Adult Competencies (PIAAC), and the Assessment of Higher Education Learning Outcomes (AHELO). The third program is the most contested because universities often argue that their results and their processes can never accurately be compared with others because of the unique nature of each institution and its students. But, of course, the market already makes such comparisons. Students and teachers choose a particular university for a particular reason, so it makes sense for their higher-education learning outcomes to be assessed so as to facilitate how they should be managed, and in which areas government spending should be made. Education is a wise investment for governments to make, but we still need more accountability and programs for comparison in this field.

Appropriate incentives are often critical to successful reform of the education sector. Take Mexico as an example of a developing nation engaged in much-needed educational reform. Until recently there were cases where a schoolteacher could hand on his job to his son. To change this culture, the Mexican Government and the OECD are working with teachers and school leaders to institute a program of performance management of education, and similar programs are being introduced in other countries. By creating an education system that rewards merit, governments can set appropriate incentives both in terms of career and in terms of payment.

An overview of contemporary reforms is not complete without discussing the issue of climate change. As the Guatemalan author Augusto Monterroso wrote in what is considered the shortest story in history: 'When he awoke, the dinosaur was still there.' The dinosaur for us is climate change, and no matter how much we talk about it, when we awake it will still be there and we will still have to address it. Climate change is the single most important challenge for future reform, and there is no way to postpone its urgency. To address climate change, we must put an economic price on emission costs and change our behaviour; there is simply no other way.

At the OECD, we regularly assess the efficacy and impact of various economic instruments (or policy responses), and we have clear evidence that taxes work better than subsidies. Subsidies tend to focus on the present and exclude new innovations, and they tend to cost too much to the government budget. As far as tax is concerned—in this case, a carbon tax—innovation to combat climate change would come from enterprises being heavily taxed for environmentally harmful practices. Trading schemes can also help to keep economies flexible, but cannot be the one and only answer.

Finding a way to reconcile ecology and economy, or achieve so-called 'green growth', is critical in the fight against climate change. In 2009, under the Korean presidency of our Ministerial Council Meeting, the OECD was mandated to achieve a green growth strategy by 2011. The OECD believes green growth is possible through a combination of taxes, innovation, education, markets, investment programs, and good governance. Perhaps most crucial is the need for international coordination for what is truly a global reform issue.

Last on our agenda for reform is the need to address socioeconomic imbalances across the globe. If global imbalances are not included on the international reform agenda then we will never succeed in having global solutions. Across the OECD, the average GDP per capita is roughly 14 times higher than that of India (7 per cent of the OECD average) and seven times higher than in China (14 per cent). Additionally, these two countries are both highly exposed to world-market volatilities in food prices, leaving them vulnerable to food crises. They also differ markedly from the OECD countries in that much of their economy is informal—with estimates claiming upwards of 85 per cent of economic activity in India is in the informal economy, not even counting agriculture. In China, the issue of informal employment is complicated by extremely complex rural land-use rights and low infrastructure, while in a country such as Indonesia we see very low levels of credit being extended to the private sector, which impedes growth. These examples demonstrate that aid is still needed to address global socioeconomic imbalances, but it should also come with coordinated efforts to achieve better regulations, freer markets, and economic climates attractive to foreign investors.

And yet, there are also many positive signs coming out of the developing world. In China, for example, the percentage of people living in poverty— defined by the United Nations as an income of $2 or less a day—has decreased in the past 10 years, from 85 per cent to 36 per cent. Correspondingly, during this period the average life expectancy in Indonesia increased from sixty-two years to seventy-one years. Further, while the percentage of people in these countries born between 1955 and 1964 to have completed secondary school is about 25 per cent, for the current generation of children it is more than 50 per cent. With the magnitude of such changes happening so fast, countries such as China, India and Indonesia will be extremely important to the future economic fortunes of Western countries. Consider that Japan and Korea together have a GDP of US$6 trillion. China, India and Indonesia have almost the same GDP but 15 times more people, so potentially this could translate to 15 times more GDP.

This is uncertain, but what is certain is that 20 years ago Korea was one of these developing countries; its transformation is a testament to the power of reform in addressing global imbalances.

Successful reform implementation: lessons from experience

As I have noted, the world shares many common interests in the international reform agenda. New global realities require new global approaches and institutions, while still taking into account the unique characteristics of individual nations. With so many reforms to make, here are a few general lessons to help make them 'stick'.

We must use the economic and political cycles to our advantage. Economic upswings are the best time to introduce labour-market reforms because the uncertainty that comes with the reforms is then balanced out by the fact that people will have more opportunities and rising incomes. As far as political cycles are concerned, the momentum that comes with a new government is often the best time to introduce substantial reforms; when governments cynically announce reforms in the year before an election they are either not serious or will not have the opportunity to properly implement them.

Reforms will be successful only if they are first supported by solid evidence for the need to reform and some degree of community acceptance of that need. If these are lacking then opponents will question the evidence on which the reform proposals are based. And even if such questioning is false or simply expedient, it will not usually be interpreted that way by the media, who will argue the government has overlooked something crucial or that it does not have a solid response to criticism of its policy.

Governments must communicate consistently about a proposed reform, because if there is an inconsistency in communication, the reform initiative will be hard to maintain. The wise policy maker proposes reforms in general terms so as to have the flexibility to adjust their instruments. If communication focuses on the goals of the reform and the instruments remain flexible then they will have greater chances of enduring success. It is also fundamental for the policy maker to monitor the process from day one because inevitably during the time it takes to introduce reform the context or some circumstances will change. Some opponents will become more powerful or less powerful. Some changes will emerge that were previously not there, perhaps relating to the international economy, changes in the labour market or whatever. In short, if we do not monitor the expected results of our reforms from the outset, the case for these reforms will weaken. In contrast, if we can prove through monitoring the results of such reforms that positive results have indeed been achieved, the case for reform can be strengthened.

Reforms are more likely to endure if strong institutions are in place to make the case or even prosecute the need for a consensus for the reform. In Australia, for example, institutions such as the Productivity Commission and the Council of Australian Governments (COAG) have successfully acted as a mechanism to create the casework for reform. Australian institutions do not, however, usually include other important stakeholders such as the business community, whereas some countries have institutions that include business and unions and can therefore make solid forums in certain areas and establish the support and involvement of business from the initial stage of the reform process.

The more you engage with your opponents beforehand, the more successful the implementation of the reform will be. This is difficult because engaging with opponents requires a clear distinction between building consensus and negotiating compensation for losses. The problem is that good negotiators—be they for business, unions, doctors or any other group—will start to make self-interested claims in the process of consultation. In other words, they want to negotiate first and build consensus later. Alternatively, they want to use the fact that they are needed for consensus as a ticket to negotiate. Take doctors or teachers as examples. These professionals enjoy a high degree of public trust. Consequently, if as a group they believe a reform proposal will inhibit their ability to provide adequate health care or educational outcomes, the public will agree, and will blame the government. This means that if reformers do not include players such as teachers and doctors in the reform process, they will become powerful opponents with the potential to generate blocking votes or veto points. And while compensating the losers is often necessary, it must be remembered that reforms are first and foremost made to correct an injustice, so subsequent losses are not always socially unjustified.

The final lesson for successfully 'making reforms stick' is the most obvious: set goals beyond election horizons, for governments to learn from each other to reduce the trial and error time. This is perhaps the wisest advice of all for authors of policy.

With these lessons in mind, I would suggest that the challenge awaits.

3. Making reforms sustainable: lessons from the American policy reform experience

Eric M. Patashnik

This chapter concerns my most recent research on making policy reforms sustainable in the US policy context, and will synthesise and build upon themes developed in my 2008 book, *Reforms at Risk: What happens after major policy changes are enacted*. What follows has four interconnected parts. First, I explore why it is important to strive for sustainable reforms. Second, I consider the puzzle of reform: why some reforms 'stick' and why others do not. I do this by introducing several concepts and by tapping into several case studies of policy reform in the United States. Third, with several cases in hand, I will identify the factors that tend to be associated with sustainable reforms. I will conclude by exploring the implications for increasing the prospects for success.

The importance of sustainable reforms

Policy reforms are often adopted with great fanfare in the legislature and among the media. It is a tremendous achievement when the political system is able to muster the will and ability to tackle an important problem and to reform it. But the struggle to recast governance does not end at the moment of enactment. The politicians who spearheaded a reform effort can change their minds about their policy goals. They might decide to do something in one year, but in five years they have a different point of view. There are always pressing priorities for any government. New problems emerge, and the one that they were so focused on in the past might no longer be as pressing; they might lose interest in an issue altogether. Alternatively, the politicians who once championed a certain reform might be replaced by other officeholders, or by new coalitions that have different values and priorities.

Policy reform usually breeds enemies. Often, a reform will tackle the privileges of some narrow constituencies, some special interest whose benefits are inimical to the larger common good. Those special interests might be the losers at the moment of reform enactment, but they do not necessarily wither or disappear. They might lose one battle, but they will be back to fight another day. For these reasons, reform must be seen as a dynamic process in which ongoing consolidation can be more difficult than winning adoption of the reform in the first place. To draw an analogy from everyday life, losing weight might be hard, but the real challenge is keeping the weight off.

But why should officeholders and citizens care whether reforms stick? When reforms unravel or collapse after enactment, several negative things can happen. First, the policy gains can be squandered; the very achievements that were fought for and accomplished in the process of enactment can be lost. Second, when a reform unravels or erodes, it undermines the ability to plan for the future. Citizens need to know what they can expect from government. They need to adapt their own private lives to the expectations of the benefit flows that will be forthcoming. When reforms unravel, people lose their ability to make long-term commitments. And finally, when policy makers work hard to reform a policy area only to see the reform collapse after enactment, it increases public cynicism about government's ability to actually solve problems. This is detrimental to building support for improved governance.

Consequently, for policy makers who care about solving problems for the public good rather than being involved in symbolic efforts that look good but do not actually achieve anything, it is crucial to consider what happens after reforms are adopted. This means policy advocates should integrate a concern for reform sustainability into their policy designs and implementation strategies. From the outset, they should consider the question: can this new policy reform sustain itself over time? It also means policy evaluators should emphasise sustainability as a criterion in assessing reform proposals prospectively. Similarly, the prospects for reform sustaining itself should be considered when gauging governmental performance. Citizens should ask themselves: this reform is working today, but will it work tomorrow?

Reforms endure not because they are frozen in time or place or because their background conditions do not change, but rather because they reconfigure the political dynamic. It is not the case that we build an edifice of reform that is so solid it cannot actually be moved. Instead, reforms must reflect the ever-changing nature of politics, where new issues are constantly emerging and new coalitions are continually forming. We need to stay afloat even in choppy weather.

Sustainable reforms achieve three key outcomes. First, they remake political institutions—the rules and sets of authority relationships by which we are governed. In this way they are not simply changing public-policy outputs; they are remaking governance. Second, sustainable reforms upset coalitional alignments and cause constituency groups to become vested in the new status quo. This is a political process that reallocates power, authority and standing to groups and interests that were previously weak. We reform government in order to empower people who were previously disenfranchised. Finally, sustainable reforms recast ideas and alter the menu of policy solutions.

It is thus crucial for policy makers to consider the capacity of a reform to maintain its structural integrity and to use its core principles to guide its course amid inevitable pressures for change. What such sustainability entails is much more than simply assembling a new policy machine and making it run, but rather remaking the political context in which subsequent policy decisions are made. In other words, a sustainable reform should change the way politics plays out—changing the debate, causing new arguments to emerge and rendering old ones that were previously persuasive irrelevant or unconvincing. This is a very powerful achievement, and it is not surprising then that many reforms lack the capacity to do these things.

The unravelling of tax reform

To illustrate some of these concepts, consider the unravelling of one very important landmark reform in the United States: the *Tax Reform Act* of 1986. This was an effort at the federal level to broaden the tax base in order to eliminate many special tax loopholes that favoured various narrow constituency interests—the oil industry and realtors, for example—but the result was a tax code that was so filled with special tax loopholes that overall rates for ordinary Americans had to be much higher than they otherwise would if the tax base had been broader and free of exemptions.

The initial reform was a tremendous achievement. It collapsed 14 tax brackets into two, eliminated approximately US$500 billion in tax breaks for various narrow interests, and shut down tax shelters for high-income individuals. The reform was also an outstanding example of bipartisanship, with President Ronald Reagan calling it 'the best job creation bill ever to come out of Congress in the United States' (*Sydney Morning Herald* 1986), and the more liberal *New York Times* editorialising: 'At last. It's a day to stop and take unashamed satisfaction on the triumph of the whole over the parts.' (*New York Times* 1986).

And yet, while the *Tax Reform Act* has never actually been repealed, the whole reform project has collapsed. Since 1986, 15 000 changes to the tax code have been made. Despite this effort to simplify the US tax code, the words in the Internal Revenue Service (IRS) code have since doubled. Further, during the first three years after the Act was signed, 80 per cent of the Members of Congress who were most responsible for passing this bill were sponsoring legislation to undo the reform. They were doing so because it was profitable. All the narrow sectional interests wanted to undo aspects of the reform, and as a consequence federal politicians were receiving campaign contributions that were creating political pressure. The initial sense of urgency to reform the tax code had evaporated; the media turned its attention to other issues. The American tax code continues to sag under the weight of particularistic interests.

The puzzle of reform: why do some succeed while others fail?

Why, then, is it that some reforms seem to stick while others collapse? I have applied this question to 10 canonical reform achievements in the United States and have found a striking variety of outcomes (Patashnik 2008). Some seemingly momentous reforms have left no permanent trace in governing dynamics; others have been repealed or eroded; others still have become deeply embedded in policy practice, changing the way in which subsequent officeholders of both major parties have had to deal with the issues at hand.

In my analysis, I define reform as a deliberate non-incremental change in an existing line of policy, intended to impart instrumental rationality on governmental activity to make it more rational, or to distribute benefits to some broad constituency. It is thus an effort to make government more effective, to create a more logical relationship between the policy tools that are used and the intended goals, and to ensure that government works for the broad majority instead of for the benefit of some narrow constituency. It is not about breakthrough policies where government is penetrating a previously unoccupied field for the first time where there was no government activity, but rather literally re-forming—forming again—an area where government is involved, but has not been as effective and equitable as it should be.

Indeed, in our age of the modern welfare, regulatory, administrative state, most of what government does today involves reform. There are not many areas where we have completely barren policy terrain, and this is why reform is often hard—as it mainly concerns altering pre-existing public or private arrangements. As Hugh Heclo has observed, there will be inevitable resistance to change from existing stakeholders who benefit from the existing arrangements. We are not simply changing government's goals; we are trying to change the way in which actors operate in the public sector and the private sector, including businesses and other types of organisations, families, and individuals.

We must thus distinguish between two phases of reform. The first is the *enactment* phase, in which initial success depends on policy advocates and experts being able to develop solutions. This can be extremely difficult. We need political entrepreneurs to frame problems, introduce new policy products, and mobilise the latent sentiment for change. What is then needed is the establishment of conditions that allow rank-and-file members of a parliament to vote for the reform. Yet the tactics used to win the initial adoption of a reform do not necessarily assure its sustainability going forward. Indeed, some of the very strategies that are most useful in helping ease the adoption of a reform can themselves cause sustainability problems. Consider the following three strategies that advocates of reforms use to make the adoption of a reform possible.

Informational strategies

This involves alerting the public that there is a problem, and thus a need for reform. This can be done by using symbols or linking the specific reform cause with a broader issue that resonates with the public. The problem with informational strategies is that they often have a short shelf life. The media might initially be useful in highlighting some pathology of government or some narrow group that is profiting at the public's expense, but the media is fickle, and might not stick with the issue after the reform is adopted. Further, it is difficult to use symbolic politics and paint with a broad brush when we enter the murky implementation phase. Advocates pushing the initial passage of a reform might be able to present it as a case of good verses bad, or it might even become a salient campaign issue for a candidate. But such use of symbolism becomes increasingly difficult when it comes to composing the detailed regulations needed to carry out the reform.

Procedural strategies

It is fundamental to frame the debate in a way that makes it hard for politicians not to vote for the reform. Consequently, policy advocates seeking to build support for the initial passage of a reform will try to create parliamentary rules that make it easy for law-makers to say yes, and make it hard for them to amend the reform or strip it away. The problem with this strategy is that after the bill has been signed into law, law-makers can submit any amendment they want. There might be a narrow interest group that pushes for an obscure provision to which no-one will pay much attention and thus it will pass, potentially undermining the original goal of the reform in question.

Compensation strategies

It is likely there will be some clientele group unhappy with a reform. A frequent enactment-phase strategy is necessary to give extra benefits or provide for transitional arrangements, to gain the group's support or at the very least to tame their opposition. The problem with this strategy is that once losers agree to accept a legislative change, if they are given compensatory benefits, what is to stop them using this precedent to demand increased benefits in the future? It might be possible to rent 'losers' in a democracy for a little while, but is it possible to buy them in perpetuity? This becomes increasingly difficult if the government is implementing a transitional scheme over a long period, promising adjustments along the way. Will losers stay 'bought' for the entirety of a transitional scheme, even if they know there is an election in between the adoption of the scheme and its final implementation date? Their acquiescence is never guaranteed.

The second stage of reform is *post enactment*. Once a reform has been passed it does not mean it has been won; all that has been won is the right to fight another day. It is rare for a reform to become embedded in an instant; consolidation takes time. During this interim period, the old policy system—which was so inefficient and inequitable that it needed reforming in the first place—must be dismantled. The old system must be uprooted, and a new one constructed in its place.

Reform outcomes are never completely settled because democracy continually adapts and responds to new pressures. There is no end point. And yet, it is possible for a reform to become so deeply embedded in governance, and in the adaptations of social actors via policy feedback effects, that its subsequent reversal becomes virtually unthinkable, even if the next parliament retains the legal ability to enact another policy that would undo it. Let me now examine how we can tell when this is likely.

Assessing a reform's prospects for success

There are several ways to assess whether a reform is likely to stick or not. First, we must look for shifts in governing arrangements induced by the reform. This involves tracing the evolution of governance institutions both before and after the reform. By doing this, we can pose the following questions: are we assembling a new system of governance? Are we creating a new agency, authority, or state capacity? Are we disassembling something, or are we simply displacing its authority? And finally, are we layering? Layering, as Stephen Skowronek has pointed out, involves a reform leading to the overlapping of two authorities. It can be a problem, as both authorities inevitably have different interests, values and cultures, so will clash. While the reform might have handed responsibility to a new authority, the old reform—its stakeholders, its expertise, and its links to the media—has not yet been eliminated.

When assessing whether a reform has changed governance, further questions to ask are: does this reform have prospects that are positive going forward? How extensive or limited are these shifts; how permanent or ephemeral? How do these shifts interact with surrounding authority? And finally, will they clash with the other power centres in that arena, or will they rather reinforce and complement them?

As an example, consider the system of public management instituted in the United States by the Clinton Administration. This involved Vice-President Al Gore trying to make the American bureaucracy more customer centred and efficient through changing the way in which the US Federal Government buys goods and services from private contractors. The desire for this reform came about partly because the American procurement process had become extremely litigious; when private firms lost a contract bid, they would often sue. Reformers argued that the agency in question was overly friendly with the Contract Litigation Bar. They proposed keeping the authority to protest and use judicial process, but taking it out of that agency and transferring it to another one.

Layering also resulted from this reform. While a less-regulated procurement system was created, this was simply put on top of the existing civil service system. The problem with this approach was that the civil servants did not have the training, resources, capacity or the incentives to carry out the new system. In this way, the Clinton Administration changed its public policy, but it did not change the state's capacity to administer the policy in a way that was going to be as robust. By layering a high-discretion, performance-oriented purchasing system atop an understaffed civil service, traditional oversight mechanisms became focused not on good performance, but on the rooting out of fraud, waste and abuse. This approach resulted in much political tension, and ultimately failed to change the way in which Congress oversees the procurement process.

Another way of assessing a reform's sustainability potential is to look at the reactions of private social actors, of businesses, families, and citizens, because ultimately, they are they actors who generate support. Private social actors determine what government does, so it is critical to consider how private actors react to what government is trying to achieve. Recent research shows that public policies are not merely the outcomes of political forces, but can also cause politics. When a policy is robust, it can change the way in which citizens vote and change the way citizens conceive of politics. Similarly, when policies have strong feedback effects—the ability to remake alignments, remake voting patterns and remake coalitions—their very existence influences and constrains governing possibilities going forward.

For this reason, we need to identify key policy feedback mechanisms, including the extent to which reforms change (or fail to change), the identities and affiliations of constituencies, and the degree to which different constituencies make investments themselves predicated on the expectation that this new policy will continue. When we see businesses and families organising their lives around the expectation that government is going to do certain things or act in a certain way, candidates must take this into account before voting those expectations away.

Alternatively, there might be no change in the positions taken by constituency groups—or in group identities and affiliations—before and after a reform. The same groups that liked a particular policy continue to like it, and the same groups that did not like it, continue to dislike it. Further, when group investments in a policy are modest—in other words, people, businesses or families are not putting significant private money or resources at stake in the expectation that reforms will continue—there is a higher probability of reversal because the reform is not rooted in society. This is because nobody is organising their lives around the expectation that the reform will continue. It is this combination of fluidity in groups and a lack of significant personal investment that presents the greatest potential for reform erosion. The original reform might stay on the books, but new public policies will be continually adopted in future years that might be antithetical. Alternatively, when we see stable and extensive investments, the reform has a high probability of becoming entrenched.

The most powerful effect to consider when assessing a reform's sustainability potential is what I call *reconfiguration*. This occurs when the reform causes new coalitional alignments to form or new interest groups to emerge that were previously not in that policy sector *and* induces such actors to make long-term, hard-to-reverse commitments based on the expectation that the reform process will continue. The combination of shifts in coalitions and the stimulation of significant investments causes the whole arena to change, because these new actors are committing their own economic and organisational resources to the reform. The policy sector has been thoroughly reconfigured, making it extremely difficult for officeholders to resurrect the *status quo ante bellum*, even if they wished to do so. All the political pressures impinging on that sector have fundamentally changed, and it would thus not be in the government's best interest to undo its decision.

Lessons in sustainable reform: two case studies from the United States

To illustrate some of these arguments, consider two case studies from the United States. The first is the deregulation of the American airline industry in 1978. Prior to that year the government regulated the airlines in the United States; it decided where the carriers may fly and how much they may charge. The only way airlines could compete was on service. The lack of price competition rendered air travel prohibitively expensive for most Americans—hardly an ideal situation for a country as geographically vast as the United States.

Many economists made the case for airline deregulation on microeconomic grounds: if the airline market was contestable, it would become more economically efficient, and fare prices would fall. To sell deregulation to the broader public, however, its advocates used symbolism. This was the mid 1970s, an era when there was concern about the increasing role of government. Consequently, airline deregulation was sold as a way of removing the heavy hand of government from the market. Additionally, the reform was pitched to the public as a solution to the high inflation America was experiencing at the time—even though, in truth, most economists would acknowledge that regulation of the airlines was not a major contributor to the overall level of inflation in the United States.

Naturally, airline deregulation faced fierce opposition from powerful and well-organised groups. The major airlines had no interest in change, having practically enjoyed guaranteed profits under the previous arrangement. All the big carriers argued their case using the symbolism of a decrease in safety standards should deregulation eventuate, and many continue to seek economic rent and protection from competition to this day. The labour unions, too, opposed deregulation, as their workers had been getting high wages in a heavily regulated sector where they did not face market competition. And yet, airline deregulation passed Congress overwhelmingly—363 to eight in the House of Representatives, and 83 to nine in the Senate.

But why has airline deregulation persisted? It is a puzzle for several reasons. First, the issues that prompted deregulation have faded. Inflation is no longer the problem in the United States. Second, the members and the coalition alignments in Congress who were responsible for enacting this policy are no longer around. Third, the deregulation did not work out as perfectly as expected, with the airline industry still plagued by problems. Planes are crowded, service is often poor, and there have been accusations of predatory pricing. Further, there are also many other well-organised losers from airline deregulation, including creditors, unions and some cities. It is certainly not the case that nobody is unhappy with this reform. And yet, despite these problems, and a frustrated public that could be mobilised on this issue, subsequent policy interventions since 1978— of which there have been many—have mainly reinforced the reform path, as Michael E. Levine has observed. Carriers have retained the freedom over pricing and routes, and despite ongoing discussion of re-regulation to capture or restore rents—or even to minimise the cost of disruption—this has never eventuated.

What, then, explains the endurance of this reform? The principal factor is that airline deregulation is an example of the politics of reconfiguration. First, this policy prompted the disassembly of the governance arrangements of the old interest-group system. The agency that regulated the airlines, the Civil Aeronautics Board, was eliminated. To be sure, there are still officials in Washington who are concerned with airlines, and some of them are in favour of re-regulation. But they are concentrated in the Department of Transportation, where they lack the bureaucratic independence and autonomy to launch their initiatives. Airline policy making today is mediated by much broader and conflicting political forces than previously because of that change in governance arrangements.

Second, the economic adaptations of social actors to airline deregulation have made the reform self-reinforcing. As Senator Jack Danforth once said, you cannot unscramble an egg. Once set in motion, these forces are not going to be reversed. Airlines and service providers have made massive investments of human and physical capital predicated on the expectation that they will get to determine where they fly. Fortress hubs have been constructed and fleets created to cater for these new management systems. All sorts of private actors have built terminals and hangars adapted to the new route structure that emerged post deregulation. It would thus be impossible to reinstate the old system without disruption. Congress still has the authority to re-regulate the airline industry, but it would be a massively disruptive move.

Next, airline deregulation has resulted in huge changes in coalitional alignments. New discount carriers have entered the market, carriers whose very existence is predicated on competition. As for the carriers that predated deregulation—the legacy carriers—they have merged, struggled to reinvent themselves, or disappeared altogether. The heterogeneity and fluidity of sectoral interest ushered in by airline deregulation have destroyed the cohesion of the old interest-group system. Previously, government faced constant pressure to maintain the system. Now the old interest group has splintered into carriers with conflicting views on whether they are in favour of regulation or re-regulation. This lack of constant uniform business pressure makes it easier for government not to do anything, because since each actor faces a different strategic situation, any attempt to re-regulate is going to encounter political resistance from some quarter.

Further, there has been a shift in the internal governance of airlines as a result of deregulation. After deregulation, the internal governance structures of the airlines—for example, CEO pay, the concentration of ownership, board size—gravitated towards the governance models of unregulated firms, because they too were now unregulated. Consequently, it would now be costly for these firms to return to their previous set-ups, because they have adapted their corporate DNA to suit the post-regulation environment. Similar outcomes have occurred as a result of other American reforms. The *Employee Retirement Income Security Act* of 1974, for example, was enacted to regulate the way in which private corporations deliver pensions and health benefits. Consequently, American private firms adapted by setting up human-resource offices and hiring tax and pension experts to rewrite and manage their own benefit plans. There is an almost Darwinian 'natural selection' process at work here: rather than powerful actors selecting the reforms that they want, deeply embedded reforms select the organisational properties of the actors who survive.

A second major factor to explain the endurance of American airline deregulation has been its ability to survive a significant exogenous shock. The ability to do this is a key test of the sustainability of any reform. When something no-one foresaw rocks a policy sector—be it a scandal or some kind of disaster—will the reform stand up or will it collapse? For airline deregulation, this exogenous shock was the attacks on the United States on 11 September 2001.

Following the attacks, it was unclear whether policy makers would abandon or maintain the reform. It is highly unlikely the American Government would have undertaken airline deregulation had the 11 September attacks occurred in 1977—there simply would not have been a push to reduce the government's role in the sector. But the attacks happened 20 years after airline deregulation had become embedded. Of course, we did see policy responses in the airline sector. Flights were grounded for weeks, then severely cut back once they resumed; the Federal Government bailed out the airline sector because it was bankrupt. In addition, the Air Stabilisation Board (ASB) was created to distribute US$15 billion in loan guarantees and cash assistance. But significantly, this new governance arrangement was given very limited authority, and it was cautioned not to slow the transition of legacy carriers to the competitive market.

Indeed, despite the personal intervention of the then Speaker of the House, Dennis Hastert from Illinois, the loan application from United Airlines was rejected three times. In other words, here we have the most powerful member of the US Congress, with significant airline interests in his district including O'Hare Airport, pleading for funding for United Airlines. Yet the ASB did not feel compelled to give it. This is a testament to the entrenchment and governance configuration capacity of airline deregulation.

By way of contrast, consider now an American reform that has *not* become embedded and the reasons why. 'Freedom to Farm' was an effort in the mid 1990s to scale back the huge amount of agricultural subsidies that the US Government gives its farmers. These agricultural subsidies are economically inefficient, inequitable, and flow mainly to large agribusinesses rather than the family farmers they were designed to protect. There is bipartisan agreement among experts that these farm subsidies are difficult to justify on the merits. They cause problems for developing countries, and contribute to obesity in the United States. But because farmers are popular in the public's eye, it was agreed Freedom to Farm could not be sudden, so it was designed to gradually transform the agricultural sector into a market system over five or seven years.

And yet, since Freedom to Farm was enacted in 1996, the United States has spent more—not less—on agricultural subsidies. This is because after 1996, the economic conditions in the agricultural sector took a turn for the worse, principally due to harsh weather. The powerful farming lobby returned to Washington and managed to secure extra funding, the excuse being that no-one foresaw worsening market conditions when the bill was proposed.

From the three principal American reforms, this chapter has highlighted—tax reform, airline deregulation and Freedom to Farm—we can identify different institutional shifts. First, airline deregulation resulted in extensive shifts in governance. The Civil Aeronautics Board was eliminated, subsequent court rulings reinforced the deregulatory path and thus created a high barrier to proving predatory pricing cases, and the post 11 September bailout was conducted by a temporary board with a narrow mission. In contrast, in the taxation and agricultural sectors, the same kind of governance shifts did not eventuate. For example, there were no shifts in power in tax policy committees, and the transaction costs for creating new tax breaks and new tax barriers were not increased.

As a sidenote, one reform was layered atop the 1986 tax reform that did briefly—unintentionally—help promote the original reform's sustainability. In 1990 Congress passed a deficit-reduction act called the *Budget Enforcement Act*. This Act had a clause called PAYGO, according to which if government creates a new tax break that loses money, it must find replacement money from somewhere else in the budget. This was a disincentive for Congress to create new tax breaks for a couple of years. The *Budget Enforcement Act* lapsed, however, in the late 1990s when the US Government briefly started running budget surpluses, removing the need for a deficit-reduction act. This example demonstrates that a reform's sustainability will be affected by whatever legislation comes after it. Subsequent laws can accidentally serve to reinforce the path of the original reform—or they can undermine it.

As far as Freedom to Farm is concerned, as with the tax reform of 1986, extensive shifts in governance arrangements did not eventuate. One need only consider that the permanent law that provides the underlying authority for the Federal Government to dole out benefits was not repealed. Instead, Freedom to Farm was layered upon this law. There was a consequent shift in congressional arrangements, but it was only temporary.

The three reforms each had different policy feedback effects. In the airline deregulation case, new constituencies were built and there was a changing of coalitional alignments and the fragmentation of interest groups in a way that helped sustain the reform. In the other two cases, however, these patterns did not emerge. In the tax arena, we did not see new coalitions or the disempowerment of tax lobbyists, and in the agricultural sector, we did not see farmers being stigmatised or public opposition to the continued provision of subsidies.

Conclusion: promoting reform sustainability

What can reform advocates do to promote reform sustainability? First, we need to anticipate sustainability problems *ex ante*. This can be done by using forward and backward mapping techniques. We need next to remember that reforms are typically most vulnerable during their early years, and that we need to use policy design to stimulate durable shifts in governance and group identities. We also need to be careful about front-loading costs and back-loading benefits, because these threaten our ability to build up a constituency for the reform.

We need to be strategic about the use of side payments and compensation schemes. Supporters should not simply be rented for the short term; ways must be found to reallocate power so that it becomes harder for the former beneficiaries to come back and fight another day. This is not easy, and can require complex legal arrangements.

We need to cultivate new reform-oriented clienteles—to create costs in subverting reforms by establishing new property rights. This is one reason the American Acid Rain Emission Permit Trading system has worked so well: there are new actors who have rights to emit sulfur dioxide, and they own those rights. These new actors do not want to see those rights taken away; the system has created new stakeholders.

Next, policy makers must not implement reforms without first establishing the bureaucratic capacity and the legal authority needed to make them work. This is a particular problem in the United States, because our state capacity is weak, and we have a difficult time strengthening it—for both cultural and institutional reasons. Further, reformers cannot rely on minimum winning coalitions. If a reform passes by two votes, its authors should seek a broader coalition to increase the likelihood of the reform sustaining itself even if the next couple of election results are unfavourable.

Additionally, to ensure entrenchment, reformers must invest significant organisational and financial resources in long-term reform monitoring and advocacy. They must recognise that reform consolidation is less sexy than reform adoption, and that the media cannot be relied on for continued coverage. Instead, it is up to the policy reformer to draw attention to the achievements of their reforms, and to make the public aware of the positive outcomes they are achieving.

We must unmask attempts to unravel the reform. Many efforts by narrow constituency groups and stakeholders to destroy reforms can take place in obscure bureaus and government proceedings when no-one is looking. Consequently, reformers must not think that simply because something is a third-tier venue, nothing is happening there; reforms are often eroded in back rooms.

Next, actors who played key roles in reform adoption should be encouraged to remain involved in the issue. Usually there are a few high-ranking people who were instrumental to the reform, be they key politicians or staff. They know the most about the issue, and they have the passion. The problem is that politicians want to remain in the media limelight, but once a policy has been enacted, it will quickly lose the media spotlight. Consequently, in America at least, their attention turns to other issues. It is thus very rare to find a politician or elected official who will stay engaged with the issue, because they always want to be near the centre of power. These actors must be made to understand that their work is not done. Their leadership is needed at least to get through that first early stage of reform consolidation.

Finally, policy reform is a long-term project, and should be considered as such. Consequently, policy evaluation should occur at multiple stages, each of which should be forward looking. Progress should be judged not simply in terms of whether the reform is delivering benefits to the public at the moment, but whether the reform has reconfigured the political context in which subsequent decisions will be made.

References

Patashnik, E. M. 2008, *Reforms at Risk: What happens after major policy changes are enacted*, Princeton University Press, Princeton, NJ.

The New York Times, 22 October 1986, 'A Tax Law to Hail. Yes, a Tax Law'.

The Sydney Morning Herald, 24 October 1986, 'Reagan Ronald stumbles over his historic 15kg tax law overhaul'.

Part II

National reform initiatives

4. How to design and deliver reform that makes a real difference: what recent history has taught us as a nation

Paul Kelly

This chapter is structured with three objectives in mind. First, it describes the current state of Australia's political culture, which prizes expediency and timidity over boldness and reform zeal—highlighting the problems this then raises for much-needed further reform efforts. Second, it identifies the contributing factors that made the previous, post-1983 reform era so successful in Australia, drawing out the lessons from that history. And third, it will examine where we ought to go from here in terms of future policy reforms. Undoubtedly, the most speculative part of the chapter will concern the future solutions, simply because they are the most difficult to discern.

Australia's present political culture: complacency and timidity

The 2010 federal election was a dramatic testimony to the shift in Australia's political culture towards policy timidity and short-term horizons. The evidence is plentiful, the most dramatic being Kevin Rudd's sudden removal from office—the first time a palace revolt has replaced a first-term Labor Prime Minister. The Australian Labor Party (ALP) now has had four different leaders over the past four federal elections: Kim Beazley in 2001, Mark Latham in 2004, Kevin Rudd in 2007, and Julia Gillard in 2010. Its intolerance towards poor polls has sealed a new intensity in impatience with a predilection not to fix problems, but to shoot leaders.

The Liberal Party itself has had three parliamentary leaders over this term: Brendan Nelson, Malcolm Turnbull and Tony Abbott. In contrast, the 11-year-long Howard era seems a nostalgic aberration in terms of its leadership stability. Volatility is now the name of the game.

When Rudd defeated John Howard in 2007, you could have managed to get betting odds of 100:1 that the next election would be a Gillard versus Abbott contest. Yet the improbable came to pass. The old norms and working rules of Australian politics have been torn up. It is not clear what the new rules are, or if 'rules' as such is the way to think about things.

My view is that the historic, post-1983 reform era—marking the Hawke/ Keating and part of the Howard governments—is largely terminated. If support for reform is to be resuscitated, it will take a different form in future. The causes of the reform era's demise were complex, although perhaps inevitable. Let me try to identify them.

A number of structural factors are at work. First, the post-2003 terms-of-trade boom, driven by China and the emergent economies, has engendered a pervasive complacency in Australia. It is often said that reform is driven by crisis, not prosperity. It is also said that the Australian character is relaxed in prosperity, and propelled into action only by crisis. Both points appear to be true.

Post 2003, John Howard and Peter Costello arguably did not grasp the scale of the new national income surge, or how to maximise its dividend. Too much was spent, and not enough was invested in reform, or enhancing a new productivity agenda. The political will to restructure and improve government programs was lost. There was not sufficient commitment to competition policy, reform of federalism, education, and better infrastructure. Costello held out many hopes, yet disappointed too often. The release of the first *Intergenerational Report* in 2001–02 was the chance for a new reform agenda but it was not properly seized.

Under the Rudd Government, Australia has survived the global financial crisis without a technical recession, assisted in part by its integration with China. This is a great result, but it has a legacy. Australia is now drifting, psychologically divorced from the crisis in the North Atlantic zone. The Australian public is experiencing cost-of-living pressures, but the political leaders feel no compulsion to offer a substantive and forward-looking reform agenda.

Ross Garnaut, in August 2010, was correct in identifying the unbroken 20-year-old Australian growth cycle as inculcating lethargy in our political system. The claim that we survived the global financial crisis through spending a significant amount of money overlooks the bigger picture. We survived because of the overall quality of our public-policy frameworks, the inheritance from our previous reform efforts, and our capacities to adopt a pre-emptive policy agenda. This relates to issues such as our financial institutions and banks avoiding the sub-prime crisis, no overhanging public debt, and the fact that our Treasury and central bank moved very quickly given the crisis, as well as our integration with China.

The second factor that should be highlighted, however, relates to botched reforms in our recent past. There are many examples, but the main ones are Howard's WorkChoices, Rudd's Carbon Pollution Reduction Scheme (CPRS), and Rudd's mining tax. The moral from these exercises is not just how difficult it is to bring reforms to fruition, but that botched reforms have counterproductive consequences. WorkChoices was misconceived. It helped to destroy the Howard

Government, and turned the public from a more flexible labour market to a more regulated labour market. It is virtually impossible even to discuss this subject in rational terms today in Australia. And it has definitely made the Coalition trigger shy on reforms across the board. Its tragedy is that Howard in his final term had control of both Houses of Parliament. And the reform dividend from this historic opportunity looks meagre in retrospect.

There are many lessons from the climate-change debacle. The single most important one was Labor's decision not to price carbon without the political cover of bipartisanship. This timidity was reflected in Rudd's paralysis after his bill died in the Senate, and again in his April 2010 decision to defer the issue for another three years. While at the end of John Howard's first term he went to an election on an unpopular goods and services tax (GST), at a comparable time in Rudd's first term, he refused to take his emissions trading scheme (ETS) to an election, despite having branded climate change the greatest moral test of the age. This was a failure of conviction.

It has left the climate-change debate in this country in a weakened and fragmented state. Note, however, there is one possible excuse for the Rudd/Gillard tactical retreat—their claim that if they had proceeded unilaterally, their reform might not have stuck.

On the mining tax, Labor broke every rule in the tax-reform book. It ambushed the industry. It misunderstood the financial impact of its tax on the industry. It shunned consultation, judging it would be advantaged politically by the confrontation that followed. It spectacularly misjudged in a failure of process and politics.

The resource-tax process had none of the industry consultation involved in the Hawke Government's petroleum tax. It could not have been more different from the Hawke/Keating 1985 tax-reform process: a taxation White Paper by the Treasury, released for debate, a taxation summit, significant modifications to the package arising from the summit, and then the final decisions. Ultimately, the mining tax cost Rudd the prime ministership. It also leaves the shadow of doubt hanging over further serious tax reform.

The third factor to inhibit reform today is the triumph of short termism in politics and in policy making driven by the 24-hour media cycle and the focus-group mentality. And this is a profound problem. The dilemma facing democracies today is the contradiction between the need for long-run, 'big picture' policy commitments to address the economy, demographic change, climate change, tax reform and infrastructural needs on the one hand, and on the other, the fact that politicians run almost exclusively according to a 24-hour media agenda. They approach each day as a 24-hour media battle, with a three-year term consisting of a thousand such daily contests.

Party faith and ideological conviction are in decline. Both major parties need incumbency to bestow patronage upon their power networks and supporters. Because their market research is much the same, they offer small variations on the same theme. Sometimes bipartisanship is desirable, but sometimes it stifles creative debate. In this timid political culture, 'safety first' is the supreme rule. The power of the negative campaign prevails. Both sides know this. Paul Keating's famous 1993 victory off the back of his anti-GST campaign set the standard. Howard's destruction off the back of WorkChoices confirmed it.

In the 2010 campaign, Gillard was not prepared to expose herself to attack from Abbott by promising a carbon price and an ETS. Instead, she said Labor would act only when there was a political consensus; in other words, when the opposition gives her a free pass. Abbott in turn walked away from any industrial-relations liberalisation—the first time in a generation when the Liberal Party has gone to an election campaign without a commitment to industrial-relations reform. The problem is obvious: the power of the negative campaign that the media will play to, and play up, and that will be reinforced by political advertising.

There are other consequences of timidity. One is the perceived need in reforms to operate by the rule 'everybody ought to be a winner'. This is a deeply inhibiting factor. It influenced the Howard Government; it influenced the Rudd Government's generous compensation in its CPRS. It was Howard's failure to honour this rule that brought him undone on WorkChoices.

The modern Labor Party is partly defined by the model of governing devised by state Labor governments, developed during the Howard era, starting with the Carr Government in New South Wales. The features of this model are control of government through the Premier's office and his/her department, a relentless focus on the media message, policy caution, using incumbency to bolster Labor's support network, and the destruction of the opposition as a viable force.

Labor's recent approach stands in contrast with that pursued by Keating and Howard. They were old-fashioned tribal warriors, both fashioned not only in the Sydney of the 1960s, but also by the Treasury. They believed that by the 1980s Australia faced a historic economic challenge and that their main mission—apart from winning office and winning elections—was to address this great challenge.

The current Labor Party is different. Kevin Rudd and Julia Gillard are not products of the economic debates of the 1980s. They came into Parliament only in 1998 and are fashioned by forces that belong to another generation. They reflect the changing nature of the political system and the pressures arising from the culture of short termism.

Related to this is the growing sophistication of the lobbying process in Canberra, and the influence of special interest groups over the public interest. The special interest group industry is now huge in Canberra. The role of lobbying has expanded enormously in the national capital; in contrast, there is no lobby for the public interest.

One final point should be raised in this section about the obstacles to reform. Technology in the twenty-first century is creating a new sense of individual empowerment. Institutions that once moulded mass loyalties—from the Church to the trade union, and from the Returned Services League to the local newspaper—are all diminished. So it is with political parties. Once they assumed voter loyalty, relying on the habit voter. Now fickle voters have to be won over or purchased. In a more diverse society with multimedia options, each person becomes an empowered focus group. The result is that it is much more difficult to build consensus for policy reform across the community.

Explaining the success of the post-1983 reform era

Let us examine some of the factors that underpinned the reform endeavour over the past 25 years. Essentially, this involves looking at what happened from the early 1980s onwards. The first point to make is that the Hawke and Keating reform agenda was driven by a sense of urgency. There was a sense in the early 1980s of national stagnation and decline, symbolised by the 1980s recession. Australia's annual average gross domestic product (GDP) growth during the Fraser era was only 2 per cent—disappointing in historical terms and by international comparisons. Unemployment rose to about 9 per cent during the 1980s recession. There was strong sentiment this stagnation had to be addressed.

Second, the era coincided with the arrival of a new government led by a popular Prime Minister, Bob Hawke, who was also astute in policy terms. The Hawke/Keating Government was remarkably free of Labor dogma, which had ruined the Whitlam Government, and was prepared to look at policy approaches with a fresh eye.

This leads us to the third factor. When the Hawke Government arrived there was a set of ideas waiting for it—ideas that had been developed over time in agencies such as the Treasury, the Reserve Bank, and the Industries Assistance Commission. These ideas had some support in the Federal Parliament, and quite a lot in the policy media. The agenda essentially involved freer trade, smaller government, deregulation of markets, lower tax rates within a fairer tax system, a more flexible labour market, low inflation, an attack on economic rent-seekers, and a more market-orientated economy. There is no doubt that the intellectual momentum of 1980s reforms was elite driven; the ideas came from the top down. It took unusual politicians, however, such as Hawke and Keating to sell them to the community.

The fourth point to make is that Hawke and Keating had a formal contract for consensus: the Accord with the trade-union movement. The decade-long Accord represented a choice by the union movement to switch from an industrial to a political strategy, to give priority to an economic reform agenda and growth strategy with the Labor Party. This meant reforms were often negotiated through the Accord—that is, with the unions first thereby creating a basis for consensus, or at least a move towards broad support.

Another element important in these reforms was the commitment to equity. For the Hawke Government, social and economic equity were vital. Equity was integral to the Accord with Labor's own constituency, and as a tactic in selling its economic reforms. But equity was vital in another sense. Equity was part of the reform agenda itself; it was an aim in its own right.

John Howard is right to argue that in the 1980s the Coalition in opposition supported many of Labor's reform directions. In fact, the opposition was usually attacking the Labor government for not going further and faster. Far from complaining that Labor was engaged in 'rip-and-tear' reformism, the Coalition's typical position was that Labor had been too cautious. This approach gave Hawke and Keating great political flexibility and the chance to occupy the middle ground, which they essentially did for a decade.

The final point to make about this period is that the Hawke Government— notably Hawke and Keating—was very effective at putting and winning the intellectual and political case for these policies. Unlike today's politicians, they actually argued the merits. They did not engage purely in spin; they did not engage in empty slogans. For a considerable time, Keating as Treasurer carried much of the media behind him and his policies. Above all, Hawke kept winning elections—and that affirmed the reforms. They worked in political terms. There is not much point introducing a new reform and then losing an election, as Howard did in 2007. The fact that Hawke kept winning elections entrenched the reforms in the system.

Even after the debilitating recession of the early 1990s, reformism remained alive. The great gain from the recession was an independent central bank targeting inflation, and a new era of low inflation. Additionally, the Keating Government advanced enterprise bargaining, increased occupational-based superannuation to 9 per cent and introduced national competition policy.

The Howard Government entrenched new fiscal rules, discharged public debt, granted full central bank independence, completed a major 'goods and services tax' reform, forced through reform on the waterfront, further liberalised the labour market with the support of the Democrats in 1996, made some decisive privatisations, and presided over a system of sound bank supervision and regulation.

The great irony of Kevin Rudd is his failure to live up to the expectations he created in opposition and in government, and to deliver on the mandate he won at the 2007 election. Rudd promised an emissions trading scheme. He pledged to revive the Council of Australian Governments (COAG) and to fix the federation, ending the blame game. He pledged a new era of human-capital investment that he called an 'education revolution'. No prime minister has ever talked so much about productivity. Ruddism was a phenomenon undermined by too many contradictions. It failed to determine its priorities.

Future prospects for reform

So where do we go from here? First, we need to rekindle our understanding of political leadership—a matter of high reflection for both sides of politics. I believe this is possible because the public is sick of spin and inaction. Today's leaders should reclaim their mission from the apparatchiks, brokers and spin merchants who have been so persuasive. They need to re-engage with reform visions. There is some evidence that as the proportion of swinging voters increases, more adverse judgments will apply to political leaders who seek merely to avoid the real issues or resort to cosmetics.

Second, an encouraging feature of the 2010 election campaign was that both sides followed a stance of fiscal restraint. Indeed, their proposed bottom lines were not very different, with neither jeopardising the return to surplus within three years. The 2010 election saw few of the big-spending commitments that characterised earlier election campaigns. Both sides seem committed to debt reduction once the surplus is achieved.

Third, we should not underestimate the groundwork laid for future policy advances. There is, arguably, recognition in the community of the problems and the challenges—for example, the need for better planning and improved urban infrastructure, the need for more investment, better transparency and higher standards in education, the need to better address environmental protection, climate change and water issues, policies to manage demographics and ageing, and the need to tackle intergenerational poverty and welfare dependency. The public is disposed to action on most of these fronts. This is important because the first step in reform is recognising the status quo is not good enough.

Fourth, in the policy community there is widespread agreement on what needs to be done in many areas. The former Secretary of Treasury Ken Henry's agenda of the three Ps—population, participation, and productivity—almost a decade ago has been vital in this process. The role of Treasury, the Reserve Bank, and the Productivity Commission in pushing ideas and frameworks for reform is pivotal. It might take five or 10 years before some ideas turn into breakthrough policy. But this is to be expected. The campaign for lower tariffs was waged for 20 years inside the policy community before the breakthrough came. Although the community might perceive that nothing much is happening, the pressure builds up and eventually the dam wall breaks.

The role of independent inquiries of intellectual standing, such as the Henry Tax Review or the Garnaut Report on Climate Change, is another important mechanism. Such reports can shape public-policy debates for years, influencing politicians, media and stakeholders.

The fifth point to make is that much of the current and emerging reform agenda is about overlapping Commonwealth–state responsibilities. Paul Keating recently said our future productivity gains will rest upon state government performance. But how do we fix the federation? How do we provide more incentives for productivity-enhancing state government policies? And how do we get better synergies between the Commonwealth and the states to tackle these overlapping issues?

Given that we are a federation, future reform is not going to succeed without the commitment of the state governments. Commonwealth–state relations have been one of the most difficult areas of our public policy. Traditionally, the solutions have involved transferring powers from the states to the Commonwealth, and letting the Commonwealth fix the problem. But it is unsustainable in the long run to have a strong Commonwealth compensating for weak states. A new model is needed. Fixing the federation requires a tremendous amount of detail, ideas and collaboration. It is true, however, that a considerable part of the national reform agenda still rests with the Commonwealth—for example, tax and welfare reform, retirement and superannuation policy.

We should acknowledge what we have learnt about reform in the past generation, because few countries have done as well as Australia during this time. We have learnt that the reform must be intellectually sound. That means potential solutions must have been debated and canvassed among policy makers and in the policy media. Consultation and dialogue with stakeholders are vital. Consensus is not easily won; sometimes it cannot be achieved. Nobody asks the government to commit political suicide. But substantive reform demands leadership, courage, communication, and a willingness to risk a government for what the leader believes is right. Moreover, we cannot do everything at once. Getting the reform priorities right is critical. Hawke did this well; Rudd did it badly. Winning the intellectual and political debate in the media is vital.

Getting the academy reinvolved has a role. Too much academic work is divorced from public policy. We need to get the wheels better attuned between the academy and policy making. The evidence suggests our universities are far too regulated when we need a greater dynamic and more diversity. Universities are bedevilled still by a one-size-fits-all model. The reward system for academics is based on research papers that are often too narrow and too remote from public policy. We need to reconnect better the academy and public policy.

Politicians must understand the limits to politics itself. They should focus on the most urgent problems, postpone those that are less urgent, and take some issues off the agenda. Take the global financial crisis as an illustration. Suddenly faced with a significant deficit instead of a healthy surplus, a rational government would have reprioritised its agenda, and not attempted everything it had previously promised. Instead, Rudd said nothing would change; he would proceed with the same agenda. No business would have done this. Such an approach created such demands on the political system that it could not deliver.

It is vital to keep our economy and political system flexible. Efficient government and effective markets go together. Sound economic policy and a decent society go together. Morality is not a government monopoly; markets also have their own morality. There is no substitute for leadership and leadership cannot be programmed. It is best produced from a wider talent pool than we are currently attracting into politics.

5. The 'new responsibility model' for New Zealand public-sector CEOs[1]

The Hon. Bill English

I approach the topic of public-sector change from a finance minister's perspective, speculating on how we might embrace further reform over the next 10 years. It is a review that comes from a number of years observing this important topic, starting with my experience as a junior Treasury official when Roger Douglas was New Zealand's Minister of Finance, developing when I entered Parliament in 1990 when the government I was part of was undertaking a program of dramatic reform, and, most recently, continuing over a number of years spent in opposition, where I had time to ponder and reflect on the lessons learned.

One of the advantages of bringing a finance minister's perspective to the topic of substantive reform and policy change is that it helps answer one basic question: why would anyone in the community choose to do what we in government want them to do? Essentially, the only reason they will agree to do what we want them to do is because we have the money and they require it. There is no shortage of public-policy talk that is attractive and articulate, but if you cannot find a reason why people should want to do it then it simply does not happen. Public services do not need to do anything in particular—that is the nature of the business.

Over the next 10 years we are going to see a revolution in public management. Governments around the world are striving to tackle the enormous fallout from the present global recession. Australia is in a somewhat unique position of being under less pressure than any government in the developed world to think hard about its public services. As for New Zealand, our fiscal and economic outlook lies somewhere between the relatively benign outlook for Australia and the extremely grim outlook for countries such as the United Kingdom and the United States with respect to their public finances. This is our challenge.

New Zealand's economic challenges

The economic context provides an important backdrop to my views of public-sector management. Consider first New Zealand's current economic challenges and how they contrast with Australia's. When comparing the Australian and New Zealand economies over the past 15–20 years—with the exception of the

---

1   This chapter is an edited version of a speech given by the Hon. Bill English MP to the 2010 ANZSOG Annual Conference in Melbourne.

Australian resources boom and the trade effect that brings—many similarities can be found. If you put aside the resources boom, you would find that Australia, like New Zealand, has experienced unbalanced growth. In New Zealand, at least, this growth has been sluggish, and too much of it has been driven by excessive debt, over-consumption and fast increases in government spending.

The New Zealand economy has become lopsided in two ways, and both need to be addressed for a rebalancing to occur. First, our trade sector has been in recession for five years, with no new jobs created in the export sector for a decade. Second, we need to address our rapid increase in external liabilities. Australia owes the rest of the world about 60 per cent of gross domestic product (GDP); New Zealand owes 90 per cent, with ours forecast to rise over the next five years. Both countries need to correct that imbalance; we simply cannot keep returning to global financial markets and asking them to lend us money. The Australian banks, which essentially finance New Zealand's external liabilities, have repeatedly told me that this is going to get more difficult and more expensive, not easier.

In an attempt to rebalance our economy, the New Zealand Government is currently embarking on a wide-ranging program of reform after a decade of stalling and inaction. To do this, we will be demanding more accountability and effectiveness from the public sector. The main reform we have made so far has been changes to our tax system. From 1 October 2010, we will be dropping income taxes considerably, with the top tax rate falling to 33 cents, the marginal tax rate on the average wage becoming 17.5 per cent and company tax becoming 28 cents. Tax on savings accounts will also be reduced. To pay for these changes, the New Zealand Government is increasing the goods and services tax (GST) from 12.5 per cent to 15 per cent, increasing the effective tax rates on property investment and closing a range of domestic and foreign loopholes. These changes are designed to rebalance the economy and increase our international competitiveness and have so far been received with a surprising level of bipartisanship. This is largely because of the policymaking process we followed, which I will discuss shortly.

As a result of New Zealand's recent sluggish economic performance, our fiscal position has dramatically reversed in the past four or five years. After 15 years of surpluses, we are now facing at least another five or six years until we resume surpluses. Even then we need surpluses of approximately 2 per cent of GDP to meet the obligations of the New Zealand Super Fund, a large sovereign wealth fund designed to offset the future costs of superannuation. Consequently, in the professional lives of most of our present-day civil service leaders there will not be a time when we have the easy money we had in the past 10 years. In other words, there will not be a time in the professional lives of our civil service when the government is free to simply increase the price it pays for public services.

To address this dire situation, we have set some tight fiscal constraints. Over the next four years there will be a 4.8 per cent real increase in government spending, or 1.2 per cent per year. This is difficult to compare with the Australian Federal Government's 2 per cent real increase per year, except that we know it is lower, partly because in New Zealand we cover all federal and state (provincial) activities under one roof. So far we have reprioritised nearly $4 billion of spending over the next three or four years from low-value and ineffective services to higher-value, frontline and more effective services. These are, however, the quick wins from a previous decade of loose management of government spending and rapid growth in government spending, particularly since 2005.

The 1.2 per cent goal will be hugely challenging, and New Zealand's public service has only recently started to understand what that might mean after a decade of 6 and 7 per cent compound annual increases. That said, whatever we do will look mild compared with the radical experimentation happening in the United Kingdom and the United States, where they are adding 10 or 12 per cent per year of GDP to their stock debt and, in some cases, shutting down entire public services. What will the community look like without public services? We will find out.

The outlook for the New Zealand public sector

Looking ahead, how are we going to live with these tight fiscal constraints? How are we going to deliver more (as the public is demanding) for less (as our finance markets are demanding)? To answer these questions, we will be looking for new ideas and directions and, frankly, I do not think they are to be found in Australia and New Zealand. That said, New Zealand will be looking at the best Australia can come up with and, similarly, we hope Australia will look to us. Around the world we will see a revolution in public service management. The prevailing literature and new public management approaches are conditioned by at least a decade of generous year-on-year increases in funding, and developed a complacency that 15 years ago was not found in our public services but has since re-emerged.

The large economic shifts that have recently occurred, particularly in the United Kingdom, the United States and Europe, mean that these governments will spend the next 20 years trying to first stop the massive increase of deficits they are currently running, and next work out how to pay back the significant public debt they have accrued. I do not believe we fully understand that while the economies of these countries will soon pick up, their public finances will be a mess for decades to come. These deficit economies face the prospect of cost-crunching innovations and dramatic downsizing of their public sectors.

The optimism of the past decade that smart people using the massive resources of government can transform society will depart these countries. That thinking has not only run out of money in most places now, but also actually achieved little that was genuinely transformational while it prevailed. New, more revolutionary experiments will have far less aspirational goals. We will have to determine which public services and income-support measures really matter—not just which ones people like, but ones that really matter. We will have to work out how to deliver those services for much less money.

At the same time another set of experiments will be undertaken. Those countries that are substantially in surplus—in our region, largely the Asian 'command' economies—are going to be developing internal demand, growth and private consumption and, therefore, demand for public services that currently do not exist in their own countries. As a result, I expect New Zealand and Australia will find themselves selling their frameworks for better management, better accountability and transparency to these emerging economies that are developing their range of public services.

Fiscal constraint and the 'responsibility model' for CEOs

In light of this, what are we doing in New Zealand, given that we have more fiscal pressure than Australia and do not have the benefit of a commodity boom to cushion the otherwise underperformance of our economy? The answer is what we call the 'responsibility model': a five-year plan centred on chief executives that incorporates some of the factors we believe will drive further change. As an incoming government in late 2008, we had a choice of ripping out 'savings' from the budget and embarking on a large-scale restructuring plan. We are not, however, doing that. We have left existing structures largely in place while establishing very clear fiscal constraints over the next four years. To do this, we are pushing the responsibility for managing resources onto our public-sector chief executives; it is not up to the Treasury or the Minister of Finance to ensure that we live within those constraints; it is up to the leadership of the separate sectors of government. We are consciously stress testing our existing, fairly devolved model of public-sector management.

There are two reasons why we are working with the existing system. One is simply that our election campaign was conducted just prior to the onset of the global financial crisis. Within days of us launching a major tax package with significant revenue costs, Lehman Brothers bank went down, the Australian Government announced its deposit guarantees, and the world suddenly changed. Despite these upheavals, we decided to stick with our original plans, having earlier specifically ruled out large-scale structural change in the public services.

The second reason we have chosen to stick with the existing models is that New Zealand's experience through the 1980s and 1990s has taught a number of people—including myself—that long-term effective change is driven by people who clearly understand the parameters they are working within and have the tools they need to implement change. That is why we are making chief executives of departments the fulcrum of change.

This 'responsibility model' requires ministers and chief executives to clarify exactly what results they want. We are using the basic tools of ministerial and chief executive accountability, and thus spend a good deal of time ensuring that discussion between the Prime Minister and his ministers exactly reflects these expectations over the next two or three years.

We believe strongly in an alignment of political and administrative expectations. The process of ensuring the Prime Minister and ministers are clear about their expectations and performance is something we value strongly. It is a process that takes time to build momentum; a culture of caution and risk management in our public sector has become deeply embedded in the decade. As ministers, we must keep demonstrating political support for change and reinforcing the mandate that chief executives can use tools and make changes without fear of political consequences. After two years, they are starting to believe us. We reinforce this message with regular oversight of the 10 different public entities that make up 80 per cent of government expenditure. Much work has been required using these very basic tools simply to slow the growth in government spending.

Continued cooperation with Australia is also critical to delivering quality services within tight fiscal restraints. Australian businesses own $45 billion worth of assets in New Zealand, so we are working with the Australian Government on everything from insolvency law through to businesspeople being able to get through customs more easily. We are developing institutions for intellectual cooperation and we have comprehensive access to Australian politicians and officials, granting us specific knowledge and relevant expertise when we want to lift that knowledge and use it. There is a much bigger body of independent policy analysis in Australia than in New Zealand, so it is practical for us to draw on the Australian experience, rather than do it all ourselves. For example, in a difficult policy area such as competition law it would be a good idea to appoint cross-membership on our competition regulators.

The challenges to further public-sector reform

There are, of course, many challenges associated with the 'responsibility model', but for experienced civil servants they will all be predictable. The first is that if we cannot generate early momentum, the public sector will doubt its politicians can stick to self-imposed spending constraints and so will hope and wait for a return to the status quo. Some in our public service are still trying to wait it out, but this approach will not work. To be blunt, hope is not a strategy for a professional civil servant. It has been tried often and has occasionally worked, but it will not succeed over the next few years because the global recession and difficulties of public finance are not going to change. In New Zealand, at least, there is strong demand from the public to see the civil service doing what they have had to do themselves: be careful with their spending and make sure they have clear priorities in their businesses or their household. There is thus popular support for our approach.

Second, in a devolved system such as ours, it takes time and effort to achieve the right balance between the collective and individual interests among ministers. I have learned the hard way that the public service will avoid doing something if ministers are ambivalent about it getting done. Even if one minister clearly wants to do it, if the others are lukewarm then that provides an excuse for stalling. In New Zealand, we spend a great deal of time getting the collective interests of ministers aligned—a significant challenge in a centre-right government in which ministers tend to come from self-employed and business backgrounds. In our system, they have considerable ministerial freedom to do or not do things. But once ministerial cohesion is achieved, that sends a clear and compelling message to the public service.

To assist with this endeavour, hard-wired accountability is essential. The complexity of the ministry at one end and the centrifugal forces of agencies trying to stay in the game at the other are not going to hold. We must develop different hard-wired models. Ideally that starts with ministers and it means that we probably need to rethink how cabinets work in order to achieve greater ministerial alignment (and reduce 'static'). Ministers need to work together to ensure the collaborative and cooperative delivery of services takes place. The New Zealand cabinet recently took 18 months to agree on a small program aimed at integrating social services at the local level. Principally, this was because, as Finance Minister, I refused to agree to it until we had a model of hard-wired accountability—not just another committee. Other ministers refused to agree for other reasons, but after 18 months we finally worked out how to integrate these services efficiently. It was a hugely instructive exercise for ministers because they are starting to realise that there is a problem out there and that problem often begins with us. At present the only powerful tool for achieving closer alignment is that ministers are ultimately accountable to the Prime Minister, who has the power to sack them. But modern cabinets require more than this punitive sanction to make them work effectively.

Our third and perhaps most important challenge is whether our public-management system permits or encourages the kinds of solutions that are now required. In the past 20 years there have been many attempts at 'joined-up' or 'collaborative' government. But solutions such as shared services, joint procurement, and joint decision making across a sector do not fit naturally into the parliamentary appropriation process, or into the traditional structures of the public service—an institution whose hierarchal accountability has not altered for many years. Most of these attempts at collaborative government, at least in New Zealand, have failed ultimately because the processes of 'joining up' are actually very inefficient. They take enormous amounts of time and effort and do not always result in better accountability. Usually, frustration prevails and all parties return to their original modus operandi.

Consequently, it is a challenge for public servants to develop strong 'internal governments' to run joint processes. In New Zealand, we are expecting them to do this without strong direction from a highly centralised process. To facilitate this, we have supported a handful of collective processes such as joint procurement and, beginning soon, administrative and support services benchmarking shared services in the health sector. We are, thus, focused on the issues associated with administrative change because we are pursuing a program of organic change. Additionally, we have also set up an internal infrastructure unit to create better capital management.

In each of these examples, our chief executives have the choice of picking up these tools or not; they are not compelled to use them. Initially progress has been slow, but the momentum is now picking up as chief executives begin to realise that when they forecast their costs against their revenues they find a significant negative gap. This financial pressure can promote the case for change; CEOs' revenues are flat, their costs are rising and over the next four years that gap will grow every month that they sit on their hands. This message is starting to have an impact.

Allowing voluntary participation in these collective initiatives maintains a healthy tension between central agencies and other policy entrepreneurs, while providing a great way of showing public-sector managers the value of spending time and effort collaborating. Essentially, if executives are not willing to enter into collaborative endeavours (and sit through the interminable meetings this usually involves) then they should not have to, but if this is the case, they must find another way to improve delivery. If they want to use new media to achieve better communication they can. We believe that voluntary participation is critical to ensuring public servants make genuine progress, rather than just ticking the box on reporting to the minister. Nevertheless, the internal governance of back-office processes is merely a first step. Admittedly, we are yet to fully achieve this, but we will.

The next major step is to determine the outcomes we want in the wider community and structure accountability and governance in the public sector around those outcomes. Yet, such an approach conflicts with our traditional model of parliamentary accountability. The fact is though, the traditional model of parliamentary accountability might account for the money, but it has singularly failed over the past 20 years to account for results. In New Zealand, for example, we have been through a long process of trying to upgrade the scrutiny of our select committees. But from a minister's perspective, it is not a fearsome forum, largely because of the huge information imbalance between opposition MPs and ministers.

Accordingly, we need to resolve the tension between accountability for results and accountability for the money. An example is the criminal justice system, which we in New Zealand are trying to make less costly and more affordable. New Zealand has one of the highest imprisonment rates in the world, but locking people away is expensive. Consequently, at a time when funding is tight, we have to find new ways to foot the bill for tougher sentences for serious criminals—something the public is demanding. One response is to examine carefully the prosecution and imprisonment rates for less serious offenders to determine what patterns are forming. So, four years ago our justice-sector agencies in New Zealand began to work together to better understand what happens in the justice pipeline—who is arrested and why, how they come to the attention of the police, how they move through the courts, how they end up in prison and what does it all cost. This has generated some initial operational solutions for a more effective and a more just and humane system.

We can get some benefits within the current justice system, but one recurring problem is that we have a series of agencies with their own statutory powers. The police are different to the courts, which are different to the corrections services, which are different to the probation people, who are different to the non-governmental organisations. Each of these organisations has a strong culture that is typically hierarchical and rigid. Having analysed the ways the justice pipeline works, the fundamental next step is not to again recite the appalling statistics about which groups are more likely to end up in prison, which has been the stuff of public policy in this area for too long, but rather to develop a governance regime that is going to allow us to drive the outcomes that we want—namely, reduced prisoner numbers.

For the existing public service, providing this type of advice is much more difficult than performing business as normal within their part of the justice pipeline, because we are asking them to fundamentally alter their relationships of power, funding and authority. They will do this only if we can develop a strong enough constituency in the public who demand fewer people in prison, for example, or less youth offending. But at the moment we do not have a suitable structure; instead, it is an amalgam of chief executives and police commissioners all trying to work their way in a similar direction. If we are really going to drive reform, so we can head off the current demand for another 3000 new prison beds in New Zealand, we are going to need a new governance structure. Our public service has not thought nearly hard enough about how it will change the accountability regimes to drive the outcomes we need with less money to spend.

In the sector of criminal justice in New Zealand, we will not meet public expectations within current fiscal constraints with the current institutional arrangements in place. We simply cannot do it. It does not add up. To do this our public service must focus strongly on how to cut through multiple layers of authority, risk management and minister management and actually put people in charge of outcomes.

This issue is not unique to the justice sector; it is far more pervasive. In New Zealand, we are currently undertaking a broad front of reform in the areas of workers' compensation, long-term welfare, social services, social housing and defence. In almost every case the key issue is not policy analysis but rather governance. Our public service finds itself on the edge of a revolution with almost none of the tools that it most needs in order to negotiate the next 10 years.

Using open policy development to anchor reform

The logic of my argument is that the entire policymaking process is going to be subject to intense pressures for change. It needs to be more efficient and have better incentives and it needs an injection of energy because the world is changing fast. The model of a large standing policy capacity available just in case the government needs it is the product of a time when money was easy. It is no longer applicable. As an incoming government, we found ourselves needing to use a different model in order to get clarity and results. We have been trying a different policy approach. Instead of relying exclusively on the public service, we have used a combination of officials, academics and private-sector experts. As an example, consider the process we have used for our tax changes.

If you imagine the political risks in putting up a GST, which we did, how then did we find ourselves in a position where we are yet to lose our heads over it? The answer is that we used a combination of expertise to enlighten a public service that had previously been too sealed off from the rest of the world. We succeeded, in other words, by using a very open process of making policy.

At the start of 2009, we decided to look at the tax system and not to do it behind closed doors. We created a 'tax working group' led by Victoria University in

Wellington and comprising academics, private-sector experts and officials—but not headed by an official or by a politician. We did not prescribe what they may or may not look at; we gave them very broad parameters. The key instruction we gave them was that every week or two they had to publish their work. This they did, publishing working papers, deliberations and minutes on the Internet, covering the wide range of topics on tax reform that reflected their very wide brief.

This real-time publication generated a high degree of media interest and diminished the role of the politicians to nothing more than keeping an open mind. To illustrate this, when the media, upon reading the first publication, asked the Prime Minister which dreadful things he had in store, his response was firm: 'Well, we're not ruling anything out.' This was probably the most critical moment in our policymaking process thus far in this term, as it subsequently enabled a high level of public discussion among the media, commentators and bloggers. In the end, after determining the problems and short-listing the potential solutions, it actually generated a consensus about which response the government would make, so that by the time we announced our solution—an increase in the GST—there was no backlash, as the many thousands of people who had participated in the public discussion could understand the reasons for it and expected it.

The government is increasingly using this kind of open policy development. Recently, we published the latest report of the 'welfare working group', which has been looking at our long-term welfare problems, including issues surrounding welfare beneficiaries and social housing. The group, which includes no officials, will next meet with the social-housing sector, and after their findings are published, we will make some decisions. Even though the social-welfare sector traditionally votes overwhelmingly against the National Party, they are giving us rich and positive engagement because they can see that we are taking the issue seriously and are listening to what they are saying. Indeed, what most people at the coalface have to say is very sensible—once they forget which party you are from. They are usually extremely frustrated by their inability to meet the needs that they see as immediate.

The only specific demand we made of the welfare working group was to ask them to determine what the problems were and what kind of changes we might need to make—ranging from how the relevant institutional arrangements interface with government through to how those affected fit into their broader communities. We put together a very challenging group of people who covered the full range of ideological views.

With this form of open policy development, the barrier for entry into the process is now zero. Anyone can access nuanced policy analysis within an hour on any topic you can think of in a way that when I was a junior official took two or three people in a team several months to assemble through a literature review. The barriers to entry are very low because access to stores of knowledge is now virtually costless. But what is more important than the knowledge is the feedback loop, and this is something the public sector is going to have to learn quickly, because if we do not get into feedback loops then those loops will just go around us. Governments coming into power will, as we did, create a loop outside, because there is nothing like the experience of opposition to teach you about this. Having spent three terms in opposition, by the time we came to power we had assembled more than 100 specific undertakings, a multi-billion-dollar tax-cut package, and a detailed first 100-day plan. We did all this with three policy advisors.

The key point here is that we do not need a big policy infrastructure to generate credible policy. The public service—certainly in New Zealand—will find that as the fiscal constraints begin to bite, it will be competing with good-quality, cheaper options for policy advice. Of course, good policy advice is underpinned by those ethics that are at the core of the public service—the professionalism, the institutional knowledge and the inherent continuity—but not at any cost. That is going to be the challenge of the next five years or so. We have learned from our experience that an externalised process with immediate, real-time feedback loops can generate high levels of energy in a policy process. Fast learning by politicians and officials provides a strong focus, and ultimately builds political support as much by the way you do the policy as by the results themselves.

Conclusion

In conclusion, the past decade was largely one of complacency. An excess of cash and confidence was ascribed to the public sector, not just in New Zealand but in most developed countries. The results of this largesse of cash and confidence are not overly impressive. Government is bigger but core social problems remain intractable; voters are sceptical that their cash was well used. The benign economic conditions of that decade will not occur again in our professional lifetime. But has the way we think about public services and public policy changed as much as the world has in the past two years? The answer is no, not yet. Our thinking will have to change.

In New Zealand, we have chosen a path of considered and consistent change over time, rather than rapid restructuring. We have engaged with the leadership of the public service because we believe they have the capability and the sense of mission to make the changes that will be required. I am confident that if we use the tools available plus a wider range of resources alongside the public service then New Zealand will succeed in this new era. There is also a moral dimension to this: we have a large obligation to the next generation. Remember, there will be fewer of them coming into the workforce as we leave it. The cost of inertia and inaction—at least in the New Zealand economy—will be a double burden for a society with not only an ageing population to support but also large public debt as a legacy of the past couple of years. We owe it to those young people to pay our own way, to pay our own bills as we go, rather than leave them with two lots of bills that they might believe they do not deserve. And because we owe it to them to pay our own way, we need to innovate, take risks and push the boundaries. The clock is ticking.

6. A portent of things to come: lessons from a reforming minister

The Hon. Lindsay Tanner

This contribution was written during the 2010 election campaign—a period when some commentators were suggesting the age of reform was over. Indeed, the first half of 2010 saw a series of extraordinary events that punctuated what perhaps would otherwise have been a steady period of reform progress in Australia. But these should not be viewed as a portent of things to come.

I was directly involved in reform efforts over the past three years in my capacity as Minister for Finance, and indirectly as a shadow minister for a much longer period. Shadow ministers have a bigger influence than many people think, because by merely defining the theatre of political combat, they and their party can play a significant role in our system. For example, what they choose to oppose the government on, what messages they choose to convey and whether they choose to be creative or simplistic all help define how Australian politics unfolds.

Of all the reform efforts I was involved in as a minister, this chapter will focus on two of the more interesting and significant: first, the process of harmonising and reforming regulation across Australia through the Council of Australian Governments (COAG) business regulation and competition working group; second, the roll-out of the National Broadband Network. I have chosen these two reforms because in very different ways they provide some important lessons for people who are interested in working out how to make things actually happen, rather than merely looking like you are making things happen without doing it, which unfortunately is the dominant dynamic of modern politics.

Reforming the federation: the COAG working group on business regulation and competition

Consider first the COAG working group on business regulation and competition. The genesis of the competition and business regulation reform agenda dates from December 2007, when under the auspices of the Prime Minister, the premiers and chief ministers met to focus on one primary objective: the harmonisation of regulatory regimes across every state and territory. This was to be no mean feat, as Australia's range of regulatory frameworks was extremely diverse, with some broad and far-reaching, but others very specific, with a focus on particular sectors or particular activities.

Twenty-seven items in the field of competition and business regulation were identified for reform and put on the agenda by COAG. Of course, being 'put on the agenda' does not imply that anything might happen, nor that anybody might actually do anything after they leave the meeting. Indeed, for many politicians, putting items on the COAG agenda serves merely as a symbolic device. Everybody involved can return to their respective constituencies and tell them that yes, the item in question is being dealt with because it is on the COAG agenda. And should anybody be so rude as to inquire what 'on the COAG agenda' actually means (which usually they are not), such politicians can resort to glib rhetoric and gobbledygook, which confuses the average person so much that they give up.

The 27 items COAG identified covered areas of concern where no progress was being made. Examples include occupational health and safety legislation, trade licensing (for example, for plumbers and electricians), personal properties security registration, environmental assessment processes, the building codes that apply around the country, rail safety laws, heavy transport laws, laws governing food labelling, laws governing chemicals and plastics, financial services (for example, the nationalisation of regulation of trust companies and margin lending), and so on.

This is just a small sample of the issues that in aggregate covered a substantial portion of total economic activity across Australia. And when we looked at each of these, what we found is a patchwork of regulatory regimes and arrangements across the country, sometimes contradictory, sometimes non-compliant. For example, in the area of food labelling, it was physically impossible for a company to produce a product that complied with regulations all around the country, because to be compliant in South Australia, for instance, automatically made it non-compliant in Victoria, and vice versa. The end result was that if producers wanted to sell their products nationally, they must produce different versions or different labels for different jurisdictions.

Thus, since its creation in 2007, the COAG working group on business regulation and competition has slowly and methodically worked through each item, in the process always inching the agenda forward. It has been a particularly interesting exercise insofar as the group is populated by senior officials of Treasury and the Finance Department, but, until recently, co-chaired by two federal politicians, Craig Emerson and myself. And, much to my amazement, all 27 areas for reform are still broadly on track. At the outset, I said privately to Craig Emerson that if, at the end of the process, 20 of the areas had been addressed, I would be satisfied. That appraisal now seems like an underestimation. And while there have been instances of slippage during those three years (for example, state and territory elections can delay the process), overall the reform process remains on track.

It will, however, take several years more until all 27 problem areas have been addressed. Why? Because first and foremost, what is required in this reform process is to reach 'in principle' agreement about what is going to occur. That could involve a single national scheme, or it could be a template piece of legislation in an individual state that other states and territories agree to implement by reference, thus creating an identical regime across the federation. Similarly, it could be mutual recognition, or it could be harmonisation. There is a variety of possibilities, often involving line agencies and line ministers.

Further, once in-principle agreement has been achieved, the process still has several stages ahead of it. First consideration must be given to the 'detail', which can be challenging. Then it must pass through individual cabinets—eight or nine of them, in most cases. Next it will usually end up on a legislative program, and once it has passed through a lower house, it must finally pass through an upper house. And although this last problem does not apply to Queensland, the Northern Territory and the Australian Capital Territory, everywhere else it does. In total, this then represents a lengthy process, and of course inevitably during various points of that process there has to be some degree of consultation with stakeholders. Thus, it is a reform process that is quite protracted.

One danger when pursuing the harmonisation of laws across the country is the tendency to race to the bottom or move to the lowest-common-denominator law. This danger arose in a number of the 27 areas. There is always a temptation to default to the easiest position under pressure from both ends of the regulatory spectrum. At one level, businesses quite validly say to us 'look, we don't want you to end up simply dragging everybody up to the most intrusive, most burdensome regulatory arrangement that applies. We don't want to be harmonised up.' Equally, we did not want to do the reverse, which was to default to whoever had the weakest laws and the lowest costs, because nobody would accept that. Consequently, it means that in some cases you enter some very complex negotiations.

A classic example of this is the unfair-contracts arrangements in consumer law, where Victoria had a much more rigorous regime than most other states. We had commissioned a Productivity Commission inquiry into this area, which had come up with a compromise model. It was not quite as strict as the Victorian arrangement, but for many states it meant that if they adopted it, it was going to become substantially more rigorous than what had prevailed previously. Consequently, the Commonwealth ended up in a position that was tricky to navigate. Chris Bowen was the line minister directly responsible for consumer law, and did a good job navigating it through the ministerial shoals across the various jurisdictions. We finished with something that is not exactly the same as the Productivity Commission proposition, but not totally dissimilar. The end result is we got criticism from the consumer movement for stepping back from the strict Victorian regime at one end, and criticism from business for strengthening consumer-protection laws in unfair contract provisions everywhere else.

You also have to maintain broad stakeholder support or tolerance for the reform directions. In the area of occupational health and safety laws, New South Wales had the toughest laws, with criminal penalties that business was completely freaked out about. If the Commonwealth had said we are going to make the NSW laws the template across the country, business groups would have then replied 'no, we will stick with the ramshackle variety we currently have'. Backsliding would have occurred.

Finally, in order to keep the COAG reform process on target, the working group established key milestones to drive progress. There was, for example, a detailed analysis in each case involving individual milestones to be achieved on a six-monthly basis; so by December 2010 we would aim to reach a certain stage, then by July 2011 another, and so on. Generally, these milestones were met.

Reform lessons from the COAG review process

I have learned a number of significant lessons from my experience in the COAG working group on business regulation and competition. First, the real enemy is inertia. One of the great lessons I have learned from being a minister—having been a shadow minister for such a long time—is that government is finite. It might look infinite when you are in opposition with one or two advisors, up against the department with 1500 people and a ministerial office with 10 or 15 people in it, but in reality government is finite. There is only so much time in the day and so much capacity to deal with issues, so many key people who can absorb challenging questions, deal with pressing issues, make decisions and implement them. As a result, either overtly or by accident, the reformer must make priority choices, with less important issues simply falling by the wayside.

So it is with the 27 areas identified by COAG for reform. The principal reason there had been no action to address them previously was systemic inertia—the fact that nobody had got around to doing anything about them. While politicians might have made noises about reforming these areas and occasionally business organisations complained about some of the particular issues, the truth was that nobody had been motivated enough to say 'we are going to make this happen'.

Even when reformers are actually pursuing a reform agenda, inertia can still be a problem. It takes a huge application of political will to maintain momentum and motivation, to keep the blowtorch to the belly of all those involved, and to galvanise a state or territory into reaction if it is lagging behind in a particular reform endeavour. Without such application, will and energy, a reform process will simply fade away over time.

Obviously, elections are a major cause of reform inertia. At any given time in Australia there will be an election happening somewhere, or sufficiently close to disrupt the ordinary business of government. Consequently, a reformer trying to gain the cooperation of every government in Australia with a particular reform program is always susceptible to being disrupted by an impending election, or indeed an election that is happening, or that has just happened.

In fact, in the majority of regulatory cases that I was dealing with during this reform process, inertia proved a greater obstacle than any serious vested interest opposition to what we were setting out to achieve. In the odd case there were minor issues to be tweaked, but most of the time the various interests involved were reasonably constructive, as we were not tackling problems where there were huge institutional barriers to reform.

A second salient lesson I have learned from this reform process is the complications that can arise from the variations across state boundaries. Consider the following examples to illustrate how complex things can get. Buying a car in Australia generally involves national organisations financing your purchase through a system of personal properties security registration. In essence, the nature of the activity does not vary across the country; after all, buying a new car, or a speedboat, is largely the same process, be it in Perth, Melbourne or Sydney. Consequently, you could be forgiven for thinking that setting up a national register to replace the existing state and territory arrangements would not be overly difficult. That is initially what I thought, until we stumbled across the fact that the fees that are currently paid—or were paid—varied enormously according to each jurisdiction. For example, some states such as Western Australia ran on the basis of cost recovery, while others such as New South Wales had arrangements according to which the fees were much larger, and were hypothecated to their fair-trading regime. As a result, the fees for personal property securities registration were being hypothecated to help fund Consumer Affairs inspectors and officers in Dubbo, Newcastle or wherever.

Unsurprisingly, this situation creates a stand-off; each side looks at this and says (in the case of Western Australia) 'we don't want to put our fees up', and (in the case of New South Wales) 'well, we don't want to put our fees down, because that leaves a hole in our budget'. An impasse prevails. And of course, as a way of ending that impasse, both parties put their hands out to the Commonwealth for financial aid. I am bitter and twisted about those issues because basically that is the default position of almost everybody in public life. Being Finance Minster, you feel the pointy end of it.

Such is the prevalence of this problem that when I used to have one-on-one meetings at community cabinet, I would jokingly suggest that we could save a lot of useless dialogue by allocating everybody a piece of cardboard that says 'give me money', and they could walk up in front of me and hold it up. This federalism-related complication is a classic example of a problem that was not immediately apparent until we really dug into the issue. Then of course we did have to come to the rescue with some incentives, at least for the initial period.

Another illustration of the problems that arise from state and territory variations became apparent when we tackled the issue of harmonising food-safety standards. This happened when we reached an agreement with the states, territories and New Zealand according to which a common regulatory framework would be created, but enforcement would remain in the individual state, territory, and New Zealand jurisdictions. Superficially, that sounded entirely reasonable; the Commonwealth did not have the infrastructure or the expertise to be on the ground inspecting or enforcing such laws. And yet, in this case, as in many others, a great deal depends on the interpretation of extremely obscure aspects such as what particular levels of chemicals might apply and so forth.

So, while we were able to create a formal regulatory structure specifying the types and levels of ingredients that could go into food, the reality was that a great deal of decision making occurred below that level at the discretion of the various inspectorates. Often these inspectorates had developed an extensive culture of protocols or arrangements through which they were actually telling manufacturers what they may and may not put in products. We then immediately came up against the challenge of ensuring there was jurisdictional harmony across decision making by the enforcers, which made the whole process infinitely more complex.

A third lesson from our experience with the 27 items on the COAG regulatory reform agenda was that there is huge benefit in doing these things as a 'job lot', not one-by-one. When you do these things on a one-off basis, you tend to force people to retreat to absolutist positions, whereas if you have a whole range of things going on at the same time, and they are broadly going through the same mechanisms, you have the capacity for implicit give and take, which broadens your scope to get good outcomes. In other words, by working across a number of areas simultaneously, the scope for negotiation between the jurisdictions becomes more three-dimensional.

Individual states implicitly understand that if they take a 'dive' on this issue then the odds are pretty good that somewhere else they are going to get looked after, and it will be somebody else who has to take the 'dive'. While I have no evidence that any explicit horse-trading or deal making was entered into, I have no doubt that the constructive tenor of the approach that all states and territories took was influenced by the knowledge that there were swings and roundabouts. Hence, in some respects, probably the most important lesson of all out of this is to have a broad canvas, and have lots of moving parts, because that gives you the maximum opportunity to keep everybody onboard. It is important that everybody thinks they are getting a reasonable deal in the totality, even if they have lost some important items along the way.

The fourth lesson I have learned during this reform process is the importance of central agencies in government to set and keep pushing the agenda. I was so impressed by their endeavours that I took to calling the business regulation and competition working group of COAG the 'central agencies club'. What is especially valuable about such agencies is the presence of senior experts who are seriously committed to reform. Such figures actually have responsibility for the big picture and want to oversee productivity improvements and the accession of genuinely national harmonised regulatory arrangements. In contrast, people in line agencies often do not share that perspective, and nor should they, as that is not their prime responsibility. As a result, if you are running the Department of Transport in South Australia, for example, your job is to worry about safety on South Australia's roads. It is not your job to worry about broader productivity issues or inter-jurisdictional harmonisation; productivity interstate is far removed from your responsibilities.

Accordingly, it is crucial to have central agency buy-in, and in this case we had central agencies driving the process. Moreover, the Prime Minister's decision to attach the deregulation responsibility to the Department of Finance was a wise move, as it put this agenda at the heart of government, not to mention at the heart of that so-called 'central agencies club'. Such a move was instrumental in driving this agenda.

The fifth lesson has been the important role of the Business Council of Australia. Every time I met with them over the past few years, I kept encouraging them to continue hitting the front pages of the *Australian Financial Review*, as there is nothing like external pressure to push issues up the political agenda. Subsequently, their role, and to some degree that of some other employer organisations and business organisations, has been crucial in keeping the issue in the public eye, and thus ensuring we are still actually doing things.

This is the great challenge in this reform endeavour: how do we popularise and get wider engagement amongst the community with these kinds of issues, especially if their content innately makes it difficult to attract attention? The best answer I could come up with was to point out in every speech I made on the subject that people in New South Wales are quite happy for me to drive on their roads and rely on Victorian authorities to tell them that I will probably drive safely and responsibly. But, if I were a Victorian plumber, they would not allow me to fix their toilets without sitting for a licence exam for plumbers in New South Wales. Clearly, it is a dangerous business fixing people's toilets, and one that is far riskier than driving on their roads. It is extremely difficult to popularise regulatory reforms of this kind because they are incremental, spread over so many activities, and because only a small number of people understand how important they are.

Despite these not insignificant challenges, the COAG business regulation and competition working group has thus far been outstandingly successful. Not only is it on track to achieve its reforms in the 27 specific areas, but it has also proved to be an effective working model for continuous cooperation and collaboration between the two levels of government, rather than occasionally coming together every six or 12 months. As a result of this working group, there is now an almost continuous dialogue going on across key players in the central agencies, both at a state and a federal level. This augurs well for future agendas, and provides a foundation for future reform.

Telecommunications competition and the National Broadband Network initiative

The second major reform I was involved in intimately over a reasonable period was the National Broadband Network (NBN). In 2002 I was shadow minister for communications, and, together with then Opposition Leader, Simon Crean, launched a telecommunications reform agenda. At the heart of this major policy statement was the concept of structurally separating Telstra's business activities from its retail services. To impose a structural separation would enhance transparency and improve competitiveness. At the time this was considered a somewhat radical proposition; the idea had been touted by various quarters for quite a long time, but this was the first time that either side of politics had seriously put it on the political agenda. Steven Conroy replaced me as the shadow communications minister in 2004, and since that time the two of us have focused relentlessly on one core objective in telecommunications: getting the industry structure right.

Telecommunications is today almost as important to our economy as financial services. It is becoming equally as significant to the lifeblood of economic activity as moving money around. And yet, because of the Howard Government's obsession with privatisation and its failure to deal first with issues of industry structure that would have created a genuinely competitive industry arrangement, we ended up with a situation where Telstra as a private monopoly was too powerful for any government to effectively regulate. One need only consider the problematic relationship between Sol Trujillo and the Howard Government as an example. As a consequence, rather than liberating its enormous capabilities for innovation, risk-taking, and being a world leader in its field, Telstra instead focused its creativity, energy and dynamism on gaining the regulatory regime and squashing competition and innovation. Telstra accounted for two-thirds of our entire telecommunications industry and yet the protective regulatory structure in place skewed all the incentives in the wrong direction.

I do not blame Telstra for that. Throughout the past decade and a half, under different leadership, the company made decisions in the interest of its shareholders, and as the management of the Telstra Board saw fit. I do, however, blame the Howard Government for failing to address these issues, and then finding itself in a position where the roll-out of broadband (principally using high-speed coax cable) in Australia was significantly behind many comparable countries, whether in terms of access, speed, price, or any other facet. This was because under the Howard Government's industry structure for the telecommunications sector, the dynamics were all skewed against rapid technological change, rapid innovation and the development of new products.

The National Broadband Network is designed to address this problem. It is not just a piece of infrastructure—huge though it is in that context. Rather, it is also a giant reform agenda that is about creating a genuinely level playing field in Australian telecommunications. Incidentally, I believe Telstra would continue to do extremely well on such a playing field, as the company's emphasis would shift from lawyers gaining regulations to more innovation, better marketing, better product development and competing from a position of genuine strength.

When I started pursuing it, the idea of a structural separation for Telstra was considered something of a fringe position. I was initially unable to garner any serious interest or support from organisations such as the Business Council of Australia or the Australian Chamber of Commerce and Industry; they were happy to berate Labor for its perceived failings on economic reform in certain specified areas such as industrial relations, but when it came to the need for serious reform in telecommunications—of fundamental importance to most if not all of their constituency—they were not forthcoming.

Further, because there was not much academic research being conducted into these issues, there was a virtual vacuum in the public-policy world about them. Graham Samuel and the Australian Competition and Consumer Commission (ACCC) were enormously important in their support, although because they are not a public-advocacy body they were constrained. Nonetheless, the commitment of the ACCC to following through on the national competition policy principles from 1995 was an ever-present pressure in the debate that always helped to focus attention on the problem.

Nor, paradoxically, was the media significantly interested in the issue. *The Australian* and the *Australian Financial Review* would occasionally cover the topic, only to forget about it for extended periods. *The Age* proved more interested in the telecommunications sector, but was relentlessly anti-reform, giving regular coverage for people such as Kevin Morgan and Ken Davidson, who do not believe there is a problem and think that competition is not a significant matter in areas such as telecommunications.

In spite of these challenges, in perhaps ways that nobody anticipated, we have progressed to a point where a new world of genuinely competitive world-class telecommunications is going to be available for Australia, and for Australian businesses. And the bill to separate Telstra should pass in the next Parliament.

Reform lessons from telecommunications and the NBN

The lessons from the telecommunications reforms are: first, build a convincing case; second, focus on the deficiencies being experienced by ordinary people and ordinary businesses, which ultimately drove the impetus for reform; third, create champions wherever you can in the political world, policy communities and in the wider community. As a consequence of this last point, the demand for serious broadband has moved from the fringe information and communication technology (ICT) world into mainstream Australia, whether as consumers or as businesses. And finally, try to mobilise the interests that support you to be as active as they can in the public debate.

All of these points are significant lessons drawn from my experience in telecommunications reform. And yet, many challenges remain if we are to introduce high-speed broadband in Australia and transform our infrastructure from the digital dark ages.

The National Broadband Network is about breaking through the inertia and resistance to create a genuinely viable, competitive, innovation-driven and risk-driven piece of national infrastructure. Under this system all-comers from Telstra down will be able to compete on equal terms, and which retail provider becomes a commercial success will be determined by the provider's capacity to innovate, take risks, provide services people want and mobilise the necessary capital.

So, there is much genuine reform taking place in Australia, despite some media commentary suggesting the contrary. But unfortunately, the majority of these reforms are of the regulatory and procurement ilk, which is not the kind of issue that sells newspapers. Be assured, even if you are not reading about it in newspapers—do not be fooled—reform is happening out there. And there will always be the need for more reform as we progress into the future.

7. The agenda for achieving a world-class public sector: making reforms that matter in the face of challenges

Stephen Sedgwick

This chapter begins by discussing some key issues surrounding public-sector reform. It will then explore public-sector change at the national level in Australia since the modern reform era began in the mid 1970s, and the implications for us today. My primary focus will be directed towards the comprehensive reform program set out in the landmark publication *Ahead of the Game: Blueprint for the reform of Australian government administration* (Moran 2010), which is in the process of being implemented, subject to the policy priorities of the Gillard government.[1] The chapter will conclude with some thoughts about what tomorrow might bring and how we can continue to work towards having a world-class public sector and maintain the momentum needed to support sustainable change.

Public-sector reform in theory and practice

Reform is essentially about balancing continuity and change, choosing between incremental change and more substantial change. As the management thinker Charles Lindblom put it, 'incremental reformers' are concerned primarily with marginal improvements that they can agree on in practice, whereas critics of incrementalism are concerned with a more systematic approach to setting objectives and achieving measurable outcomes (Lindblom 1959:79–88, 1979:517–26). Lindblom identified this dichotomy and the implications of each approach more than 50 years ago, but it still has resonance today. The challenge for reformers is judging when fundamental, rather than incremental, change is required.

In a recent publication, the Organisation for Economic Cooperation and Development (OECD 2010:27–8) identified five generic lessons to emerge from a study of global public-sector reform initiatives

---

1 In September 2009, the then Prime Minister, Kevin Rudd, appointed an Advisory Group chaired by the head of his department to develop a blueprint for major reform of the Australian Public Service (APS). The Advisory Group's report, entitled *Ahead of the Game* (Moran 2010), contained 28 recommendations across four themes. The current government has accepted all of them.

1. the importance of raising citizen awareness of, and support for, reform through public debates and consultation strategies

2. the need to consult extensively with public servants affected by reform

3. the requirement to reduce uncertainty, and therefore opposition to reform, by allowing it to proceed in stages—that is, 'incrementally'

4. the need for permanent, independent organisations for steering reform, especially after the initial stages in order to prevent incrementalism giving way to inertia and reform stalling

5. the importance of individual national jurisdictions supporting and collaborating with international public-sector research organisations in information sharing and evaluating reform approaches and progress.

All of these elements are to be found in previous reforms to the Australian Public Service (APS), but it is fair to say they certainly figure prominently in current thinking and initiatives and no doubt will continue to loom large in future. There is another important aspect to designing sustainable or fit-for-purpose reform approaches: the little-explored conception of a nation's 'administrative tradition' (Painter and Peters 2010). A sound understanding of the influence of a country's administrative tradition is needed in framing sustainable reform initiatives and charting their progress.

Exploring the key issues in Australian public-sector reform, 1976–2010

During the past four decades, successive Australian governments and the public sector have been called on to address the challenges of a rapidly changing world. They have done so by revising existing policies and programs and developing new ones. Public service leaders have sought to learn from past initiatives when framing new reform proposals. The outcomes of the recent review of the APS reflect elements of continuity and change with key themes from earlier public-sector reforms as far back as the 1970s. Successive generations of public servants are constantly called upon to adjust their thinking and practices to respond to the changing needs and expectations of their communities and to exploit new options to solve problems as technology (including administrative technology) changes.

Let us explore these issues by looking at the evolution over time of three major themes. The first concerns the public sector's stewardship role; the second, its success in centralising or decentralising its various functions and the effect this has on its operations; and the third, the effectiveness of the APS accountability framework. In each case, I will focus principally on the human-resources components of the reforms.

Two pieces of major legislation—the *Public Service Reform Act 1984* and the *Public Service Act 1999*—and the findings of a number of inquiries and task forces attest to the determination of successive governments to create an efficient and effective APS. The most recent of these is, of course, *Ahead of the Game* (Moran 2010), a far-reaching blueprint for the reform of Australian government administration, released in March 2010 and formally approved in May.

In examining the three key themes outlined above, I will be looking at this legislation and these inquiries as carefully considered responses to new demands on the public sector. It must be said, however, that we have been more successful in some areas than in others. The process is always one of learning and adaptation, of reconciling continuity and change, of managing expectations and making the best use of the available resources.

No single reform approach ever has all the answers—partly because our external environment is never static and neither should the public service be static; and partly because the balance between centralisation and decentralisation shifts over time as technology changes. Our most recent reforms—some of which have moved us back a little compared with earlier initiatives—are best viewed in that light.

Several forces have shaped public-sector change over the past four decades—a period marked by what one commentator calls 'a major re-conceptualisation of the role of government' (Nethercote 2003:12). The main influences have been

- new service-delivery opportunities, cost-saving opportunities and accountability demands created by advances in information and communications technology
- globalisation
- a more contestable policy formulation and service-delivery environment
- increasing community expectations of government—not just for high-quality services and efficient regulation, but also a palpable sense that 'government' should be able to solve almost any problem, no matter how complex it might seem, or how intractable it had appeared in the past—and growing intolerance of poor performance whether in direct provision of services or through regulation.

This has led to what has been called a 'reinvention of government'—one characterised by a more agile and flexible approach to public policy and a high level of responsiveness to society's needs (Albrow 2001:158, 162).

The stewardship role and the need to be *Ahead of the Game*

The findings of the Royal Commission on Australian Government Administration, known as the Coombs Inquiry, are well known. The Coombs Inquiry, which reported in 1976 (Coombs 1976), was the first large-scale inquiry into the Public Service since the 1920s (McLachlan 1920).[2] It took two years to complete and called on the APS to

- increase its responsiveness to the elected government
- improve its efficiency and effectiveness
- foster greater community participation in government.

Indeed, these themes have been reflected in successive APS review and reform processes since the *Coombs Report* was released in 1976—an important element of continuity in our reform process.

Coombs called for, amongst other things, stronger policy coordination across government through the Department of the Prime Minister and Cabinet and more positive steps designed to enhance the flow of information to the community. There were concerns at the time that departments were operating too independently of each other and possibly of government and that the APS was less responsive to the government of the day and their interpretation of changing community needs than it should be.

These themes were developed and enshrined in the *Public Service Reform Act 1984*, which stipulated that a portfolio secretary should exercise their responsibilities for the general operations of his or her department under a greater degree of ministerial direction than in the past. This emphasis was taken further in the *Public Service Act 1999*, which gave portfolio secretaries considerably more flexibility in administering their organisations and serving the public, but with greater accountability for results.

The key point for our analysis here is that by 2010 questions were being raised about whether our understanding of the role of the senior leaders of the Public Service had become too narrow over time. Compared with Coombs' times, now there is a strongly embedded acceptance that the APS must be responsive to the government of the day, and manage risk and deliver results for citizens (and not simply comply with processes). All of these were matters that, in Coombs' time, were in need of repair.

---

2   McLachlan was a retired Public Service Commissioner.

While not losing sight of those essential qualities of public service, some had begun to shift their attention to another question—namely, whether public service thinking had become too reactive, too government centred and too short term. This sparked a debate about what historically has been termed the 'stewardship role' of senior public servants. This role requires public servants to be more proactive and forward thinking—both in their management of the APS workforce and in their development of policy thinking and models of service delivery. Some of this is about the responsibilities of today's leaders to build the capability needed within the APS to respond to tomorrow's problems; some relates to the importance that should be attached to having strategic policy-advising capability within departments to advise governments about what the policy issues and approaches should be.

The domestic and international environments in which nations now operate present political and public-sector leaders with a number of pressing challenges. These have become known as 'wicked problems' and include, in our case, nationwide water shortages occasioned by an unusually long drought; concern about some seemingly intractable, multifaceted social issues such as Indigenous disadvantage, homelessness and mental health; and growing international attention to 'diabolical problems' (to use Ross Garnaut's term) such as global climate change and security challenges, including those related to several large-scale terrorist attacks on a number of continents.

The recent *Ahead of the Game* report (Moran 2010) picked up these themes. It set out a comprehensive change strategy for the APS, which, first and foremost, re-emphasised that the needs and requirements of citizens have to be at the centre of policy design, service design and delivery; it also challenged the Public Service to be more forward looking. The report called on the senior leaders of the APS to look again at how programs are designed and delivered to ensure that they meet the needs of citizens in ways that are convenient for them rather than for public servants, and to minimise regulatory burdens. These require more 'joined up' approaches to government and a re-examination of how we hold agencies accountable for results that need several of them to work together. Some of these proposals challenge our traditional accountability models, which I will discuss below.

Ahead of the Game placed specific responsibility on a new public service leadership forum—a Secretaries Board—to find better ways of joining up government services and articulating an accountability framework that reflected contemporary understanding of how government needs to interact with citizens. It will also involve strengthening the capacity of the APS to provide strategic, big-picture advice that addresses the most difficult challenges of the day, among them the capacity to identify fundamental rather than incremental change when the situation requires it. Agencies have been challenged to assess their capability in these matters and to systematically set about building capability if they are currently deficient.

The performance of agencies and individuals should be assessed in a number of ways, notably through the introduction of systematic capability reviews that will be conducted centrally using teams and approaches to be developed by the Australian Public Service Commission (APSC). Importantly, *Ahead of the Game* put renewed emphasis on the fact that the APS is a long-lived institution with responsibilities to the future and not just the present; that the APS workforce needs to be resilient in the face of the unexpected, and to develop policymaking capability ahead of predictable need—in other words, to look towards tomorrow and see what issues might emerge in future that we should begin to research today, ahead of need.

The new Secretaries Board, comprising portfolio secretaries and the Public Service Commissioner, along with an expanded senior leadership forum (the APS 200) will be central in driving the stewardship function. For example, a small group has been formed from within the APS 200 to take forward the APS capability and service-delivery improvement agenda set out in the Management Advisory Committee report *Empowering Change: Fostering innovation in the Australian Public Service*, released in May. Along with its responsibilities to identify better ways to 'join up' government for citizens, the board also has responsibilities to oversee the development of the APS workforce, including through more centralised approaches to leadership training and talent management.

The APS blueprint will have far-reaching consequences for Australians and public servants. It represents a recognition that many traditional approaches to public policy no longer work as consistently well as they once did. Consequently, governments and public servants increasingly have to review and, as necessary, refresh their models of policy formulation and service delivery in response to the expectations of citizens. And APS leaders cannot perform this role well without managing their organisations in order to ensure that they are adaptive, self-critical, outward oriented—that is, especially citizen focused—and forward thinking. *Ahead of the Game* sets out how they can go about this internally and in their relations with citizens.

Striking a balance in centralisation and decentralisation

The 1976 Coombs Inquiry reaffirmed the need for centralised oversight of public-sector employment legislation by the then Public Service Board, the body responsible at the time for the APS industrial-relations and human-resources functions (and a predecessor of the APSC). In the interests of achieving a more open but better integrated public service, Coombs, however, called for the creation of a separate cadre of APS senior executives and the beginnings of devolution from the centre—more specifically, from the Public Service Board—of greater responsibility for agency operations to agency heads.

This began a process of devolution of human-resources management that played out over many years and culminated in the abolition of the Public Service Board in the late 1980s and the introduction of the current *Public Service Act* in the late 1990s. The board was replaced with a Public Service Commission with a relatively limited role. It was responsible for developing the Senior Executive Service and training, consulting and advising government on public-sector change, and some human-resource systems and human-capability alignment functions such as recruitment, promotion, dismissal, mobility and retirement matters. Under the provisions of the *Public Service Act 1999*, agency heads were given all the powers of employers over staff, subject to a new ethics framework enshrined in the Act in the form of legally enforceable APS Values and a Code of Conduct.

Parallel reforms had occurred in respect of financial management so that agency heads and their senior managers were now provided with full responsibility for reconciling their organisation's budgetary, performance and accountability, and risk-management priorities with those relating to recruitment, training, employee development and leadership. Eventually, agency heads also received power to determine pay and conditions within their agency, subject to only light central oversight.

Some centralised elements remained, however. In the case of human-resources management, the APSC's role, for example, was to be one of promoting and reviewing APS employment policies and practices across the Public Service, as well as quality assurance in the areas of people management, training and career development, and leadership. The essential point is that these centralised elements were very light handed. The commission was to promote and encourage good practice but had limited authority or leverage to enforce compliance.

Again, the 2010 reform blueprint recommended a subtle change of direction. It proposed an amalgam of past, existing and new approaches to the challenges we face, many of which call for more innovative thinking. In the human-capital area, for example, *Ahead of the Game* moved beyond 'people management' as we have traditionally defined it to a more holistic philosophical approach, which recognises that the short and longer-term capabilities of our organisations need to be planned for and systematically developed.

This reflects a realisation that good people management underpins an effective human-capital strategy, which in turn underpins the capacity of the APS to achieve its strategic objectives and meet the evolving demands of citizens. It also proposes, in essence, a degree of re-centralisation—but not of the same order as we knew in the past. It proposes that agency heads retain all the powers of an employer, but that these powers should be exercised within a more consistent, centrally determined and monitored framework. The commission will have more and stronger levers to promote good practice and to expose poor practice.

Current government policy is that greater consistency will be reflected, for example, in new arrangements for better aligning pay and conditions across agencies and, on efficiency grounds, in a continuation of the trend towards more centralised information and communication technology (ICT) management. Moreover, *Ahead of the Game* requires the APSC, for instance, to

- establish APS-wide frameworks for human-capital management, including in respect of workforce planning
- simplify APS recruitment processes so as to attract the best applicants from the public and private sectors
- revise the legislated APS Values to a smaller set better able to influence workplace behaviour
- revise the APS's performance-management frameworks to ensure not only that poor performance is identified and managed but, for the first time, that high-potential individuals are systematically identified and their development accelerated
- establish a Strategic Centre for Leadership, Learning and Development to achieve stronger strategic alignment between the commission's leadership development and talent-management activities and contemporary human-capital priorities of the APS
- undertake human-capital benchmarking, capability reviews and a citizens' survey.

A Human Capital Priority Plan is to be developed for consideration by the Secretaries Board to assist in implementing these initiatives and, over time, identify emerging systemic workforce issues for the APS at large. Additionally, the longstanding emphasis on APS-wide, whole-of-government collaboration as a means of generating optimal outcomes will be strengthened. These reforms challenge the Public Service to adopt a more systematic and consistent approach to workforce planning and to developing its people. At the moment only 30 per cent of agencies undertake systematic workforce planning and only 8 per cent actively engages in talent-management activities. More consistent approaches are to be developed and promulgated, and performance routinely assessed and supported by the commission. The aim here is to avoid both excessive interference from the centre and the development of a compliance or 'tick box' mentality in agencies.

The important element of this reform is to provoke debate within agencies and at the level of the Secretaries Board about the needs of the APS workforce, and to embed active management of the workforce into agency practices by concentrating on strategically relevant issues that add value to an agency's management. These issues will need to be established and periodically updated through dialogue with agencies and their leadership. A central element in this process will be to build a workforce that reflects the diversity of the population whose needs the APS seeks to anticipate and serve. In a couple of critical areas—especially in respect of the representation of Indigenous Australians, those with a disability or, at senior levels, women—the APS certainly has room to improve. Improved performance and talent-management processes will be put in place; clearer work-level standards designed to enable better alignment of skills and training to job requirements are to be introduced; and salaries and conditions will be better aligned.

It must also be noted that there has been a degree of re-centralisation over time in respect of some financial-management functions. But these changes have essentially responded to new opportunities presented to exploit economies of scale using centralised purchasing—for example, in respect of travel—or common services or ICT. The fundamental thrust to devolution of financial management, the flexibility of agencies to reallocate resources and the use of program budgeting remain unchanged.

Effective accountability: from the Financial Management Improvement Program to horizontal coordination and performance assessment

If we look back once more to the Coombs Inquiry, it called for greater agency accountability by means of a strengthened annual reporting process for departments. Coombs also advocated a higher level of accountability for individual public servants. An ambitious initiative designed to improve departmental financial management—a recommendation of the 1983 Review of Commonwealth Administration—also occurred at this time, with the establishment in 1984 of the Financial Management Improvement Program. It encompassed a broad range of change initiatives in the areas of corporate and program management, program budgeting, and performance evaluation. These reforms were designed to improve strategic planning and policy formulation and to ensure the more efficient use of resources. They were to be realised through better framing of goals and objectives and improved management and measurement for results and outcomes.

A central theme of the *Public Service Act 1999* was that public administration, including systems and human-capability alignment functions, would be improved by strengthening the accountability—and integrity—of government. This was in part a response to the increased availability of online data that could be used to make judgments about public-sector performance. The *Ahead of the Game* report took the accountability issue a step further. It proposed that secretaries devise a coordinated response to develop more variegated accountability and performance arrangements better suited to the new modes of policy implementation and service delivery that the APS must increasingly deploy. Initially, this calls for an accountability model that will ensure effective oversight, without stifling innovation and preferably while also reducing the web of unnecessary rules that saps employee initiative. Some of these rules are devised within agencies and seem to add no value. But it goes further than that.

A major challenge for a citizen-centric service is to present a more joined-up face to citizens—one that respects the convenience of the users rather than the providers of services. There are many aspects to this issue. For example, traditionally we have defined accountability through a single minister and the public servants who deliver a specific program on his or her behalf. But some problems cannot be addressed through a single program or minister, such as Indigenous disadvantage in remote localities. Better outcomes for these Indigenous Australians require improvements in health, housing and schooling, amongst other things, that are mutually reinforcing. Yet, traditionally we have assessed these programs separately, and no-one has accepted responsibility for the overall outcome—failure to advance the life chances of these Indigenous peoples has been seen as someone else's problem; in effect, they have fallen between the cracks in our accountability framework. The fact that responsibility for some of these issues is shared across several levels of government in a federal structure simply compounds the degree of difficulty.

The new reform agenda challenges the Public Service's leadership to work systematically through our service-delivery models and accountability frameworks to find solutions to how we can better hold agencies and individuals accountable for their contribution to achieving desired outcomes when a number of programs, portfolios or jurisdictions are involved. In parallel with this, the APS intends to establish more robust and effective risk-management systems, as well as new monitoring and reporting arrangements. These include an improved performance-assessment framework for secretaries—one that is to involve a higher level of feedback from their peers and subordinates as well as stakeholders. *Ahead of the Game* proposed that feedback should be sought about all of the roles that agency heads are to perform, including their stewardship responsibilities, their management of their department and outcomes achieved, and the quality of their policy advice. Moreover, the APSC has also been given a formal role in monitoring and reporting on the implementation of all *Ahead of the Game* recommendations. Together with the introduction of human-capital benchmarking, capability reviews and the citizens' survey, these represent a significant increase in the leverage available to the APSC in effecting change.

Delivering reform: reflections to date and into the future

Today's reform agenda is the latest manifestation of the reform imperative whereby policies and practices are redefined in response to a changing national and international governance environment. Three specific developments have been significant in changing the environment in which the APS functions

1. improvements in civic participation as a result of increasing education levels, leading to more specific citizen expectations of government

2. continual economic pressures and the need to produce better outcomes with fewer resources

3. Australia's ageing population and workforce (including the APS workforce).

Moreover, our challenges are more numerous and their nature more complex than in the past, leading us to rethink how the Public Service can work better internally and engage externally with citizens and with the best contemporary thinkers to find solutions. What lessons have we learnt from four decades of reform?

APS leaders must be clear about their objectives and ensure that the effort they are expending remains commensurate with the benefits they expect to generate. Sound reform should be defined as the delivery of sustainable change over time. This change is as much about human capability and alignment as it is about administrative change; it is about achieving the right balance between systems and people; and it is about balancing the needs of the present and the future (including stewardship obligations), centralisation and decentralisation of functions. I also believe that incentives and the accountability framework matter. Effective change requires behavioural changes. This requires good communication of the case for change and the nature of what is expected; however, in addition, the incentives structures and the accountability regimes have to be aligned with the objectives of the reforms. And, as we all know, in applying incentives and administering accountability, what the regulators and public service leaders do is more important than what they say—their actions will drive an organisation's culture and its approach to the acceptable standards of work, values and focus on clients.

It is also important to recognise that the various elements of a specific reform process need not be undertaken or completed all at once; establishing priorities for change and realistic time frames is a significant component of sound reform. In the tradition of our predecessors, we should continue to enrich reform approaches through self-critical evaluation, research and knowledge of international best practice—in short, with evidence; and, as *Ahead of the Game* advocates, do this by forging better links with public administration research and training institutions such as ANZSOG as well as other think tanks. This applies to all aspects of public-policy activity.

Ahead of the Game has rightly drawn on recent developments in the United Kingdom, Canada and New Zealand to adapt and borrow new techniques to foster accountability and improve links with citizens and others to achieve better outcomes. The citizens' survey and capability reviews are examples of this. But it has also learnt from our experience with past reform about the need to get the balance right between immediate needs and longer-term ones, and between too loose and too tight approaches to devolution of authority to act. These are reflected in the heightened attention to be paid to the stewardship responsibilities of secretaries and the stronger emphasis on approaches in the blueprint to managing human capital that acknowledge that we are 'One APS' (Management Advisory Committee 2005) united by common values and expectations of performance.

A further reflection is that reform is about people—their motivations, the incentives they face, their flexibility and willingness to change. It is about focusing and refocusing on factors such as employee engagement. Kenneth W. Thomas, for example, has identified four central elements in what he terms 'intrinsic motivation': a refinement of the traditional conception of engagement, and one that produces better organisational outcomes. It does so primarily because the greater autonomy employees often enjoy compared with in the past allows those with a high level of intrinsic motivation to perform very effectively. These elements are: a sense of meaningfulness; a sense of choice; a sense of competence; and a sense of progress (Thomas 2009). In the APS context, we professionalised our financial-management processes long ago but so far have not achieved the same degree of professionalisation of our human-capital approaches—perhaps because they are too difficult to quantify and therefore address.

And the final observation based on our experience since the 1970s is the central importance of good leadership; this imperative recurs in review after review. In each generation, we need to develop leaders who embody the best values of public service; who look outward to identify the needs of those whom we serve; who look forward to anticipate emerging issues and build resilient organisations; who are not afraid to take on the tough issues; who are accountable; who know how to communicate and manage change; and who are prepared to respond to and seek to influence the agenda of the government of the day. Building such a leadership cadre is a fundamental precondition for sustained reform and high performance.

Conclusions: reform as invention and reinvention

The reform initiatives undertaken by successive Australian governments and the public sector since the mid 1970s attest to their desire to better serve Australians through more flexible and agile responses to changing national and global imperatives. They also demonstrate that, as Australia's place in the world changed and we were called upon increasingly to function in a globalised social, economic, governmental and public-sector environment, we learned to develop more agile and responsive approaches to meeting the needs of governments and citizens. This imperative remains—perhaps to a greater extent than in the past. According to one commentator, the most critical question for every twenty-first-century organisation is this: 'are we changing as fast as the world around us?' (Hamel with Breen 2007:42).

Highly functional public-sector organisations that effectively align their human-capital and structural arrangements stand the best chance of successful adaptation. Such organisations will also be efficient stewards of their resources, adept at achieving the right balance between centralisation and decentralisation of their functions, and guarantors of effective accountability. They will maintain their capability only if they address internal challenges such as those associated with the growing 'virtual' workplace—for example, the pressures on workers such as isolation arising from tele-working (already a trend in the United States). And we can fulfil our role effectively only by keeping a close eye on how society is changing and by equipping ourselves to deal with societal change. I am certain that we never can get to a final point—there is always room for improvement in what we do now, and the reform process itself is essentially a matter of invention and reinvention.

Charles Lindblom in 'The science of "muddling through"' declared that incrementalism as an approach to public administration did not lack rigour; it represented a legitimate and considered response to addressing challenges and delivering outcomes in the actual forest of events public-sector managers face daily. Twenty years on, he had not changed his mind, writing that we were 'Still muddling, not yet through' (Lindblom 1959:79–88, 1979:517–26). As Lindblom recognised, the enterprise is not about conquering but about persevering, continual adaptation and change. And therein lies the challenge— and the excitement—of being a career public servant.

References

Albrow, M. 2001, 'Society as social diversity: the challenge for governance in the global age', in *Governance in the 21st Century*, Organisation for Economic Cooperation and Development, Paris.

Coombs, H. C. (Chairman) 1976, *Royal Commission on Australian Government Administration Report*, AGPS, Canberra.

Hamel, G. with Breen, B. 2007, *The Future of Management*, Harvard Business School Press, Boston, Mass.

Lindblom, C. E. 1959, 'The science of "muddling through"', *Public Administration Review*, vol. 19, no. 2 (Spring), pp. 79–88.

Lindblom, C. E. 1979, 'Still muddling, not yet through', *Public Administration Review*, vol. 39, no. 6 (November–December), pp. 517–26.

McLachlan, D. C. (Chairman) 1920, *Royal Commission on Public Service Administration Report*, Government Printer, Melbourne.

Management Advisory Committee 2005, *One APS—One SES: Senior Executive Service of the Australian Public Service*, Australian Public Service Commission, Canberra, <http://www.apsc.gov.au>

Management Advisory Committee 2010, *Empowering Change: Fostering innovation in the Australian Public Service*, May, Australian Public Service Commission, Canberra.

Moran, T. (Chairman) 2010, *Ahead of the Game: Blueprint for the reform of Australian government administration*, Advisory Group on Reform of Australian Government Administration, Department of Prime Minister and Cabinet, Canberra.

Nethercote, J. R. 2003, 'Australian public administration in perspective', in Australian Public Service Commission, *The Australian Experience of Public Sector Reform*, Commonwealth of Australia, Canberra.

Organisation for Economic Cooperation and Development (OECD) 2010, *Making Reform Happen: Lessons from OECD countries*, Organisation for Economic Cooperation and Development, Paris.

Painter, M. and Peters, B. G. (eds) 2010, *Tradition and Public Administration*, Palgrave Macmillan, Houndmills, Basingstoke, UK.

Thomas, K. W. 2009, *Intrinsic Motivation at Work: What really drives employee engagement*, (Second edition), Berrett-Koehler Publishers, San Francisco.

8. Collaborative reform: lessons from the COAG Reform Council, 2008–2010

Mary Ann O'Loughlin

During the 2007 federal election campaign, Kevin Rudd pledged to reform Commonwealth–state relations if elected—an unusual mandate to request, given that Commonwealth–state relations have rarely garnered much community interest.[1] But Rudd was very experienced in this field, having worked in both the Commonwealth Public Service and the Queensland Public Service, as well as serving as chief of staff to former Queensland Premier Wayne Goss. In the lead-up to the election, Rudd promised to 'end the blame game', with a primary focus on health. This message resonated with the community, allowing Rudd to take a reform agenda for Commonwealth–state relations into office.

The Labor Government was elected in November 2007 and Rudd held his first Council of Australian Governments (COAG) meeting in December. The meeting agreed 'to a new model of cooperation' and identified seven areas of reform for its 2008 work agenda. COAG also agreed to change the nature of Commonwealth–state funding arrangements, with treasurers to report on proposed reforms. To drive reforms, COAG agreed to meet four times in 2008.

Reforming federal financial relations

The COAG meeting of November 2008 welcomed a 'new era in federal financial relations', with the *Intergovernmental Agreement on Federal Financial Relations* coming into effect on 1 January 2009. There are three main elements of the new financial arrangements

1. National Specific Purpose Payments supported by new National Agreements

2. National Partnership payments associated with National Partnership Agreements

3. a performance and assessment framework to support public reporting and accountability.

---

1 References to the 'state' or 'states' include the state governments and territory governments.

National Specific Purpose Payments and National Agreements

Under the new framework for federal financial relations, the previous more than 90 different payments from the Commonwealth to the states for specific purposes—many containing prescriptive conditions on how the funding should be spent—have been combined into five new National Specific Purpose Payments. National Specific Purpose Payments are ongoing financial contributions from the Commonwealth to the states to be spent in the key service-delivery sectors of schools, skills and workforce development, health care, affordable housing, and disability services. The states are required to spend each National Specific Purpose Payment in the service sector relevant to the payment but they have full budget flexibility to allocate funds within that sector as they see fit to achieve the agreed objectives for that sector.

National Specific Purpose Payments are associated with National Agreements between the Commonwealth and state governments. National Agreements establish the policy objectives in the service sectors of education, skills and workforce development, health care, affordable housing, and disability services. There is also a National Agreement on Indigenous Reform, which does not have an associated Specific Purpose Payment, although it links to other National Agreements and National Partnerships, which have associated funding.

National Agreements set out the objectives, outcomes, outputs and performance indicators for each sector, which are agreed between all jurisdictions. The agreements also aim to clarify the roles and responsibilities of the Commonwealth and states in the delivery of services and the achievement of outcomes. They do not include financial or other input controls imposed on service delivery by the states, and there is no provision for National Specific Purpose Payments to be withheld in the case of a jurisdiction not meeting a performance benchmark specified in a National Agreement.

National Partnership Agreements and payments

National Partnership Agreements outline agreed policy objectives in areas of nationally significant reform or for service-delivery improvements, and define the outputs and performance benchmarks. They cover a wide range of service sectors and reform areas, from health, education and housing through to business regulation and competition. National Partnership Agreements differ from National Agreements in that generally they are time limited and the associated National Partnership payments for the states are linked with specific reform activities or projects. The Commonwealth provides National Partnership payments for three purposes: to support the delivery of specified projects, to facilitate reforms, or to reward those jurisdictions that deliver on nationally significant reforms.

Performance and assessment framework

The third main element of the new federal financial relations arrangements is a performance and assessment framework to support public reporting and accountability. Under the Intergovernmental Agreement, the Commonwealth and states have agreed to greater accountability through simpler, standardised and more transparent performance reporting, and 'a rigorous focus on the achievement of outcomes—that is, mutual agreement on what objectives, outcomes and outputs improve the well-being of Australians' (COAG 2008).

Devolution and transparency

The remainder of this chapter looks more closely at COAG's collaborative reform of federal financial relations. It uses a framework put forward by Michael Barber, the expert partner in McKinsey's Global Public Sector Practice, who was previously head of former UK Prime Minister Tony Blair's delivery unit. Barber identifies three paradigms of public-sector reform

- command and control—top-down management
- devolution and transparency—devolution of responsibility, public accountability for results to drive performance, and incentives to encourage improved performance
- using markets and quasi-markets—including privatisation and contracting out.

COAG's reform of federal financial relations is a good example of the devolution and transparency paradigm

- responsibility is devolved—in this case from the Commonwealth to the states
- there is a strong accountability framework, with the COAG Reform Council responsible for public reporting of the performance of governments
- there is a range of incentives to drive performance, particularly public accountability under the National Agreements and financial rewards for the achievement of benchmarks and milestones under a number of National Partnerships.

For all paradigms of public-sector reform, Barber argues that there are three underlying requirements for effective reform: strategic direction, performance management, and the three Cs—capability, capacity and culture.

Strategic direction: focus from research and dialogue

Barber argues that a sustained, well-thought-through strategy is needed to guide reform. The COAG reforms of 2008 had the advantage of being guided by a strong sense of strategic direction. This was true both for the policy agenda in the areas of productivity, human capital and competition and regulation, and for the reform of the architecture of federal financial relations.

Much work had been done in 2005–06 to develop what was then called the National Reform Agenda for COAG. This agenda focused on human capital, competition and regulatory reform streams. The COAG reform agenda of 2008 built on this previous work.

In the area of federal financial relations, the strategic direction guiding the reforms was the outcome of a long process of research, consultation and debate. Although Kevin Rudd brought the issue of federalism reform to the fore in 2007, there had long been discussion and debate around the issues, informed by academic research into the problems with our federal financial relationships— particularly the problems of the overlapping roles and responsibilities of the Commonwealth and the state governments, and of vertical fiscal imbalance.

In a speech given in November 2009, Terry Moran, Secretary of the Department of Prime Minister and Cabinet, himself a strong advocate for the Commonwealth– state reforms, described the intensive work involved, and the resulting new arrangements. He said the reform process was:

> Long and painful; I played a role in Victoria and then at the Commonwealth level. Hear me when I say that the states and territories got what they had campaigned for. That includes a new basis for financial relations—96 Specific Purpose Payments reduced to six, saving the states and territories from much micro-management. It includes a new basis for accountability—agreed objectives, strategic outcomes, outputs and measures to guide these new streams of money and free the states to innovate in health, schools, vocational education and training, housing, Indigenous matters and other areas…And it includes a new independent umpire—the COAG Reform Council—to assess the performance of governments against the goals of the COAG reform agenda. (Moran 2009)

Moran's insight demonstrates that when the appropriate research and development work are conducted, a clear strategic direction for the reform can follow.

Performance management: moving to a new level

The second factor underpinning public-sector reform identified by Barber is performance management. This is where we at the COAG Reform Council come in. The council is central to the new accountability arrangements. The Intergovernmental Agreement gives the council significant responsibilities for assessment and reporting of the performance of governments under National Agreements and National Partnerships.

For each of the six National Agreements, the COAG Reform Council provides annual reports to COAG based on a comparative analysis of the performance of governments against agreed indicators. The first-year reports establish benchmarks against which progress in reform and improvements in service delivery can be measured.

For National Agreements, the Reform Council's performance-review process is a fairly intense exercise. The performance information for each National Agreement is received from the Steering Committee for the Review of Government Service Provision. The council's report on the National Agreement is due to COAG within three months of receiving the data, and the council must formally consult with the jurisdictions on the report during this three-month period.

The COAG Reform Council's main accountability role for National Partnerships is to independently assess whether performance benchmarks or milestones have been achieved before the Commonwealth makes reward payments to the states. As of November 2010, there were seven National Partnerships with reward payments agreed by all jurisdictions: six reward National Partnerships in health and education, and the *National Partnership Agreement to Deliver a Seamless National Economy*, which has 36 streams of regulation and competition reform. The council publicly releases all its reports about a month after submitting them to COAG; they are available on our web site (<www.coagreformcouncil. gov.au>).

Effective performance management depends on being able to measure results and change. This is acknowledged in the Intergovernmental Agreement, which notes that 'the success of the new framework for federal financial relations depends crucially on the development of robust performance indicators and benchmarks' (COAG 2008). A significant challenge for the council in undertaking its accountability role is the availability of performance indicators that are meaningful, simple and comprehensive for members of the public, as well as robust data to support these indicators and allow for analysis of change over time. After all, a key purpose of performance monitoring and reporting is to inform the general public about government performance and overall progress.

In its first-year reports to COAG on the National Agreements, the council highlighted the many problems with data and performance indicators that were hindering effective performance reporting. For example, the *National Healthcare Agreement* is a very complex agreement with 15 output measures, 20 progress measures and 70 performance indicators. For the baseline report, data were available only for 58 indicators in a comparable form. Many of the indicators are output rather than outcome measures. There are also no quality and safety measures, measures of patient satisfaction, or data on the extent to which the services are actually meeting need. The council has identified similar types of problems—although not on such a scale—with all the National Agreements.

The good news is that COAG, at its December 2009 meeting, requested the heads of treasuries to undertake a review of National Agreements and National Partnerships, covering the clarity and transparency of objectives and outcomes and roles and responsibilities, and the quantity and quality of performance indicators and benchmarks. The report was submitted to COAG at the end of 2010. We look forward to seeing the results of this work.

Reform culture: focusing on outcomes and performance

Barber's third underpinning for effective public-sector reform comprises three interrelated challenges when effecting change: capability, capacity and culture. Here I will focus on culture. The late management consultant Peter Drucker once famously said 'culture eats strategy for breakfast'. In other words, while strategic direction and performance management are important ingredients for effective reform, if the necessary culture for change is not in place, the reform agenda will not be achieved. There are two key points to be made here.

First, significant cultural shifts are necessary to ensure public servants—at both the Commonwealth and the state level—move from an input-orientated focus to an outcome-orientated one. This requires a new way of thinking, planning and measuring, and can thus be difficult to adopt. It is much easier and more comfortable to measure inputs (for example, the level of funding) than outcomes (for example, what results are being achieved with the funding). There is a risk that people will revert to command-and-control input measurement if outcome measurement proves too difficult. Strong leadership at the Commonwealth and state levels is essential to direct and support the necessary cultural change.

Second, we must move away from a culture that equates accountability simply with sanctions and punishment, be it by supervisors, the media or interest groups. Greater transparency in public accountability for governments' performance is a potentially significant achievement of COAG's reform agenda.

But it is essential that those whom we want to hold accountable have a clear understanding of what accountability means. Accountability should encompass not just monitoring, feedback and reporting, but also the extent to which governments are allowed the opportunity to act constructively on feedback about their own performance.

Concluding remarks

According to the contribution in this volume by Aart de Geus, Deputy Secretary-General of the Organisation for Economic Cooperation and Development (OECD), the confluence of two factors is necessary for significant reform: a broad-based popular sentiment that things have to change; and leadership that is able to translate this broad dissatisfaction into concrete reform proposals. Both these factors are often difficult to achieve, but the degree of difficulty increases with collaborative reform.

In Australia, collaborative reform involves nine jurisdictions, requiring the engagement of nine sets of popular sentiments and the commitment of nine frequently changing political and bureaucratic leaderships. And while Kevin Rudd garnered much public support for ending the 'blame game' during the 2007 election campaign, this support was focused on improving service delivery rather than identifying institutional requirements to do so. Additionally, it is difficult to build an evidence base around institutional reform, so it is harder to make the arguments and gather support for reform. For many reasons, popular support can be difficult to mobilise for what can seem like the arcane topic of reform of federal financial relations.

Regarding leadership, there are many associated issues that make collaborative reform difficult. First, the nature of our federation and form of government can pit Commonwealth leaders against state leaders; prime ministers, treasurers and premiers against line ministers; and, at the bureaucratic level, central agencies against line agencies. These key players often face very different pressures, including from interest groups.

In the public sector, we are also faced with the problem of the reformer bearing the brunt of the reform. In effect, we are asking public servants to design and implement their own reform, imposing measures on themselves that might significantly impact on how they have done their business in the past. This can result in a loss of power as the power shifts somewhere else.

These are interesting times for collaborative reform in Australia. As Julia Gillard begins her first term as elected Prime Minister, what can we expect her approach to be towards what Terry Moran calls 'the bold experiment'? Moran's view on the current exercise in collaborative reform is that if we do not see improved outcomes for Australians in service delivery then the opportunity will be lost and the future direction of the federation will change. On the positive side, there has been great progress in a short time through political and bureaucratic leadership at all levels—through the Commonwealth and states, across central and line agencies, through commitment and persistence, hard thinking and hard work. There is definitely momentum. The view of the COAG Reform Council is that the challenge is to stay the course and gain the benefits.

In his book *The Intelligence of Democracy*, Charles E. Lindblom argues that democracy is superior to other political systems because of the greater number of incentives to encourage intelligence and learning in the process of policy making. If this is indeed the case then the greatest opportunity for intelligent policy making across a federation of nine jurisdictions is to be achieved through collaboration with, and learning from, one another.

References

Council of Australian Governments (COAG) 2008, *Intergovernmental Agreement on Federal Financial Relations,* Council of Australian Governments, Canberra.

Lindblom, C. E. 1965, *The Intelligence of Democracy*, Free Press, New York.

Moran, T. 2009, Speech delivered at the Don Dunstan Oration, Institute of Public Administration Australia, Adelaide, 6 November 2009.

9. Entrenching 'Rogernomics' in New Zealand: political and academic perspectives

Jonathan Boston and Sir Roger Douglas

This chapter looks at the case study of public-sector reform in New Zealand in the 1980s and early 1990s, and what underpinned the success in moving this significant reform forward. I will briefly outline the nature of the reforms in question, then propose some explanations as to how these comprehensive, radical, and rapidly introduced reforms were made possible. I will conclude by analysing the outcomes of these reforms, before finally drawing some lessons from the experience. In the second half of the chapter, Sir Roger Douglas will offer his observations from the reform process, as one of its major architects.

Most readers will be aware of the radical changes that occurred in the New Zealand economy, public sector, and many areas of policy, health, housing, and the environment in the 1980s and early 1990s. In essence, we had a major reform period of about nine years—from 1984 to 1993. This fell into two categories: first, those reforms introduced by the fourth Labour government from 1984 to 1990; second, the reforms introduced by the fourth National government from 1990 to 1993.

Since then we have not experienced reforms of a similar magnitude. We have had minor reforms, but they have been of an incremental and sporadic nature. Of course, the fact these recent reforms can even be compared with those of the nine-year period is a testament to the longevity of that initial wave of reforms. Indeed, if the success of a reform is measured by its sustainability, one would have to say the New Zealand reforms have been largely successful. For the most part, they have been sustained over the course of several different governments, of different political persuasions.

In terms of the actual reforms, obviously there was a range of economic reforms that took the form of macro and micro changes. In essence they were about economic liberalisation, covering virtually every area of economic policy: trade policy, industry policy, competition policy, labour policy, tax policy, capital markets, major fiscal consolidation, monetary-policy reform, and so forth.

And it was in that context of radical economic liberalisation that we had a remarkable period of public-sector management reform. The significant legislative changes of that period included: the *State Owned Enterprises Act* of 1987, the *State Sector Act* of 1988, the *Public Finance Act 1989*, and then the *Fiscal Responsibility Act* of 1994.

As pieces of legislation, these acts anchored in place the reforms. Further, they radically changed the nature of our public sector in New Zealand in terms of our financial-management systems, human-resource management systems, the structures of our institutions and the accountability framework. We underwent a significant process of corporatisation, commercialisation, privatisation and contestability.

And in very broad terms, the key features of these new public-management changes included the remarkable speed with which they were introduced, the radical nature of some of the changes by the standards of New Zealand at the time, and, by international standards, the comprehensive nature of the changes. Nor were these one-off changes. They were part of a 'job lot', in the phrase used earlier by the former Australian Minister of Finance Lindsay Tanner. They were also relatively coherent. They followed a particular paradigm or ideological framework, being largely market orientated and liberal by nature.

But how were these changes made possible? Changes of these kinds rarely occur in democratic regimes internationally. How then was it possible to introduce these sweeping economic and public-sector reforms, and to do it so quickly, and effectively, and in a sustained manner? An explanation can be found in the work of John Kingdon, and his idea that in thinking about reforms we need to think in terms of three streams of activity: problems, solutions, and politics. In essence, during the period of radical reform beginning in 1984, these three streams came together in a rather unique way.

First of all, New Zealand was provided with a window of opportunity. This came about by an exchange-rate crisis in the middle of 1984 associated with the election, coupled with protracted economic difficulties—decades of economic decline creating a window of opportunity for people who were prepared to seize that window. In a sense, it was no longer possible to continue pursuing this approach. Something had to change.

Second, we had some ready-made solutions. For at least a decade, the Treasury had been planning ways to transform the New Zealand economy. As part of this process, they had prepared a series of thoughtful papers, and indeed at the time of the 1984 election, had produced a book advocating significant reform called *Economic Management*. Subsequently, at the 1987 election, a second book, called *Government Management*, was launched. So there were ready-made solutions to complement the work that the political parties were doing—not least Roger Douglas in the Labour Party.

The political stream emerged when the Labour Party came to power in 1984, thus completing Kingdon's trifecta. This new government contained an energised ministry of people who were prepared to take risks, and who were prepared to provide leadership. Had the government not had that willingness to take risks and the leadership capabilities of the people at that time, these sorts of changes would not have been possible.

But there is one other element that is critical to understanding the reform process in New Zealand, and that is the constitutional framework. Unlike the federation of Australia, New Zealand is a unitary state, making for a much simpler political system. Moreover, we have a unicameral parliament, so there is no Senate to block or divert reforms. Again, that is critical. And at that particular time we had first-past-the-post voting, enabling changes to be made quickly if you had a determined government with a clear majority in Parliament. Those conditions obviously do not apply in Australia, and they do not apply in most other democracies—or at least not to the same degree.

What about the results? Well, critically it would be fair to say in terms of the economic outcomes they have been mixed. While the economic reforms produced the positive outcomes of low inflation, a fiscal surplus from 1994 through to 2008, substantially reduced public debt and reduced unemployment, only relatively modest economic growth was to follow, at least in terms of gross domestic product (GDP) per capita.

The real wage gap with Australia has continued to widen, particularly in the past couple of years, and accordingly New Zealand faces the continuing problems of being a relatively poor neighbour to Australia. Why, then, were the economic reforms not more successful? That is probably the subject of another chapter, but there are a number of reasons, some of which will be discussed later in this chapter.

What about the state-sector reforms? From the evidence I have seen, and that I have been involved in helping to generate, it would appear these reforms were successful at least to some degree, if not to a significant degree. Evidence of improved efficiency, effectiveness and profitability of our state-owned enterprises certainly occured. Moreover, New Zealand continues to boast a low-corruption and high-trust environment for its citizens and businesses. Evidence from the two-yearly Kiwis Count survey suggests the services provided by the public sector are generally regarded as satisfactory, if not of good quality, by the consumers of those services.

And there has been relatively little pressure to revisit the fundamental features of the new public-sector regime. That is not to say there are not problems with it, but there is not huge pressure to reconfigure the regime. Together, this suggests that the reforms have been relatively successful.

There is, however, one unintended result of the new public-management reforms of that period of which we should not lose sight. Because of the huge public dissatisfaction with some of the ways in which these reforms were introduced, and some of the early consequences, we ended up with constitutional change. As a result of a series of referenda, we moved from a first-past-the-post majoritarian system to a mixed-member proportional system, otherwise known as proportional representation. This ramification was clearly not intended, and it has created an environment in which the reforms that were introduced during that period of 1984–93 could not be rolled out with such speed today. There is an irony in all this. Recently, we have seen evidence of this loss of reformist capacity over climate-change policy. Any reform proposal is now complicated by the system of proportional representation we have adopted.

Finally, let me identify five brief lessons from this reform experience. First, we could say the reform of some of the sectors of the New Zealand public sector has been more easily achieved than in others. Reforming the health sector has been particularly difficult, but also reforms in education, welfare, and environmental management have been much more difficult than in some other areas. And it is not difficult to understand why. Partly it is because of the inherent complexity of these issues, and partly it is because of the powerful interests that are at stake. It has also been because of a lack of leadership and vision.

Second, we have had far too much emphasis in New Zealand on machinery-of-government changes, which has been both costly and disruptive. Further, continual restructuring has tended to remain a feature. One of the drivers has been a situation whereby because chief executives have a significant amount of autonomy, they have the capacity to undertake reform. Consequently, when a new chief executive is appointed, you can almost guarantee that within six months there will have been a restructuring of the department. This restructuring fetish associated with the particular incentive structure in relation to chief executives has been one of the unfortunate aspects of our reform program.

Third, we have not given enough attention to the problem of size. We are a country of 4.3 million people trying to do everything that a country of 20 million does, or even one of 200 million. And that creates some very significant tensions, not least because we are essentially a second-world economy, rather than a first-world economy. How we address that, I do not know, but there are some interesting questions here that are relevant to the states in Australia.

My fourth lesson is that the reforms placed unduly high expectations on ministers, as the authorising agents, the principals and purchasers of services. The model we developed assumed that ministers would be competent and discerning purchasers, and, moreover, that they would be willing to specify their desired outcomes clearly. While I am not meaning to suggest that all ministers are incompetent or lacking in discernment, we can be reasonably confident of the fact—from 20 years of experience—that very few ministers are prepared to specify their desired outcomes with a high degree of specificity. And without that we have a fundamental flaw in our public-management system, which is predicated on the specification of outcomes, leading to the purchase of outputs, and then a purchase of inputs to achieve those outputs, all with the objective of achieving the desired outcomes.

And finally, through these reforms, we have created in New Zealand a public sector that is relatively risk adverse. There are a number of reasons for that, and I am not sure what the solutions are, but we have created a disincentive structure that actually tends to reduce the willingness of the public sector to provide the kind of leadership it did 25 years ago when Sir Roger Douglas became a minister.

Embracing the politics: the lessons from 'Rogernomics'

Sir Roger Douglas

In the remainder of the chapter, I will reflect on my experience as a principal architect of the reforms in question, but first I will elaborate on the aforementioned point about the comprehensive nature of our reforms. It is my firm view that if we are going to undertake reform, unless we aim to undertake it in a comprehensive way then it is probably not worth doing in the first place. If we are simply going to fiddle around the edges, or do ad-hoc reform, we are probably better to leave it alone, because the cost of what we are implementing is probably equal to any benefit we would get from the changes. There is no point, for example, reforming the financial-market area, if we leave the goods market, or the labour market, and the public sector itself, alone. So, reform needs to be done in a comprehensive way.

Turning to the politics of major reforms, this is of vital interest to the politician as opposed to the occasional commentator. Reforms start with the politicians. In fact, we often need a group of politicians who are prepared to lose, because often undertaking reform might be unpopular, or it might take a while to engender benefits for the public. So politicians need to ask the question 'why am I in politics?' And if it is because you want to be in perpetual power, you are not going to champion reform. And if you really want to achieve something then get on with the job.

Looking around the world (and certainly in New Zealand at the moment), most politicians ask themselves the wrong question. That question is: 'what can I get away with; what will the public accept?' And when a politician asks that question and designs a program accordingly, we will always get the wrong answer. The question politicians need to ask is: 'what should I do in the interest of the country?' And then one might ask a second question: 'how do I market that particular policy to the public?' It is at that point that some adjustments might be made.

I agree with the point made earlier by Jonathan Boston about ministers acting as purchasers, and authorising agreements with their departments covering the required outputs for the year. Most ministers simply sign what the department puts up to them. I always had the view—and it was one that I was pushing well before I got offside with the Prime Minister and left the ministry—that ministers need two or three outside advisors in order to be sure that they can clarify exactly what are their goals and priorities.

When I was Finance Minister, what we in Treasury did was quite simple. We listed under various headings or sets of activities the issues that were likely to come up, or that we wanted to come up. Then we would put in the next column what our approach to this issue was in the interest of the country. We then asked if we were to develop policy along those lines, how long would it take—usually how many years. We then tried to estimate the benefits for the nation. We then said: 'how do we market these ideas within the government and to the public?' And that determined our work program, but because there were always a lot more things on the list that we wanted to do we had to establish priorities. For example, port reform was considered to increase GDP by 1–2 per cent. We estimated what chance we had of getting it through, which we said to be 20 per cent. In the end, we actually did get it through.

Looking back at the New Zealand experience, wherever we introduced what I call quality policy, the policies lasted. Wherever we went for reform and went for the best options, and were prepared to take the heat upfront, those policies are still in existence today and are not the subject of much popular comment. Contrastingly, where we undertook less than optimal reform, such as in education, health and welfare, the problems still exist to this day. They are still on the agenda, and they will not be solved until we go for a more radical policy.

Strong leadership is required for reform not just in the political sphere, but also within the public sector. Yet consensus and support for major reform are unlikely to occur until it is actually implemented. Consensus comes when you make a decision, you implement it, and it actually works, and then people agree with you. In my case, if I had gone along to the trade union representing forestry workers and said to them 'we are going to reform you; you currently have 7000 members and on 1 April you will only have 2700', it is highly unlikely they would have agreed.

Therefore, one of the key factors behind our success in implementing our reforms is that we packaged the changes, and we aimed for quantum leaps. For example, we removed all the subsidies to farmers. They were getting approximately one-third of their income via the government in one form or another, and we eliminated virtually all the subsidies over a couple of years. But this would have been impossible to do had we not at the same time had microeconomic reform in terms of eliminating import licensing and lowering tariffs, so their inputs were cheaper, as well as reform of transport and the ports so the cost of getting their products across the wharf was halved.

So there was a package, and that was absolutely fundamental. Whilst some people lost their privileges, they actually gained from the fact that everyone else lost their privileges as well. And overall these people were probably better off because government was no longer the middleman.

I can well remember a meeting with a range of interest groups after my first budget. They had come to the view that our radical reforms were in the interests of the country, and therefore in their long-term interest—all, that is, except the road-transport operators, who thought that putting up their road-user charges by 48 per cent in one hit was excessive, but they were howled down. We did that because we wanted to end some of the monopoly rights the railways had. Hence, packaging reforms is absolutely vital to their success.

Further, speed is absolutely essential in any program of reform. Many people say that our program in New Zealand was implemented too quickly; I do not think we went fast enough. It is not too much speed that kills reform but rather uncertainty. The times when our government found itself in trouble were due to uncertainty. For instance, we were persuaded by the States Services Commission shortly before an election to visit and consult on the West Coast of the South Island. We were reforming the coalmines, causing them to lose half their staff, and the forestry sector, which lost two-thirds overnight. These were big employers on the West Coast, one of New Zealand's poorer areas. So we went down there to consult, leaving the affected families in limbo for three or four months. No-one knew if they had a future job or whether they would receive a generous redundancy payout. During this period, we went down to being 5 or 6 per cent behind in the opinion polls. Many people in cabinet were nervous about pushing on with such reforms, but we decided to go ahead. A month later, we were 15 per cent ahead in the polls again; what damaged us at the time was uncertainty, not the speed of the program.

But to act quickly we have to be sure of the reform principles and to have done the work program. Governments have only a limited time frame or window of opportunity. So if governments are thinking about a political time frame, they need to get their programs launched in order to see some benefits down the track. If they drift for too long then the motivation disappears. If we had not taken decisive action in 1984 then the consensus we built would have evaporated.

Another important lesson to remember is that in the midst of a major reform program the reformers should not allow themselves to blink. Everyone will come initially and want the decision makers to change their minds, but if they give any impression that they might then all the opponents' efforts will be focused on getting a change of mind. If, however, they think the reformers do not intend to change then they go away and get on with their own jobs. And we should remember that unless they get on with their jobs, we are not going to get any benefits, because it is not the politicians who create the real benefits it is those producers who change the way they do things.

Consultation is also important and it is important not to sell the public short. We should be upfront; we must tell the public what we are trying to achieve and why our approach is better than others. But we should consult against decisions that have broadly been made. We undertook a major round of consultation when we introduced a goods and services tax (GST), but the people who did that for us went out and consulted. They knew we had made a decision to adopt the GST; they were helping us work out how to do it in the best way.

If we are introducing substantial change, we should not be afraid to tell people the downside. If governments sell only the good side, they will not succeed. If there is going to be a downside—such as half the people in a particular industry losing their job—there is no point not communicating that. We must tell short-term losers why the reform is of benefit to the nation and ultimately of some benefit to them. It is also very important to tell the public about the reform program as far in advance as possible, because there are individuals and businesses out there who have to make the necessary adjustments. For example, when we undertook tariff reform, we announced a program for three or four years so that businesses actually knew the end point. There was no point announcing, say, a reduction in tariffs of 10 per cent if ultimately we were going to take 30 per cent off them. They needed to know. Some businesses might say they could live with a 10 per cent cut, but if they knew it was going to be 30 per cent in three to four years they would then decide on their business strategies. Maybe they would get out of certain lines, or import those lines, or concentrate on manufacturing a smaller range of products. So, the more notice we can give of our intentions, the better.

Where we did not succeed and what to do about it now

Some of our reforms failed or we ran out of time to pursue them properly. As in Australia and the United Kingdom, in New Zealand, the problems in health, education and welfare are yet to be adequately addressed. Over the past 20 years in New Zealand, we have thrown billions of dollars at these areas, and yet performance has not improved. In fact, productivity in health (after rising in the mid to late 1990s) over recent years has now dropped dramatically. Nor can anyone in New Zealand be happy with the outcomes of education, where 20 per cent of our kids come out of school unable to read, unable to do simple mathematics, and up to 40 per cent are not adequately prepared for today's world. Clearly, if other industries had such poor performance, they simply would not survive.

The problem is that over time politicians have created a rod for our own backs. We have arrived at a position where the actual institutional means of delivery—public hospitals, public education and public schools—have become the objective and the goal, rather than quality health care, an operation for anyone who needs one within a reasonable time, and a quality education for every child.

Moreover, if reformers decide to make some efficiency change, they are labelled as delivering a loss of equity, when in fact the truth is that we cannot have increased equity without improved efficiency. It is not a question of equity *or* efficiency. It is simply that we cannot have improved equity without improved efficiency.

So, what would I do about it now? The solution is relatively simple. We must open up the supply side; we must provide consumer choice, introduce competition, and get rid of the monopoly aspects of provision. For instance, I would provide the people of New Zealand with the existing option of staying within an education system that fails 20–40 per cent of the people it serves, but also provide new options, such as different incentives to parents. We might allow parents to receive the first $35 000 of their income tax free if they choose to opt out of the public system, putting an extra $6000 or $7000 in their pocket to invest in their choice of schooling and health cover. The same could apply for sickness or accident cover or unemployment insurance. But if we elected to do such things then two things would have to be ensured. First, people would have to subscribe to an educational provider for schooling, and would need to buy an approved health cover, and accident, sickness and unemployment insurance. Some of these insurances would be subsidised by employers—at least the accident and sickness parts. We would also encourage people to save so that they would have sufficient savings to look after themselves in retirement and in aged health care as well. Those already nearing retirement would not have time to build up their savings, so might need a percentage of the current pension to enable them to subsist.

If we undertook such reforms, we would transfer some 30 per cent of the economy—which is now largely delivered in New Zealand in a monopoly way—into a competitive model. I do not personally care whether it is the public service that provides it, or the private sector; I simply want quality services such as kids being able to learn. I want choice. If the new competitive schools do not work, they go broke, and someone else takes them over or offers the services.

Paradoxically, the key ingredient in being able to deliver such competitive services is some form of collective property. To undertake this reform, I would put all the schools—primary schools and secondary schools—into a single property company. We would next create a board charged with ensuring that competition took place. The fixed infrastructure would be maintained but choice of delivery providers would be given to parents as to where to send the child.

If we did that in New Zealand, we would see the same improvements in productivity that we saw in forestry, coal, telecommunications and the postal system in the 1980s and 1990s. In some of those cases, we saw productivity improvements of 100 per cent, and where real prices dropped by as much as 50 per cent. If it can be done in these areas, it can be done in the health and education sectors as well. But it cannot be achieved under the current bureaucratic system that we have in New Zealand.

10. Institutional renewal and reform: the challenge of the Commonwealth of Nations

The Hon. Michael Kirby

In July 2010, I was appointed to the Eminent Persons Group (EPG) established by the Commonwealth Heads of Government Meeting (CHOGM) held in Trinidad and Tobago in 2009. At that meeting were gathered the leaders of the 53 Commonwealth nations. They decided to establish the EPG in order to investigate, and report on, the essential ingredients of reform to the institutional arrangements of this global family of Commonwealth nations. There was a sense that in this era of institutional reform, there might be lessons applicable to the Commonwealth of Nations for the attainment of desirable identified objectives. At the least, this global challenge will identify some of the impediments that must be overcome if lasting reform is to be attained. This is always a complex and challenging task when it involves the creation of new structures and the disturbance of long-settled and comfortable ways.

This chapter will address the challenge of reforming the Commonwealth of Nations. I want first to examine some of the institutions that make up the Commonwealth of Nations, to identify the important role that these institutions play in a reform process, and to examine the new initiatives that will be necessary to assist the Commonwealth of Nations as it undertakes the present process of renewal. I will reflect briefly on the options for institutional reform of the Commonwealth generally and, of course, the views that I express are my own and not those of the EPG.

Second, I will seek to examine the importance of the common values that are probably still shared in the former British Commonwealth. Historically, this organisation has evidenced success both in changing and evolving its own characteristics and in influencing change in member countries where a clear and coherent voice can be found to that effect. The struggle against the oppressive apartheid regime in South Africa, and its later counterpart in Rhodesia (now Zimbabwe), constitutes an example of such success. I will show, however, that the Commonwealth has not always found a commonality of will in facing later challenges. In particular, the failure of the Commonwealth to adequately address serious human rights problems in member countries is an example of where the organisation has fallen short of the defence of the values that it ostensibly espouses.

My purpose is ultimately twofold: first, to demonstrate that the process of institutional renewal and ongoing reform is critical to ensuring effective policy development and implementation in the organisation in question. Second, I hope to show the importance of the constant evaluation and re-evaluation of policy objectives, based on identified institutional values. Only if those objectives are clear and coherent will true reform be proposed, sharpened, put in concrete form, delivered and maintained.

Shared British history and dialogue

The Commonwealth of Nations grew out of the British Empire—the largest, most diverse and successful imperial exercise in human history. The sun never set on the Empire in its heyday, early in the twentieth century. It comprised more than one-quarter of the land surface of the world and about one-third of its population; it was truly a time when the Royal Navy ruled the waves. Australians of my age grew up in the last decades of the British Empire, after it had survived the challenges of its enemies in World War II. Every 24 May, on Queen Victoria's birthday, my school celebrated Empire Day. It was to some extent a triumphant reminder of the warrior character of the British race, of its economic, intellectual and industrial inventiveness, of its strong institutions of law and government, and of its sense of racial superiority and destiny— ultimately shattered only by the drain on its manpower and treasure in the global war of 1939–45.

The Commonwealth of Nations was eventually formed in April 1949 to replace the British Empire and British Commonwealth. It was then, at the Commonwealth Prime Ministers' meeting attended by Ben Chifley of Australia, that the formula was worked out between Earl Attlee and Jawaharlal Nehru whereby India could remain a member of the Commonwealth without allegiance of its citizens to the British Crown. Until then, it was that allegiance that had been the cement that kept the British family of nations together. Unwilling to accord allegiance, Ireland departed, as earlier the United States of America had done. But in an inventive solution, it was agreed that thereafter the Commonwealth would be a community based on 'free association'. The British Monarch would be accepted as a symbolic head. In this way, King George VI added the title 'Head of the Commonwealth' to his royal titles. On the accession of Queen Elizabeth II, she was recognised as Head of the Commonwealth, an office she takes most seriously (Mayall 2010:26). In witness of this role, the first meeting of the EPG, held in London in July 2010, concluded with an audience with the Queen, as Head of the Commonwealth, at Buckingham Palace.

Various former links that once held the Empire and early Commonwealth together successively fell away, including judicial appeals to the Privy Council—finally ended in Australia in 1986 (*Australia Acts 1986* [Cwlth and UK]:s. 6) and in New Zealand in 2003 (*Supreme Court Act 2003* [NZ]). In addition, Commonwealth preference in trade declined after the 1960s. In a recent speech to the Commonwealth Legal Forum, Sir Shridath Ramphal, second Secretary-General, declared that 'Language, Learning and Law; these three are the most precious heritage of the Commonwealth; but the greatest of these is law' (Ramphal 2010:359).

Certainly, these are the fields in which, over my professional life, I have come to know and appreciate the work of the Commonwealth and of its Secretariat housed in the royal palace of Marlborough House in London.

There are nearly 100 associations that have the word 'Commonwealth' in their name. They bring together professional, institutional and other colleagues whose nations have substantially shared the experience of British rule and institutions. The Commonwealth Parliamentary Association, for example, taps the deep reservoir of experience found in the legislatures of Commonwealth nations. Because one of the core values of the Commonwealth is accepted to be electoral democracy, it is natural that the nations that substantially follow the traditions derived mainly from the British parliamentary legacy should find unity in an ongoing conversation between parliamentarians of Commonwealth nations.

As well as establishing the EPG, the *Affirmation* agreed at the 2009 CHOGM conference contains an extensive elaboration of the belief of the Commonwealth in 'the inalienable right of the individual to participate by means of free and democratic processes in shaping the society in which they live' (CHOGM 2009:12). The same document recognises 'that parliaments and representative local government and other forms of local governance are essential elements in the exercise of democratic governance'. Today such legislatures also participate in the Inter-Parliamentary Union (IPU) with its broader global membership and operation. There is, however, something especially comfortable and friendly in a meeting of personnel who share a common language, common history, many common institutions, common laws, common traditions and interests. Often these are unspoken. Sometimes they are even unconscious. But enough survive to make the dialogue capable of proceeding without so many adjustments for the differences that must be recognised in the United Nations and other circles.

In addition to professional and governmental bodies, and the regular meetings of ministers of Commonwealth nations holding similar portfolios, a very large number of civil-society organisations that have flourished within the Commonwealth enjoys representative bodies that focus on this connection.

Thus, the Royal Commonwealth Society (RCS) plays an important function in stimulating and maintaining the lines of connection that exist within the Commonwealth. In recent times, the RCS has taken a lead in exploring the attitudes of Commonwealth citizens and their knowledge concerning the Commonwealth, their criticisms of present arrangements, and their suggestions for the ways in which the Commonwealth links could be strengthened (Royal Commonwealth Society 2009).

Last year, the RCS conducted a so-called 'Commonwealth Conversation'. It was a hard-talking, candid, disparate and impressive dialogue identifying what is wrong in the Commonwealth and how its citizens might go about trying to improve it. A repeated feature of the comments that emerged was a criticism that the 'Commonwealth is just too timid; that's the problem' (Royal Commonwealth Society 2009:20); that 'the Commonwealth isn't serious about human rights' (p. 23), and that it must be more articulate and forthright in declaring what its values are and establishing frameworks to hold the member nations and their citizens to their obligations of upholding the shared values proclaimed at regular meetings of CHOGM (p. 24).

I cannot think of a single other international organisation that would welcome, encourage and support such a critical and public introspection about its own strengths and weaknesses. In the final published version of the RCS document, the Secretary-General of the Commonwealth, Kamalesh Sharmar, welcomed the enterprise. He said:

> I support the Commonwealth Conversation. It is extremely important that discourse takes place within the Commonwealth so that it is no longer seen as working along rigid paths or as being something belonging to the past, rather than something that belongs to the future. A future that is being shared. A future that is being shaped through discourse about expectations and possibilities. (Royal Commonwealth Society 2009:6)[1]

In some ways, the RCS seized an opportunity and took an initiative akin to the intensive public consultations in which the Australian Law Reform Commission engaged under my leadership in the 1970s and 1980s. The commitment that this then extracted from the Secretary-General is a welcome and fresh approach— certainly unusual in international agencies. It has also been welcomed by participants in the Commonwealth Conversation. In my opinion, there must be more such dialogue (Royal Commonwealth Society 2009:6).

---

1 Also see the very candid conversations in the Report of the Commonwealth Round Table Conference. See *The Round Table*, vol. 99, no. 408 (June 2010): '"A great global good?" Reviewing the modern Commonwealth' by Stuart Mole, pp. 321–4; and especially the contribution by Anwar Choudhury, p. 23.

There have been several investigations of ways to revamp the Commonwealth and to improve its institutional structure. A common theme of past inquiries has been the emphasis placed on the need to improve performance of the secretariat in London. This was recognised by CHOGM in 2009. The Port of Spain *Affirmation* expressed a demand for

> efforts to improve the Secretariat's governance, its responsiveness to changing priorities and needs, and its ability to enhance the public profile of the organisation. We commit ourselves to supporting the Secretariat in this endeavour. We also underline the importance we attach to intensifying the Secretariat's commitments to strategic partnerships with other international organisations and partners in order to promote the Commonwealth's values and principles. (CHOGM 2009:par. 14)

By the standards of other international agencies (even of the much less effective French rival, La Francophonie), the Commonwealth Secretariat is small in size, diverse in background and varied in experience. Observers sometimes complain about the variability of performance and the inordinate delays in addressing communications. Whatever the reasons, the need for improvement in the secretariat is clear. The inability in the RCS poll of two-thirds of those interviewed to name a single activity that the Commonwealth undertakes was especially discouraging (Llango, 2009:2.). At least one might have expected citizens to name the Commonwealth Games!

The ways forward for Commonwealth renewal were suggested in part by the CHOGM leaders themselves in establishing the EPG and affirming the Commonwealth values and, in part, by the suggestions of the RCS and other commentators. Common themes in contemporary proposals include

- the need for the Commonwealth to prioritise its activities more effectively
- the need to concentrate on those activities that the Commonwealth does best without replicating the activities done elsewhere by the United Nations, the G20, the Organisation for Economic Cooperation and Development (OECD) and so forth
- the need to avoid the delusion that the Commonwealth can be a global fulcrum for political, business, educational, economic, human rights and developmental activities
- the need to embrace greater openness in the bureaucratic style of the Commonwealth, which, in some ways, reflects the old colonial tradition of secrecy and non-transparency
- above all, the need to walk the walk, and not just talk the talk of so-called 'Commonwealth values'.

Several countries of the Commonwealth have been seriously in default in their maintenance of the core values of electoral democracy, independence of the judiciary, and adherence to fundamental human rights. Yet in the past, little or nothing has been done by the Commonwealth or its Secretariat to redress these defects.

Searching for shared values

In repeated meetings of CHOGM, the leaders of the Commonwealth governments have attempted to state the values for which the Commonwealth stands and which are 'guaranteed' for their citizens. Thus, in 1971, the statement of the Singapore CHOGM affirmed a strong stand against racism and, in particular, apartheid—then dominant in the Government of South Africa. There is little doubt that the pressure from the Commonwealth and facilitation by an earlier EPG hastened the demise of that regime and the return of a democratic South Africa to the Commonwealth table.

In 1991, in Harare—in happier times in Zimbabwe—the CHOGM meeting contained an assertion of the centrality of

> [d]emocracy, democratic processes and institutions which reflect national circumstances, just and honest government and fundamental human rights, the rule of law and the independence of the judiciary, freedom of expression and the enjoyment of such rights by all individuals regardless of gender, race, colour, creed or political belief (Oke 2008).

These statements were in turn reaffirmed in 1995 by the Millbrook Declaration adopted during the Auckland CHOGM. That declaration accepted the need for improved machinery in the Commonwealth by a subcommittee of foreign ministers in the Commonwealth Ministerial Action Group (CMAG). It was hoped that CMAG could respond quickly to perceived dangers to, or departures from, declared Commonwealth values. This body was declared to be the 'custodian of the Commonwealth's fundamental political values' (CHOGM 2009:pars 8, 10; see also Commonwealth High Level Review Group 2002). Whilst it has been partly effective in responding to the military takeover of elected regimes (for example, Fiji) and to serious infractions in democratic elections (for example, Zimbabwe), CMAG has been far less effective in investigating and responding to persistent abuses of civil, political, economic, social and cultural rights for all. Sometimes, despite the rhetoric, the inhibition of non-interference in domestic affairs seems to have been at work. Yet if that rule still prevailed in the Commonwealth, South Africa would still be an apartheid state.

The human rights challenges facing the EPG

This, then, is the challenge that currently faces the EPG. Although the United Kingdom is a nuclear power, it has neither the means nor the will to reassert imperial rule. On the contrary, the United Kingdom has never had the fascination for the Commonwealth or its former imperial legacy that many had in the Commonwealth nations themselves. The growth since 1949 of countless international agencies and groupings, of the power and influence of the United Nations, and of economics as a precondition for good governance and effective achievement of human rights make the challenge before the EPG today a very large one.

Nonetheless, if we look to those times in the past when the Commonwealth has been most effective, they would undoubtedly include the times when the Commonwealth could agree on a significant moral cause based on Commonwealth 'values' founded in the essential notions of human dignity shared by people everywhere. The Commonwealth was never stronger than in responding to the oppression against people on the ground of their race in the southern African countries that had been part of the British Empire. The question now is whether—grounded in the strong assertions of fidelity to universal human rights—the Commonwealth can recapture the same unity of purpose around basic ethical principles. And whether it can revamp its institutional structures to ensure the attainment of the goals so eloquently stated, and restated, in successive CHOGM declarations.

If the Commonwealth is to be simply a congenial club of mostly middle-aged men who attend its meeting every second year, enjoy the royal ambiance and then depart to continue oppressive regimes, it will probably fade away— perhaps deservedly so. Yet that would be a tragedy for the utility of the official, professional and other shared experiences that the Commonwealth facilitates, and for the utility of having an organisation of 54 states of all sizes and degrees of power, which can meet together in comparative friendship and harmony and share experiences and viewpoints on a basis that (formally at least) is one of equality and mutual respect.

One ethical issue upon which the Commonwealth of Nations has evidenced an obvious blind spot is a peculiar legacy of British rule. I refer to the anti-homosexual laws that remain in place in 41 of the 54 member countries of the Commonwealth. In our world of nearly 200 nation-states, only 86 states still criminalise consensual same-sex acts in private involving adults. And nearly half of those states are members of the Commonwealth. This is because the common and statute law of Britain in colonial times imposed a criminal offence for such conduct throughout the Empire. Napoleon's codifiers had abolished the

offence in France in 1803. The result of that action was that the countries that
derived their penal codes from the codifiers (France, Spain, the Netherlands,
Belgium, Germany, Russia and Scandinavia) never exported the sodomy offence
to their colonies. So this was a peculiar British export. And whereas the United
Kingdom and the older Commonwealth members have repealed such laws during
the past 40 years, they remain firmly in place in most developing countries of
the Commonwealth of Nations.

In Zimbabwe (presently suspended from the Commonwealth), President, Robert
Mugabe, has voiced many attacks on homosexual citizens, describing them as
'un-African' and 'worse than dogs and pigs'. Reportedly, he told crowds: 'we
are against homosexuality and we as chiefs in Zimbabwe should fight against
such Western practices and [demand that they] respect our culture.' (Johnson
and Walker 2000). At the same time, former Kenyan President Daniel arap Moi
declared homosexuality was 'against African tradition and biblical teaching'. In
Zambia, a government spokesman in 1998 declared that it was 'an abomination
to society'. The previous President of Nigeria, Olusegun Obasanjo, in 2004,
declared that it was 'definitely un-African' (BBC news online 2004). In Malaysia,
Section 377 of the country's penal code has been invoked twice to prosecute
former Deputy Prime Minister and now opposition leader Anwar Ibrahim. The
potential for misuse of this law is large. Its impediment to the battle against HIV/
AIDS is significant. The attempts to reform the law in Commonwealth countries
have failed. Even in modern Singapore, where the former Prime Minister Lee
Kwan Yew supported the reform, the legislature rejected a Law Society proposal
for reform. The government contented itself by saying there would be no
prosecutions. But the law remains on the books to harass, shame, belittle and
endanger citizens.

In Malawi, two young men were sentenced in 2010 to 14 years' imprisonment on
conviction of sodomy following the conduct of a symbolic 'wedding'—probably
only a party. Only the intervention of the Secretary-General of the United
Nations led to a presidential pardon (see, for example, Husain 2010). In Uganda,
a bill has been introduced that, if enacted, would impose the death penalty
for various homosexual acts.[2] Despite this sorry record, the Commonwealth
Secretariat has publicly remained silent and apparently inert and ineffective. It
has been left to UN officials to take the running in defence of the human rights
that are repeatedly declared as core values of the CHOGM declarations.

In the face of populist politics, religious passions, spiritual competitions
between religions, alleged cultural and regional attitudes and unwise public
health strategies, how does a body such as the Commonwealth of Nations find

---

2   Opinion for Commonwealth Lawyers' Association by Mr Timothy Otty QC, Judith Farbey and Gemma
Hobcroft, 9 March 2010.

the resolve and the institutional machinery to deal with such issues? At least on one footing, in the light of modern scientific knowledge about variations in human sexuality, the attitudes of Commonwealth member states to their homosexual citizens are a kind of sexual apartheid. But where is the leadership and institutional machinery to intervene and to ensure that the Commonwealth can make a difference in a truly modern way on this and other human rights issues? Is the Commonwealth of Nations condemned to stumble along as an ineffective body, publishing grand declarations of human rights every two years, but, when tested, lapsing into public silence and failing to take any effective remedial measures?

Conclusion

Achieving institutional reform at a global level is an extremely difficult endeavour. So much is demonstrated by the endless arguments about reform of the United Nations and the comparatively little progress that has been made under successive secretaries-general to achieve such reform. The project now facing the EPG for the reform of the Commonwealth of Nations presents a mighty challenge. Agreeing upon and securing proposals that will gain acceptance at the CHOGM meeting in Perth in October 2011 will be difficult. Success is by no means assured. It might be expected that smaller and developing countries of the Commonwealth (which are very numerous, being 31 of the 54 classified as small states) will demand recognition by the EPG and the Commonwealth of the integral role of the 'right to development' as an element in universal human rights, and a demand that the Secretary-General of the Commonwealth become a kind of spokesperson for smaller Commonwealth states at the meetings of the new groupings of the world's richer and more powerful countries—specifically the G20. Five nations of the Commonwealth (the United Kingdom, Canada, Australia, India and South Africa) have a seat at the G20.

The proposal for a more active Commonwealth role might, however, run into resistance from the G20 themselves because of its ramifications for other potential participants. It might also run the risk of diverting the Commonwealth's attention from the present institutional challenges—namely, the better implementation of the declared values of the organisation and their translation into regular effective practical action. Should the Commonwealth not concentrate on improving the machinery it already has in place in the CMAG? Should it not first strive to uphold the values it has regularly proclaimed before it takes on other, larger economic and geopolitical challenges, however integral they might be in theory and even in practice for attainment of human rights for all Commonwealth citizens?

This is the tricky problem that must be addressed by the EPG. Perhaps in the contrasting demands of the older, developed countries of the Commonwealth and of the younger, developing countries might lie the seeds of a common agreement. The long-term attainment of practical human rights for Commonwealth citizens will never be assured whilst poverty, homelessness, and lack of access to water, education and basic health care remain features of daily life in some Commonwealth countries. By the same token, in the face of the activities of human rights-denying countries of the Commonwealth, it might be better to exclude some of the more egregious offenders for a time until they get their human rights record and conduct into better shape. Yet, is the Commonwealth willing to face up to and decide that such action should be taken?

The dialogue of the EPG continues. Its report will be provided to the CHOGM meeting in 2011. And even when the report is produced, the adoption of any reform and its successful implementation throughout this global community will be a huge challenge. To focus on the way ahead requires concentration by the EPG on what is attainable and what can be achieved by strategic decisions. The EPG needs to heed the warnings of Eric Patashnik (2008) in his book *Reforms at Risk: What happens after major policy changes are enacted*. Although stated in the political context of legislation enacted by the Congress of the United States of America, much of what he says is relevant to the deliberations of the EPG in the still more difficult challenge of reform in institutions—such as the Commonwealth—that function at a global level:

> 'Like a child's room', writes former Treasury official Eugene Steurele, 'one has little expectation that when [the reform] is cleaned up, it will stay tidy forever. By the same token, permanent improvements can often be made along the way'. Just as parents learn to pick some battles with their children and avoid others, so idealistic yet savvy reformers must reflect on which potential reform targets are worth the effort…Because battles over reforms sometimes get caught up in broader partisan and ideological conflicts, it is easy to lose sight of the fact that reform decisions also reflect normative tensions between the values of commitment and discretion, and between the pay-off from the avoidance of foreseeable policy mistakes, on the one hand, and the pay-off from the preservation of the flexibility necessary for beneficial social learning and policy evaluation on the other. The often circuitous paths that reforms take matter not only because they create winners and losers at certain moments in time, but because they shape the possibilities for governance in the future. Strategic leaders will want to think carefully about the reform legacies they leave to their successors. (Patashnik 2008:180)

These words, written in the context of securing lasting reforms to the tax code of the United States of America, have a more general relevance. They carry a general instruction for national reformers, but also for those who seek to change international organisations to reflect more clearly the altered world in which those organisations now operate.

The alternative world of the Commonwealth of Nations is one in which the trappings and realities of British power—which once held the family together— have retreated almost to vanishing point as a relevant consideration. Even the trappings of British symbolism are no longer particularly potent. What is left is a body held together by history, sentiment and perceived current utility. Yet, it is a body that proclaims its allegiance to values that are vital for peace, security and equity in the world.

That is what universal, fundamental human rights represent. It is why the Commonwealth so gladly embraces these rights and asserts them as the 'core values' that it upholds. It is why it has created an organisational structure to ensure the attainment of such important values. It is difficult, in an ever-watching world, to get away for long with grandiose declarations, followed up by seriously inadequate performance. Yet this is what the Commonwealth has so far stumbled along trying to do.

Reform certainly cannot be imposed against the will of the organisation. Effectively, it must be agreed to. At the heart of securing agreement is the need for conviction that—at least in a sufficient number of participating governments at CHOGM—it is in their interests, and right, that they should do so; or that the game is up and they cannot continue to go on declaring one thing and doing another: to declare human rights as a 'fundamental value' but to deny them repeatedly and so publicly in domestic policies.

The time is fast approaching when the Commonwealth must make a choice. Upon the choice that is made could depend the survival of the organisation— certainly in anything like the form it presently manifests. So much seems to be inherent in the many responses of disillusionment and despair expressed in the Commonwealth Conversation conducted by the Royal Commonwealth Society and in many other contributions urging effective institutional reform.

As a useful connection between many states and peoples that history has fortuitously presented to us, the Commonwealth of Nations is certainly worth preserving. It needs effective and lasting institutional reform, however, if it is to survive. If there is sufficient will, it should be possible to secure such lasting reforms. But is that will attainable? Or would its members rather that it atrophied into insignificance, because they were unwilling to face the painful and competing realities? If there is the will, there is the way.

References

BBC news online, 27 October 2004, 'Obasanjo backs bishops over gays'.

Commonwealth Heads of Government Meeting (CHOGM) 2009, *Trinidad and Tobago Affirmation on Commonwealth Values and Principles*, Commonwealth Heads of Government Meeting, 27–29 November 2009, Port of Spain, Republic of Trinidad and Tobago.

Commonwealth High Level Review Group 2002, *Report by the Commonwealth High Level Review Group to the Commonwealth Heads of Government, Coolum, Australia*, Department of the Prime Minister and Cabinet, Barton, ACT.

Husain, M. 2010, Commonwealth Lawyers' Association condemns Malawi gay couple imprisonment, 20 May 2010, Statement by Commonwealth Lawyers' Association President.

Johnson, R.W. and Tom Walker, March 19 2000, 'Mugabe makes new 'gay Britain' attack'. *The Sunday Times*.

Llango, R. Iniyan, 2010, 'CHOGM 2009, Detour or Dead End?' *Commonwealth Human Rights Initiative Newsletter*, vol. 17, p.2.

Mayall, J. (ed.) 2010, *The Contemporary Commonwealth: An assessment, 1965–2009*, Routledge, London.

Oke, Ayo, 2008, 'Democracy and Good Governance in Africa', Speech presented at the United Nations Workshop On Promoting Democratic Transitions in Africa, Banako, Mali, 24-25 November 2008.

Patashnik, E. M. 2008, *Reforms at Risk: What happens after major policy changes are enacted*, Princeton University Press, Princeton, NJ.

Ramphal, S. 2010, 'A Commonwealth of laws: at 60 and beyond', *Commonwealth Law Bulletin*, vol. 36, p. 359.

Royal Commonwealth Society 2009, *Common What? Emerging findings of the Commonwealth Conversation*, November 2009, Royal Commonwealth Society, London.

Part III

Tackling and anchoring reform initiatives

11. Tackling cartels: lessons for making and entrenching reform

William E. Kovacic

My background is teaching law and my natural habitat is the university, but for nine of the past 10 years I have been tackling national and international cartels and seeing theory meet practice at a federal institution, the Federal Trade Commission. For me, the deepest education in that process has been realising how hard it is not only to get seemingly straightforward things done, but also to make certain that changes or adjustments in a policy stick. This chapter will focus on those experiences.

I think often of the work of my historian colleague Ronald Spector, who writes about organisations and public services with a particular focus on defence organisations. In his book *At War at Sea* (2001), he analyses the desperate efforts of the Allies to develop effective convoying systems in the beginning of the Battle of the Atlantic in World War II, and out of absolute necessity they were pressed to put very junior and inexperienced people into positions of command. In the book, Spector cites the experience of a young Canadian officer who had never been to sea, only to find himself commanding a Corvette that is weaving dangerously through the convoy. Observing the situation, a senior British officer of a destroyer sent a blinkered message to him: 'What do you think you're doing?' And the answer that came back from the Canadian officer was: 'Learning a lot.'

To me, one of the greatest elements of 'learning a lot' has been to see how difficult it is to make reforms stick. In this chapter, I wish to discuss a reform that has been seen largely as a policy success: the development of a global consensus favouring substantial attacks on cartel behaviour. I will first cover some recurring phenomena that are formative preconditions for making reforms stick, then discuss a change inside the anti-trust system that involves the ramping up of criminal enforcement against cartels. I will next discuss the larger set of policy relationships that determines whether or not reforms taken inside a single discipline are effective over time. Finally, I will explore the individual implications of this for larger public-policy changes.

Formative preconditions of which policy makers ought to be aware

There are three recurring phenomena that determine whether reforms stick. The first of these formative preconditions is the fact that it is rarely the case that a single element of policy is absolutely independent of others. This suggests that if we were all to map out the policy space in which our institutions operate, we will find they share boundaries with a host of other government agencies, whose decisions basically bring us into what is an interdependent equation with different variables. A change in one will send ripples throughout the system, and interest other institutions.

This is the 'policy archipelago': a web of interconnected reefs and islands. It exists across disciplines, and across jurisdictional boundaries. And needless to say these relationships are not always amicable and agreeable across agencies.

There is a famous story told about Curtis LeMay during the time he was the head of the Strategic Air Command of the US Air Force (1948–57). He was getting a briefing from a junior Air Force officer, who referred to the Soviet Union as an enemy. LeMay interrupted and said: 'No! No! No! The Soviet Union is an adversary. Our enemy is the United States Navy.' As this quote illustrates, in many instances, we often find enormous amounts of tension across public institutions, where you might assume from a distance that because they are part of the same public service architecture they will have shared interests.

The second formative precondition is that regulated entities that are the subjects of reform, especially those whose behaviour is being constrained, are remarkably resilient and adaptive. They are geographically mobile in many instances. They will move to different jurisdictions within a country, or across borders, that do not have the same controls. They are highly adaptive in pursuing their own objectives through other means, so that if we were to impose an effective regulatory reform with respect to one dimension of their behaviour, they do not then surrender, throw up their hands, and say 'I give up'; they try to circumvent the new rules.

This feature has to be seen as a version of an 'arms race' in which any single adjustment by the public-sector body is going to be matched with counter-strategies by the other institutions. Hence, in any thinking about introducing significant reforms, a necessary element of the policy-development process must be to ask: 'what is going to be their next move?' They are not going to stand still and do exactly what we hope they might do.

And last, there is a tremendous benefit to public institutions of economic and historical precedence, which can be assembled only through a profound process of retrospection. The evaluation of outcomes, and the learning from the experience base, can happen only if there is enough institutional memory, continuity, and commitment to do this kind of difficult assessment inside the body.

Enforcement against antitrust behaviour

The recent development of a widespread anti-cartel norm across society has been one of the most striking elements of public policy experienced throughout the field of competition law. Take an example from the beginning of the US experience with competition law—now 120 years old—that illustrates the dramatic evolution in the form of criminal sanctions brought to bear on producer cartels that covertly seek to reduce output at increased price.

For such wrongdoers, the basic fine level in 1890 was $5000—a little bit more money than it is now, and the offence was a misdemeanour, which is a relatively light-handed criminal offence. It stayed that way for 65 years. In 1955, Congress took the bold step of raising the maximum fine to $50 000, but left the offence level in place. That might have seemed quaint in 1955, but by 1974 it was a laughable deterrent. In other words, imagine going to a significant price-fixing organisation such as Archer Daniels in Midland and saying 'that will be a $50 000 fine, please'. They would reach into their pockets and say: 'I think I've got that right here. See you the next time, for the next defence.' In 1974, the offence was again boosted, to a $1 million maximum fine—still quaint—but it was changed to a felony, which is a much more serious offence, with three years' maximum prison term for individuals.

In 1987, the law was ramped up further—doubling the fine and with the possibility of recovering the proceeds. Effectively, it permitted multi-hundred million-dollar recoveries in individual cases. In 1990, it became a $10 million fine per offence, plus allowing higher damages to be awarded by the courts ('double the loss' for violators, 'double the gain' for victims). And in 2004 the law became a $100 million maximum for each offence, as well as 'double the loss, double the gain', and a felony with a maximum prison sentence now of 10 years. That is what criminals now get for bank robbery. Price fixing in the United States is now treated as an extremely serious criminal offence, with comparable civil and criminal trends taking place elsewhere. This represents a great policymaking success.

But, stepping back, there are equilibrating tendencies that have to be taken into account when assessing progress and asking 'will things stick'? As we raise sanctions and compensation in the legal system, and as the ante is upped, a couple of things happen. We have to convince courts and juries that it is worth taking away the freedom of the violating individuals—and this was a big cultural shock when we go back to 1974, and the US system became much more serious minded about doing this.

First, we had to convince juries that price fixing was a serious offence worthy of criminal punishment; but juries were not accustomed to defining 'anti-competitive' behaviour in this way. Crimes against individuals involving harm to body and property—these were thought of as serious offences. In antitrust cases, the accused person sitting in the courtroom was someone typically wearing a suit and white collar—someone who looked like your uncle or your father. And what was the offence? Well, price fixing. What was that? Who cared? In the eyes of many juries, this was nowhere as serious as entering a bank with a ski mask and a revolver. Moreover, the moment we started to bring forward these cases, the firms in question quickly adapted and used counter-strategies.

The effectiveness of the US legal-enforcement practices depended on addressing both of these concerns: jury attitudes and counter-strategies by the accused. And there were a number of very successful strategies devised to tackle these concerns. US prosecutors—and often their counterparts in many other counties—realised that we had to establish a norm that accepted criminal punishment as routine for antitrust violations. So what did they do? Well, they built on an academic consensus that cartels were almost invariably harmful, and carefully picked the right cases to prosecute at the beginning. And what were the first cases for which we pushed for more powerful sanctions in the United States? They involved public procurement, and in particular public procurement for such basics as milk, involving such things as bid rigging against school authorities. So what was the case? Perhaps the person accused looked like a sweet uncle, but here is what he had done. He had artificially raised the price of the milk the children were meant to consume. This meant for our popular campaign that these dear little children were going to go hungry in school, because the school district could not afford to pay for the milk. As prosecutors, we were building public outrage.

Other cases involved price fixing for municipal supplies. So, for instance, the terrible roads that motorists were driving on remained in poor condition because the local municipal authority tasked with maintaining them could not afford to because the suppliers set the price for the concrete and the paving services. These price fixers might not have been wearing ski masks and waving revolvers about, but they were nevertheless thieving from the public purse. And, it was argued, as law-abiding taxpayers, the citizenry should not feel bad about taking their freedom away.

The development of those early procurement cases created a social expectation and community acceptance of the idea that price fixing was a serious offence. This was a deliberate, careful strategy that resulted in the successful implementation of the program. In many respects, the procurement-first strategy changed social attitudes such that people began to accept such prosecutions as a useful application of serious, powerful sanctions.

A second key element involved examining closely the empirical data that were being uncovered by the prosecutions. What one often finds in cases where public policies are inherently interdependent is that the root cause of some sanctionable behaviour in one sector lies in some other collateral area of decision making. And so it was with many of the prosecution cases taken up against bid rigging and anti-competitive offences.

What was discovered? We found that one of the main contributory causes of cartels were restrictions that require public procurement authorities to buy only from domestic sources. In the commercial world, if you want to draw a bullseye on the back of public purchasing authorities, make sure that their domestic content restrictions are extremely onerous. Consider the example of a successful prosecution of a company that sold frozen fish to the Department of Defence. What soon became clear was that there were only four firms able to supply such fish, and that there had been only four firms for about 30 years. Why was this? We found that there was an absolute prohibition on buying frozen fish from companies outside the United States, such as in Canada, Iceland and the United Kingdom. If we had allowed firms from these other countries to bid for these public contracts, the United States would probably have been covered with frozen fish up to a depth of about 20 m, shore to shore. But by limiting the market to the US producers, we did them a great favour. They knew that no entry of other suppliers was permissible. And they knew that every time, in every procurement, these four US companies would confront each other again and again. So they got to know each other very well and colluded on price. In this way, by imposing the 'buy-American' requirements, the US Government did a great favour to facilitate cartels.

Similarly, in markets where foreign suppliers were not excluded, it soon became apparent that existing cartel members resorted to anti-dumping processes to try to keep these foreign suppliers from lucrative procurements. In effect, national and international trade rules and conventions were a great ally of cartel participants. Moreover, public procurement procedures, for example, required all bids from suppliers to be laid out on a table for all to see. It was a basic requirement that in an open tendering process, the sealed bids of all of the bidders are subsequently disclosed for transparency and scrutiny purposes. But what occurred in many instances was that there was a rush from participants to come to the front of the room to look at the table. Why were they so interested?

If cartel participants were part of a bid-rigging scheme, it was a great way to establish whether or not their counterparts did what they promised to do. And it was a perfect way to detect deviations.

Another consequence of this international situation was that cartel firms that were getting hammered in North America simply decided to put together these cartels in other countries that did not view such behaviour as a serious offence. Firms could go from jurisdiction to jurisdiction selecting those that simply did not care, re-establishing their cartels without fear of challenge. For prosecutors and antitrust regulators, if we looked carefully at our experience base, we knew where these counter-strategies and pressures were coming from. It also gave us insights into how other public policies had to be changed inside North America and elsewhere in order to get a good solution.

We also observed that another way in which price-fixing businesses responded was to seek substitutes. Executives of firms soon realised that if they formed a private agreement with their counterparts, they risked going to prison. But if they could get public agencies and legislators to form the cartel for them, and it became mandatory, then the government agencies would in a sense unwittingly enforce the cartels on their behalf. Consequently, firms observed two options— one that said 'go to jail', the other that said 'great success awaits you through manipulating public policy'—and they simply moved their strategies from one to the other. An example that comes to mind involved state legislation that forbids in many instances sales of wine on the Internet across state boundaries. The 'public policy' justification for such restrictions is that Internet trading would be likely to promote underage drinking, so it has to be banned. Now, each of these states that adopted the ban still allows consumers to use the Internet to buy wine from vineyards produced *inside* the state, but not across state borders. It is hard to imagine that there is any empirical evidence showing that drinking wine from within the state produces less drunkenness than drinking wine from outside the state! The regulation is premised on a fallacious rationale and done to stymie competition.

Who are the beneficiaries in this case? What was the public interest or public-safety issue at stake? The public issue at stake was the income of the producers inside states. And many states acquiesced in this kind of legislation. Likewise, states have also misused their regulatory apparatus in other ways to prevent competition, such as by using land-use controls and challenges to new store openings to keep out external entrances.

The broader policy consequences

So, it is clear from where I stand that the would-be cartel members never give up—they just adapt their strategies. Any single reform initiative aimed at improving the effectiveness of the antitrust law enforcement could easily be negated by these counter-strategies. What does this imply for substantial policy reform over time? What does the individual agency have to do? First, it has to foresee dynamic readjustments by firms, whether they are related to environmental policy, labour policy, competition policy or whatever else. The economic actors so affected will adapt and readjust. This creates an imperative for the public agency to think about how that adaptation might go on and, by means of *ex-post* evaluation, to observe how it is actually taking place.

The individual agency must commit to the process of looking back at actual experience, and asking: 'How are we going? Are reforms working? What are we learning from what we are seeing? And, is there some pathology that resides in some other collateral area of policy making that still needs to be fixed?' Otherwise, as policy makers, we are basically left picking the tops off weeds after they come out of the ground, and not getting to the roots to fix the real problems. This self-reflection can be done in part only through such internal diagnosis and examination. It will also involve examining connections to the larger world of policy development, once one sees the interdependencies and linkages. Such a situation results in effective advocacy before other public institutions, linked to public agencies with shared interests.

In the United States, we have found in the Federal Trade Commission that, as a federal agency, we have had to form cooperative relationships with state governments to keep them focused on the ongoing need for competition reform and ensure they act as the 'coast watchers'. We know that many would-be cartel firms are now going to state capitals to lobby for the adoption of legislation they hope will override other competition-policy commands. In return, through developing cooperative alliances with state government agencies, we hope to be able to persuade their legislatures not to adopt such measures, pointing out if they do the costs to economic efficiency. We have to be continual advocates. And, in mounting our advocacy, it is also important to draw upon the knowledge we have acquired and the types of economic precedence with which we have experience. Similarly, at the Federal Trade Commission, we have striven to build solid relationships with procurement officials across the jurisdictions in order to prevent them from becoming inevitable targets of effective cartels. In particular, during the recent stimulus program in the context of the global financial crisis, there was a dedicated effort to provide this kind of support and guidance.

So, to conclude these reflections, in many respects the key element to making reforms effective and sustainable in the longer term comes down to how they were conceived initially and calibrated over time. Reform adjustments made within a single frame of reference (a paradigm, academic discipline, an agency 'mind-set') might not always be the most effective unless examined in a larger context of interactions with other areas of public policy. Moreover, perhaps the most important element of this diagnostic process is to undertake a dedicated effort to examine one's own patterns of experience—in short, the painful process of asking how and why things have worked or not worked. We need to go back and ask in a deep and meaningful way how and why things have turned out the way they have.

As a final reflection, one of my colleagues at George Washington University has an insightful sign on his office wall. It says: 'It's what you learn after you know it all that really counts.' We cannot beat experience, expertise, diagnosis and, of course, ongoing learning—that is the only way we will continue 'learning a lot'.

Reference

Spector, R. H. 2001, *At War at Sea: Sailors and naval combat in the twentieth century*, Viking Press, New York.

12. The overhaul of Australian immigration practices, 2005–2010

Andrew Metcalfe

Over the past five years, the Department of Immigration and Citizenship (DIAC) has sought to reform and transform our culture and business practices. This endeavour has come about as a direct result of the department's previous history of maladministration in cases such as Cornelia Rau's unlawful detention in 2004 and the subsequent *Palmer Report* her case provoked. This chapter will analyse the progress that we are making, characterised by attempts to build stronger visa, migration and citizenship services. It will also explore the challenges we have faced in implementing this organisational change, and our future plans for the department.

Immigration: the complexity of operational practices

First, we need to consider where the department has come from and where we are planning to go. In addition to our core business enrolled in managing the entry and settlement of people from around the globe, the department's activities cross a number of key policy areas, including: economic policy; social policy; and national-security policy. In addition, we are vitally involved in a number of emergent debates—for example, in Australia's future population options, an issue of discussion in the community and the 2010 election campaign, and an area in which we have done significant work. Moreover, we are an organisation that does not simply deal with 'policy issues', but one that is also involved in client service delivery, whether it be directly through our own offices or through service-delivery partners or outsourcing arrangements.

My department serves millions of clients across a range of programs each year, from tourists coming to Australia to the hundreds of thousands of students studying here from overseas; from temporary and permanent workers coming to Australia to refugees and people seeking Australian citizenship. The complexity of our work and of the policy design that has gone into these programs is reflected in the simple fact that as of 2010 there are now more than 150 visa categories for both short and long-term stays in Australia, including making provision for New Zealanders coming to Australia.

The figures of our work speak for themselves: in the year 2009–10, nearly 120 000 people became Australian citizens, the department granted more than 4.3 million visas, and staff in our service centres answered 1.73 million telephone calls. Moreover, during this period, 29 million people crossed Australia's borders, and that was facilitated by visa programs and by services provided by my department and by the customs and border protection service on our behalf. Roughly half of those 29 million were Australians, and roughly half of those were people coming to Australia and half leaving Australia. Even so, that represents approximately seven or eight million non-Australians coming to Australia and leaving again. This is an indication of the sheer size, scale and integration of our economy with other economies, manifested through tourism, the international student sector, overseas workers and people coming here to settle permanently. To process this workload, we have approximately 7000 staff, of which about 1000 are based overseas across 100 offices. We are very much a multinational organisation.

We make decisions in often sensitive, complex and deeply personal areas, sometimes involving a person's character, their criminal record or whether they pose a threat to Australia's security. We also take into account their relationships, and whether these relationships—a parent–child, husband–wife, de facto, parent—are in fact genuine or whether, as occasionally occurs, relationships are entered into or assumed for immigration outcomes rather than for family outcomes.

Immigration status and, of course, refugee status are other critical issues. Refugee status involves a complex interrelationship of international law, Australian domestic law (both statutory and case law), the personal circumstances a person faces should they return to their homeland (that is, would they be persecuted), and assessments as to the credibility of people and whether or not they are in fact telling a correct story. These difficult tasks are complicated by the fact that many people who come from refugee situations might be traumatised or deeply affected and consequently unable to communicate effectively. This is a complex area of decision making, and the public debate often underestimates its complexity.

In addition to those previously mentioned roles, we as a department provide services for people required by law to be in immigration detention, and Australian law requires that people who arrive here without a visa are detained. At the moment this means well more than 3000 people are currently detained in various centres around the state capital cities and in other places such as Christmas Island and the Curtin detention centre in Western Australia. Detention involves the department in other responsibilities, because we are responsible not only for a person's status and the determination of whether they should stay in Australia or go home, but also the provision of facilities (often through service providers) including accommodation, and medical or mental health services. It is a hugely complex area and one that we have put at the core of the framework we established post 2005. As we are a service provider in regards to immigration detention, we do not talk about inmates or prisoners; we talk about the people as 'clients'—clients of the department who deserve our respect, and from whom in turn we seek to be respected.

Thus, we are profoundly involved in extensive policy work and operational activities—both in Australia and overseas—to support Australia's response to the issue of irregular maritime arrivals. In the past 12 months, for example, we have seen almost 6000 people arrive in Australia by boat unlawfully—a subset of the aforementioned 29 million border crossings and, in international terms, a very small figure. When you look at the number of asylum-seekers moving to Europe and to North America, for instance, in global terms, Australia's figure—while certainly not small and certainly significant in our historical terms—is miniscule when compared with the world. And yet, the department acknowledges that decisions regarding irregular maritime arrivals often involve complex assessments of Australia's obligations in relation to individual claims—and all of those activities can be the subject of great public interest and of course debate.

The department's core values are essential to the way in which we conduct our business. We are professional public servants and are accordingly committed to the values of the Australian Public Service (APS). Moreover, in recognition of the specific work we undertake as a major department within the Commonwealth, we have developed and promote specific DIAC values to reinforce key aspects of the way we do our work. These include commitments to

- service excellence
- being open and accountable for our actions
- listening and responding to the needs of our clients, our stakeholders and each other
- fostering teamwork and ensuring integrity in decision making and business activities.

Further, such values are universally applied throughout our department, regardless of where we are conducting our work—whether in the national office in Canberra or in Christmas Island Detention Centre, in Brisbane or in Beijing. Similarly, our values are applied regardless of the nature of the business activity—whether we are interviewing a client for a visa, or confirming citizenship, whether our staff are organising a compliance visit to a factory where it is suspected people are working illegally in Australia or have overstayed their visa, or whether we are engaged in any of the many other tasks that we do. The adoption of these values—and the way we have embedded them in all parts of our work and business planning—has not only integrated the culture of the organisation, but also helped to raise the level of trust in our work by government, clients and any other stakeholders in the wider community.

Reformation: towards a new values-based culture

I was appointed Secretary of DIAC in July 2005 following the tragic cases of Cornelia Rau and Vivian Alvarez and indeed many other people who had been unlawfully detained. It was a deeply bruising time for the department, with its failures regarding these unlawful detentions all over the media and highlighted in major reports by the former Australian Federal Police Commissioner Nick Palmer and the former Chief Commissioner of the Victorian Police Neil Comrie.

For me, that time was about restoring confidence in the department, regrouping and establishing a clear set of values and forward actions that would prevent a repeat of those tragic mistakes. This approach was best articulated in a 2007 Ombudsman report by John McMillan entitled *Ten Lessons Learnt*, which basically summarised the lessons learnt from the various reports the Ombudsman issued in relation to those immigration cases.

When McMillan launched that report, I suggested there was in fact an eleventh lesson: the need for a strong and positive culture and values base for public officials. It is essential that we do not forget those lessons of the past, and they are not exclusively applicable to DIAC; anyone working in public administration could usefully regularly refer to that Ombudsman's report from August 2007. Indeed, in our department's business planning, as part of the individual business plans for work units, we require our managers to address the various lessons in that report and to make a self-assessment as to whether they are at risk of forgetting those lessons.

My task and that of the senior leadership team of the department was to create an integrated department united by our common, historical purpose of building the Australian nation and sharing a common culture based on the APS Values and Code of Conduct as well as our own specific business values. This period was the beginning of the journey to drive and integrate the reformation of DIAC through a values-based culture. A key question for any successful change process is how to sustain change over time, because it is one thing to have an initial rush of enthusiasm, but quite another to genuinely change an organisation and ensure that change endures beyond the tenure of a particular leader or set of leaders.

The success of the change of an agenda also lies in the ability of leaders to communicate their claims effectively; to engage all the employees in the journey, to make this a shared experience, to ensure the people understand the reasons for the change, and ultimately to own that change. This required involving our people in each step of the journey and harnessing their own goodwill and creativity as part of that journey.

Back in 2005, we analysed the *Palmer Report* and adopted its three key themes to inform our work into the future. Five years on, those key themes still remain relevant. Essentially, what Palmer's report said was that the Department of Immigration had to become an open and accountable organisation; it had to have fair and reasonable dealings with clients; and it had to have well-developed and supported staff. In our department, we refer to these three themes as 'the triangle'.

The importance of these three simple themes is of universal relevance across public-sector organisations. The values they encapsulate provide the principles for sound decision making and good administration. The values also provide a framework within which plans can be interrogated. It is fair to say that every aspect of our work could be traced back to these values. Additionally, we cannot and should not ignore changes in our operating environment, and a solid evidence base is crucial to avoid reactive decision making. We have also done a number of things over the past few years beyond looking at values, such as looking at culture, analysing our attitudes and surveying staff. Then of course there have also been some specific business measures that have been adopted to try to change and create a better operating environment for the department.

One of the most significant aspects—certainly the most expensive in terms of expenditure of public funding—has focused on improving our capability through information technology (IT) innovation. We call this the 'Systems for People' program, and it is essentially an IT transformation strategy—a redesign of our business processes aimed at providing better management and use of information as well as modern technological support. Indeed, it has been one of the largest technology-enabled business transformations undertaken by the public sector in Australia, with our budget forecasting the overall bill over four years to come in at $600 million.

A strong evidence base for policy making and operational decisions is also critical to the sustainability of any organisation, so recently we established a specific policy innovation research and evaluation unit to identify and analyse long-term issues. We found as an organisation we have become very focused on the short term. But given that the issues we deal with are essentially long term in nature—for example, the lasting impact of immigration on Australia's population and our integration into the global economy through the movement of people—we needed to shift part of our focus to longer-term issues.

To achieve this, we commissioned a new research program to cover the settlement outcomes of new arrivals, the contribution of humanitarian entrants to Australia and the long-term impact on Australia of the migration program. The research this program conducts is now instrumental in informing the government's work on sustainable population for the future.

We quite deliberately sought to extend this research program beyond the traditional focus on the migration program and actually sought to extend it into areas of refugee resettlement and community cohesion. We developed the ideas for the program through much internal discussion to ensure it was not just captive of one particular area. To do this, we also held consultations with stakeholders and with the minister himself. He was interested in what we would be looking at, and the results of that research will start to become available to us and hopefully will contribute to sound decision making, rather than simply basing issues on gut feelings or anecdotes.

Another move we made was appointing a chief economist to the department—a position that had previously not existed. Despite the fact we have had a chief lawyer, a chief information officer and a chief auditor, we did not actually have someone focusing on economics as a policy skill. In retrospect, this seems like an obvious skills gap, so now we have a chief economist and support staff who have greatly strengthened our capability in the critical area of government policy decision making. Examining the improvements that have been put in place in the past couple of years around the policy design program (the design of the migration program, the interrelationship between international student policy and the migration program), it is pleasing to note that there has been a much sounder evidence base drawn from economic principles than might have been the case some years ago.

Restoring trust in the department was obviously another crucial challenge. After the damning cases of Cornelia Rau and Vivian Alvarez, there was arguably a complete loss of trust in the department among the general public; these two unlawful detentions seemed to act as a lightning rod for broader concerns in the community about the management and detention of asylum-seekers. In 2010 we again have many people back in detention, yet so far the department has largely escaped criticism over the matter. This is a sign that we have been successful in restoring trust in our administration. This has been achieved through the reform program, but also through extensive stakeholder engagement, both at a community level amongst advocates, critics and the media, and at the political level.

One of the best pieces of advice I received in my first days in the job was from a colleague who suggested we identify and meet the 20 people who hated the department the most. Some were quite surprised to get a letter from me! By meeting these people, we were able to restore communication channels, thus restoring a semblance of trust in the department, even if we do not always agree with these people.

I have also attempted to restore trust at the political level—an endeavour supported by former minister Amanda Vanstone and her successors, Kevin Andrews and Chris Evans. I usually make an opening statement at the beginning of any Senate Estimates hearings, and talk about the department's activities and what we have been doing. This open and accountable approach has been important and also involves working closely with the Ombudsman.

Organisational reform requires some form of external validation—for while we had been getting some constructive responses and some important anecdotal feedback from key stakeholders such as the Ombudsman and the Human Rights Commission, it was essential for us as an organisation to have our progress assessed by an outsider. That is why, three and a half years into the post-Palmer reform program, I commissioned a respected organisational consultant, former secretary of the Victorian Premier's Department Elizabeth Proust, to undertake an independent review of DIAC's achievements.

Fortunately, in 2008, Proust concluded that the department had made substantial reforms and progress since 2005, forming the view that the implementation of the post-Palmer reform program was essentially complete. She identified the entrenchment of these reforms as a key issue for the future, and did not shy away from criticism, pointing to some areas for particular activity including the finalisation of our technology changes. Overall, the Proust review was of great assistance to us in providing a frank health check from the perspective of an outsider well versed and experienced in public administration and the difficulties involved with managing large organisations.

Proust's assessment gave us confidence to believe we had largely put in place measures to ensure we did not repeat the tragic mistakes of some years ago, while acknowledging that in a big department involving thousands of staff, operating in numerous locations and dealing with millions of clients every year, mistakes do happen. One of the key aspects of our cultural change was to have some very clear expectations that if mistakes are made, we immediately identify them, out them, and address them. Such an approach stands in contrast with the tragic situation of Vivian Alvarez's case, where there was a cover-up involving a couple of middle managers.

While many of us at the department were simply mystified as to how and why such a cover-up could occur, the fact is that it did occur, and one of the key areas of our post-2005 reforms has thus been to ensure that we accept the fact that mistakes are made. Accepting that if a mistake is made it needs to be openly dealt with and addressed does not mean we are always happy with the mistake, but it is much worse if a mistake occurs and no-one does anything about it.

From reformation to transformation: the second stage of DIAC's overhaul

Having gained confidence we were heading in the right direction, by 2009, the department felt ready to move into the next stage of its development. This coincided with the commencement of another period of high operational tempo in the department, for not only were we running big migration programs and responding to the effects of the global economic crisis in adjusting some of those programs; not only were we dealing with serious issues relating to the overall welfare of overseas students in Australia and working closely with the Department of Education and state governments and others in relation to that, but during this period we also saw the re-emergence of irregular maritime arrivals coming to Australia. We also recognised that the department had been experimenting with new ways of doing business, had produced some good ideas, and had done a lot of work in developing a stronger client-service culture. My then Deputy Secretary, Carmel McGregor, should be singled out for bringing a great deal of insight and energy into re-energising the department's client service strategies.

While many features of our reform agenda were starting to be realised, we needed to incorporate them into a cohesive and united forward plan that built on the post-reform base. We had reformed the department, but we now needed to *transform* the department. This initiative will help strengthen Australia's borders, and enable us to provide far better services in migration, visa provision and to citizens.

We are now one year into this transformation. Presently, we are seeking to conceive what DIAC should look like in terms of service delivery, policy capabilities and internal business services well into the future (five, 10 or 15 years out). We are seeking a well-planned, carefully conceived vision that we can not only populate with initiatives, but also ultimately end up being a genuinely modern and strong organisation that provides excellent services to government and to our clients.

We have set ourselves a challenge of being nothing less than the best immigration agency in the world, and, given the capabilities of some of our counterparts, we are probably quite close to that mark. This does not mean, however, that we cannot improve, because there is still much room for improvement. We do not simply want to benchmark ourselves against other immigration services; we want to benchmark ourselves against the best in the public sector and indeed against the best in the private sector. We decided that we needed to do this notwithstanding the high operational tempo of the department; indeed, we cannot hope to manage such a high tempo without transforming into a more efficient and effective department. Consequently, the transformation is essentially aimed at ensuring we are both financially and operationally sustainable in the long term. To do this, we have focused on three elements: policy, client services and internal business services.

Many agencies are now attempting to become citizen centric, but in DIAC we first needed to recognise that many of our clients were not citizens—some were perhaps on a pathway to becoming citizens. Consequently, we talked about delivering services to 'clients'. Additionally, as a policy *and* delivery agency, we were interested in demonstrating effective implementation of policy through integration with service delivery. Today there are not too many departments in Canberra that have both a policy and a service-delivery aspect; the functions are often separated. We see our combined roles as an asset, because it gives us internal integration. Consequently, it should enable us to perform better than some of our colleagues. The priorities leading our transformation are all in alignment with the Moran blueprint for the reform of the APS and with the Government's Web 2.0 technology agenda.

I previously mentioned steps we have taken to improve our policy and evaluation performance and increase our client-centric focus; our agenda is very much about program and individual case integrity, about service delivery and about efficiency. In seeking greater levels of efficiency, it became evident that we actually needed to restructure the organisation, and to do this we have now grouped together all of our policy and program management functions under one deputy secretary. Such functions include visa services, citizenship services and refugee status determination services. By the same token, we have also grouped together the areas of internal business services, technology, property, finance and legal issues.

The shift to a global operational structure is also something that we are seeking to achieve. For the first time, the department has shifted its thinking from geographic management and service delivery organised within the Australian states to global service delivery, whereby senior officers have responsibility for a business line and the delivery of services for that business line anywhere in the world. At the same time, we have based those global manager positions largely in the states, using our state directors to oversee them. We are increasingly confident this is a much smarter way to deliver genuine client services and decision-making integrity without people getting different treatment in different offices depending on where they happen to turn up. We are also using new technologies to aid decision-making processes and record keeping as well as moving to provide global access to electronic visa applications.

So how have we integrated risk analysis into our global management structure? As part of our innovative organisational structure, we have formed a specialised division to focus on risk, fraud and integrity issues. While we have always had a strong focus both on integrity of individual decisions and on broader program integrity, we needed to ask ourselves whether we were managing some of our specific programs effectively. This new division in Canberra—dealing with risk, fraud and integrity—is not only responsible for identifying and analysing key risks across the department, but is also setting our overall risk-management framework, policies and procedures. To do this, we have some high-end expert services in this area, but at the same time we have assigned one of our global managers to be solely responsible for operational integrity.

We did this because we had a specialised unit based in Adelaide that looks at operational integrity issues, so a global manager of operational integrity works closely with the Canberra-based risk, fraud and integrity division and with key policy and program management people to provide pre-decision support to the global service-delivery network. In addition, this team provides post-decision sampling and checking to ensure that our visa and citizenship outcomes align with policy intent. Such a position ensures that our integrity-control framework is integrated.

Through this approach, we aim to consider risk and any ventures associated with risk in a global manner. This could involve high-end investigations that have a close working relationship with the Federal Police, or the monitoring of employers as to whether or not they are in fact giving people the correct entitlements. It can also include our overseas network of what we call integrity officers who are involved in managing risk issues at overseas posts. This is the first time we have brought them together in one cohesive way. We are already seeing the benefits of this global approach in terms of integrity decision and in our service delivery to clients.

Additional benefits of this global structure are that our service centre staff are trained to work within a range of programs to apply principles for consistent decision making and provide a seamless client service regardless of location. This involves doing increasingly more work with clients by email, electronically and on the telephone to create strong organisational units that manage that type of work. To help us achieve this, we should look at best practice from the public sector, and from the private sector, to learn how we can create career structures, organisational units, learning and development opportunities and the monitoring of performance. Ultimately, we aim one day to become a far more accessible organisation where people can contact us any time of the night or day and speak to us in their chosen language.

Currently, we have 'contact centres' in Sydney and Melbourne, but in the past they were seen largely as useful recruitment centres for people who would then move to other jobs in the department. We hope to expand these centres to include Australia's west coast, because Perth's time zone is beneficial when engaging with clients in China, India, and other parts of Asia. In addition to our existing Australian call centres, we have an effective call centre operating in Ottawa, Canada, where we provide services for parts of Europe and North and South America in a range of languages including Spanish, Portuguese, French and English.

Reorienting our organisation to be client focused led us to appoint a global manager for service centres. To get the best in performance, we specifically recruited someone with expertise in effectively managing contact centres. As a result, we are already seeing a significant improvement in performance independent of those other changes yet working their way through.

An integral part of this transformation was sustained, effective communication. By effectively communicating and engaging with departmental staff to secure their buy-in and ownership of the change journey, we have created a shared view and vision of where the department is going. In my view, the progressive nature of the roll-out and ongoing engagement with staff have been similarly successful in entrenching DIAC's transformation program.

Throughout the department, we have especially stressed the importance of listening, for while it is tempting and sometimes inevitable to get stuck in the office and buried in emails, we want our organisation above all to be one that works through issues with people. For our departmental leaders, this means having a constant presence to get the best out of their team. Essentially this involves working with staff to understand their problems, so they know what the agenda is—both short term and long term. Ultimately, it requires establishing clear and consistent messages and expectations.

Improving communication also involves regular staff surveys. Previously, this rarely occurred. Prior to 2005, 10 years had passed since the last staff survey. But since the reforms began we now survey our staff every 12–15 months to try to shift people out of passive resistance into a much stronger engagement, and we have been largely successful in this undertaking.

An integral part of the planning and preparation stage was the development of comprehensive communication and stakeholder engagement strategies that include targeted individual communication plans for effective business areas. We deliberately tried to do this by the book so as to understand, identify and map our risks and to make sure the medium and long-term objectives of improving client service, enhancing efficiencies and ensuring decision-making integrity were met. The lead times for each element of the roll-out have been deliberately long to ensure we are able to continue business as usual, particularly at a time of high operational tempo, while at the same time developing and maintaining the momentum for longer-term change.

The third and final part of this overall transformation has been to group together all of our services for managing business and corporate services. This includes payroll and personnel centres or training units in each of our state offices, property managers or other business services. We have grouped them together to create a mixed corporate business-services area. Consequently, we now have a unified central legal-services area, a unified central technology-services area and a unified central communications and public affairs area. And yet, our people and our financial services continue to be spread widely across our states and territories and our divisions.

We believe we can provide better services and drive better efficiencies through a shared service model. We commenced this journey only in mid 2010, and the first thing we are focusing on is being able to account for all the people involved—quite a challenge indeed. The process involves bringing them into a single budget group before starting to examine how we can actually provide the best services. This does not mean all our services will come out of Canberra; it means rather that they can be done and distributed through a range of different models. By doing this, we believe we can improve efficiency, the value of people's work and the value of their work satisfaction. We also believe it will help us deliver benefits in value for money back to government, and do that in a way that will ultimately benefit the long-term future of the department.

Ultimately, transformation is about better services: better services for the Australian Government regardless of its policies; better services for our clients, be they visa applicants, potential citizens, immigration detainees, people who overstay visas or any other clients; and, last but not least, better services for our staff to ensure their job is an enjoyable one.

Concluding remarks

In 2010 DIAC celebrated its sixty-fifth birthday. We were created in 1945 by Prime Minister Ben Chifley, with Arthur Calwell becoming our first minister in July of that year, before the end of the War in the Pacific. Over those 65 years, we believe we have been a major force in helping build modern Australia and, indeed, are a vital part of Australia's economic and security infrastructure. As a result, Australia is now a country in which nearly one in two of us was either born overseas or has a parent who was born overseas.

And while there has generally been bipartisan support for migration policy, the history of immigration in Australia has been controversial at times. Often competing views and interests have to be carefully weighed, be they policy related, legal, operational, or indeed the needs of individuals. There has been significant public interest in immigration and citizenship matters in the

Parliament and in the community since the earliest days of the department and often right back to 1788. Many issues have been strongly debated in the Parliament, in the courts, in the media, in academia and in the court of public opinion. Such is to be expected from a vibrant, modern democracy such as Australia. Successive governments determine different levels of migration to suit Australia's needs at the time, and debate on such matters will continue in many forms.

Against this backdrop, the department has recently undertaken a significant overhaul. The progress of our initial reform program from 2005 to 2008 following the *Palmer Report*, and the subsequent transformation program that followed, can give us some confidence that we are an agile and forward-looking organisation. We have had considerable positive feedback from staff and I have been extremely encouraged by the support we have been receiving from senior colleagues in other departments.

But the best indication yet that we are succeeding in our endeavour has been the feedback we have received from our clients and stakeholders. For example, in August 2010, I announced to staff the results of the first research commission run by the department to gather intelligence on the experiences of our clients. It showed that about 82 per cent of our clients were satisfied or highly satisfied with our services—and that includes those who do not want to be our clients, such as those in detention, so it is a gratifying result. I can say those unintended clients are probably less pleased with our services than others, but it was not about the quality of the service; it was about whether they wished to receive the service in the first place.

As this transformation process continues, the Department of Immigration and Citizenship will strive to provide the best possible visa, migration and citizenship services to the Australian community by continuing to examine our services and operations. I am genuinely excited by the opportunities and benefits the department's long-term transformation program will provide to our direct clients, the Australian Government and the wider Australian community. I look forward to continuing to be a part of this journey.

13. Getting integrity reforms adopted internationally

Jeremy Pope

Throughout the Cold War, the topic of corruption on the international stage was virtually taboo. Development agencies could not or would not discuss it; international financial institutions closed their eyes to it; representatives of Western governments engaged in it when it suited them; and the private sector saw it simply as an unpleasant but increasingly expensive way to get things done. The silence was deafening. There were no reliable estimates of the extent to which development aid in particular was being siphoned off into bribes and kickbacks, let alone any analysis of the impact on fundamental human rights of what economists would euphemistically describe as 'leakage'.

There was a cosy coterie of elements profiting from the system in both developed and developing countries. Aid money had to be dispersed or parliaments would cease to provide it. Corrupt officials in the developing world were doing aid donors a favour simply by taking their money. The World Bank depended on lending to generate its own income, profiting as it did on the margin between the rates at which it lent and the slightly lower rates that it could borrow money given the benefits of according lenders a sovereign guarantee. Advancement within the bank depended on a staff member's ability to push money out the door, with no brownie points for stopping a loan simply because corrupt elements would benefit. No-one in senior management seemed to be exhibiting any desire to upset a mutually beneficial state of affairs, notwithstanding that their researchers were later to estimate that about $1 trillion was involved annually, or about 3 per cent of global income (Rose-Ackerman 2004).

In the meantime, development was to a significant degree being stymied. Developing countries were incurring needless levels of debt from suppliers who could recoup their kickbacks either by over-charging or short-changing on the delivery (and quality) of goods and services—or both. In addition, the prospect of massive bribes completely distorted the decision making about which projects should go ahead and which should not; ambitious infrastructure projects were always to be preferred over those with large labour components. The distortion of much-venerated international competitive bidding, too, had reached the status of being an art form.

One could see a country such as Tanzania apparently absorbing large-scale flows of aid over a period of decades, yet leaving its people no better off—and its education and health systems failing palpably. Only this year it finally surfaced that in 2002 the United Kingdom's biggest arms supplier, BAE Systems, paid a $12 million commission into the Swiss account of a middleman in a deal that led to Tanzania—one of the world's poorest countries—buying a controversial military radar system (*The Guardian*, 20 January 2010). The backdoor payment represented 30 per cent of the contract value. The East African state had to borrow to finance the deal, which was strenuously opposed by its citizens.

Underpinning this sorry state of affairs was the conceit in the developed world that it was more moral than the rest—that others 'did things differently', so it was 'not for us to impose our standards on others'. It was a comfortable way in which to defend the status quo. A leading African (Olusegun Obasanjo) was later to decry:

> Others are wont to argue that the African culture of appreciation and hospitality encourages corrupt practices. Again, I shudder at how an integral aspect of our culture could be taken as the basis for rationalizing an otherwise despicable behaviour. In the African concept of appreciation and hospitality, the gift is usually a token. It is not demanded, the value is usually in the spirit rather than in the material world. It is usually done in the open and never in secret. Where it is excessive, it becomes an embarrassment and is returned. If anything, corruption has perverted and destroyed this aspect of our culture (Obasanjo 1995:27).

The parlous situation in the developing world continued into the early 1990s, and it was in this unpromising environment that Transparency International (TI) first saw the light of day. It was greeted by a cartoon in Spain depicting TI as a latter-day Don Quixote astride his donkey, with a lance skewering a pile of documents.

The emergence of TI as a civil-society movement

How did Transparency International come into being—an international non-governmental organisation (NGO) with national chapters now in about 100 countries and one that is quoted daily in the press around the world? Transparency International's genesis dates from a discussion within the Global Coalition for Africa in 1992 that continued in a number of 'retreats' involving a World Bank official, Peter Eigen. It was there that Eigen hatched the idea of naming and shaming the corrupt corporations in the North by publishing an 'International Business Monitor' exposing those involved on both sides of corrupt international dealings. He outlined his plan for a bulletin to expose the activities of corporations behaving corruptly in the Third World. But the approach was recast into a less combative one, which was adopted as the only practicable way forward. We believed we should focus exclusively on corruption in international business transactions and seek to bring about change by identifying and working with those within the private sector who were unhappy with the 'competitive corruption' auctions that were taking place. Instead of being essentially confrontational in nature, we chose coalition building, and rather than simply criticising from a distance, we decided TI should join in a search for solutions and connect up those who might be won over to a reform movement.

Our focus on corruption in international business transactions emerged because of a belief that if international procurement could be tidied up, the worst effects of prevailing corruption could be moderated. The danger we saw was that corruption would become so widespread so quickly that it could undermine and destroy growth in developing nations. And even if corruption was consistent with economic growth under some conditions, this did not imply that it facilitated growth or that it did not have other negative political and social consequences.

None of us ever imagined that TI would so quickly be transformed from a small, ginger group addressing a part of the corruption agenda into a truly global movement addressing corruption in all its manifestations. Initially, at least, our small non-governmental organisation would have the limited aims of

1. breaking the conspiracy of silence about the issue of corruption in the private sector of the Western world (a topic broached only within the cloistered confines of gentlemen's clubs, and even then in whispers)

2. having the World Bank change its policy towards corruption from denial to one of active engagement

3. persuading development agencies to address the problem head-on (and not being afraid of upsetting their Third-World client governments and their First-World exporters).

We would do this

1. through public advocacy in breaking down the myth of Western moral superiority, so making it easier for developing-country leaders to discuss the issue and at the same time raising the awareness of citizens in the Western democracies of the harm those in their countries were inflicting on the developing world

2. by building coalitions among key constituencies of leaders and organisations who were on the side of change (making full use of the personal contacts each of us had built up over the years).

Later, when our mandate expanded, we were to add a third strategy: breaking the taboo that surrounded the issue in the developing world and challenging feelings of apathy and complete helplessness.

From the outset, we thought of ourselves as creating a very small 'ginger group' that, with active support from key individuals in a range of countries, would position itself as an advocate for the poor in the developing world. The support we already had from significant figures in the developing world gave us some legitimacy to be a champion of its interests. Our own small group represented something of a coalition, as there was a variety of agendas within it, not least a private-sector one.

We envisaged a small and temporary secretariat supported by active groupings in perhaps 15 key countries. Setting this up in Berlin would make sense. As a veritable tadpole in the international NGO pond, we would merely be one among many were the secretariat set up in London, New York, Washington or Paris. In Berlin, we would be unique, and an object of curiosity. As such, we would have a distinctive personality.

One of our group, George Moody-Stuart, had already privately circulated a small book entitled *Grand Corruption: How business bribes damage developing countries*. He laid bare the methods used by exporters around the world. For the first time, a respected business figure was talking openly about the role of the private sector in undermining governance in the developing world and countries in transition. He also labelled the phenomenon 'grand corruption'— an expression that quickly acquired use worldwide. His book was controversial; some emerged to support him, others moved to end some of his remaining directorships. Unbowed, Moody-Stuart soon proved a valuable asset in explaining to a bemused world across Africa and beyond just how bereft of moral superiority the developed world really was. 'We, too, are part of the problem', he said, 'and the developed world must join with you all in finding solutions'.

Getting the show on the road

The formal launch of the fledgling organisation, in May 1993, attracted a number of prominent personalities who agreed to attach their names to TI. Frank Vogl, a founding member and former correspondent with the *London Times*, secured a degree of global publicity for our launch event at which two of our advisory council members spoke—one a Nobel Laureate, the other a former African president. Some press attention was generated and the reaction from around the world was encouraging. A number of letters arrived in Berlin giving thanks for the fact that someone, somewhere, was at last trying to do something about corruption.

Funding was, of course, a problem. A handful of staff was hired on the clear understanding that if the money did not come in they would not be paid. Fortunately, a director in the German aid agency GTZ had recently discovered that its own officials had bribed the Education Ministry in Indonesia to win an aid contract. Appalled, he agreed to underwrite our rent. Two British charities, the Rowntree Trust and Nuffield, provided some seed money but although there was strong support from some within the World Bank, its then President, Lewis Preston, personally blocked any financial support from that quarter. A former World Bank President, Robert McNamara, pleaded our cause with Preston in vain. The bank's legal department was implacably opposed to us, and counselled others to avoid us as being mad, bad and dangerous to know.

Nor was the World Bank the only opposition. In Berlin, we had moved in to offices recently vacated by the Berlin Olympics Committee, whose bid to host the games had failed, and with the offices came an antiquated telephone system that had been given to the committee by Siemens. We thought it only polite to let Siemens know that we had inherited the telephones—only to have Siemens immediately claim them back. They said 'it would be bad for TI to be reliant on support from the private sector'. (For the record, in December 2008, Siemens ended up paying $1.6 billion in the largest fine for bribery in modern corporate history.)

On the media side, we started to garner support in some quarters such as the *BBC World Service*. By November 1994, *Newsweek* was running a cover story on 'Corruption: how bribes, payoffs and crooked officials are blocking economic growth', and stating that TI 'has given real visibility to the fight against graft'. In the meantime, we were warding off suggestions from some in the Berlin Senate that TI should oversee the integrity of the procurement processes being used for the redevelopment of one of the city's airports. Others wanted us to vet the voting in a worldwide poll they were planning to determine the world's top-10 tourist sites! We had to resist being drawn away from our principal focus.

We delighted in drawing outrageous responses, as they exposed the barefaced yet comfortable effrontery of the bribers, such as the following letter to the United Kingdom's *Daily Telegraph* (26 June 2000) newspaper:

> Having been involved in exporting to various countries in the Middle and Far East and in Africa, I have bribed government ministers and officials

of all grades, in the form of cash payments, commissions, introductory fees, new cars, hospital treatment and so on for more than 40 years. If I were not now retired I would continue to do so. That is the way one does business in those places…We expect people from overseas to conduct their business affairs in this country according to our laws and customs; it is both grossly impertinent and extremely naïve to suggest that we should not then respect their customs and conduct ourselves in their country as they would wish.

We were less enthused about consistently being labelled a 'CIA front' by the French journal *Le Monde Diplomatique*, which consistently declined offers to have free reign of our accounts. Others suggested additional links to MI5 and regularly referred to the fact that TI's earliest corporate supporter, General Electric, had been heavily fined for its part in international corruption in 1992. The expression 'the opacity of transparency' was a favourite in several languages. There have been continuing attacks on the organisation on various web sites. Making a virtue of necessity, our take on what was being said was that corporate interests unhappy with our creation were getting their retaliation in first. If some people were *not* unhappy with us then clearly we were wasting our time.

Some academics were also among the unhappy, seeing us as intruding into what had been their exclusive domain. Two of us went along to an international meeting of political scientists, held in Berlin, only to have a motion moved that we be ejected from the room. The indictment was one of being 'activists', not 'academics'. There were economists, too, who argued that corruption was not necessarily a bad thing, and that it introduced an element of certainty in what could otherwise be a very uncertain world.

Some have argued that corruption can have beneficial effects, such as access to government affairs and administration when political channels are clogged, or as a means of lessening the potentially crippling tension between the civil servant and the politician by linking them in an easily discerned network of self-interest. A German Catholic priest was paid handsomely by German companies to lecture managers on the morality of bribery—companies had a duty to ensure there was work for their employees to undertake, and if this meant bribing to get the contracts, there was a positive duty to do so. We, however, viewed corruption as tending to lower the general welfare of the populace. Of the priest, we asked whether it was moral to make martyrs of employees of companies whose management was honest.

We also considered as misleading an often-quoted equation espoused by a US professor, Robert Klitgaard, who argued that 'corruption is a crime of calculation, not of passion. People will tend to engage in corruption when the risks are low, the penalties mild and the rewards great.' (Klitgaard and Parris 2000:28). Klitgaard proposed a simple formula: $C = M + D - A$ (Corruption = Monopoly + Discretion − Accountability). We knew we had a lot to learn ourselves, but the equation beloved of many academic writers ignored the human element: integrity. A person can control a monopoly, not be accountable and still exercise discretion without being influenced by corruption. So we argued we had to rewrite the equation as Corruption = Monopoly + Discretion − Accountability − Integrity.

Other than approaching persons of influence, we were unsure just where and how to begin. We had to tackle a very steep learning curve and in this were grateful for the guidance of the academic Susan Rose-Ackerman. We chose to focus initially on corruption in sub-Saharan Africa. With support from the African Leadership Forum, roundtables were held to discuss the issue in several African capitals. We started organising integrity workshops and journalists' training courses in Uganda and Tanzania. The first integrity workshop in Tanzania made huge waves when, in opening the workshop, the country's Chief Justice, Francis Nyalali, stated emphatically that the approaching first-ever multi-party election of 1995 would be the most corrupt event the country had ever witnessed.

It was in Tanzania that we first tried out the concept of 'integrity pledges' to which all those present would be invited to subscribe. In Tanzania, the pledge challenged candidates for the presidency to commit themselves publicly, and in advance, to programs of reform and to declare their personal assets and those of their spouses upon election. Benjamin Mkapa, newly elected President in 1995, subscribed to the pledge and lived up to it. When at our suggestion he disclosed his assets publicly, it created a tidal wave of interest not only within Tanzania, but throughout sub-Saharan Africa and beyond. His hope that his cabinet colleagues would do likewise was, however, thwarted. The Attorney-General, whether innocently or otherwise (and himself later implicated in scandal), issued a press statement to the effect that disclosure was not required by the law, seeming to imply that the President had in some way acted illegally. Meanwhile, in Washington, two of us participated at 'brown-bag lunches' inside the World Bank that were quite literally crammed well beyond capacity and spilling out into the corridor, showing that many of the rank and file within the institution were hungry for change.

Building intellectual property: the first TI 'source book'

Just when we reached the stage of having to juggle our bills between paying the phone company and paying our landlord, the Ford Foundation came to the rescue. What, they asked us, is your intellectual property? This was an opportunity for us to inform ourselves much more deeply about the nature and extent of the corruption problem—critical if we were to claim any credence as being knowledgeable.

We recognised that it would not be enough simply to chant 'corruption bad, integrity good'. We needed to find some answers. At that stage, our focus had been restricted to finding a solution to the 'prisoner's dilemma' in the context of international competitive bidding in procurement. The prisoner with the dilemma can escape from prison only if other prisoners help him, but he has to decide whether he can trust the other prisoners. This translated for us into: 'I want to stop bribing, but if I do, can I trust my competitors to stop bribing, too?'

To respond to the challenge from the Ford Foundation, we went to work on producing what was described as a 'source book'. At the Commonwealth Secretariat, I had gathered a collection of the publications from the Australian Attorney-General's Department prepared under the guiding hand of Tom Sherman, who was then in the course of addressing the aftermath of Joh Bjelke-Petersen's catastrophic tenure of office in Queensland. Reading these from start to finish, it became apparent that what was being repaired was not an independent or discrete set of institutions and practices, but rather a single holistic integrity system in which the interplay and relationships of many made up a single whole. In this way, the concept of the 'national integrity system' was born. It was clear from this that there was no silver bullet when it came to countering corruption.

From TI's perspective, major corruption represented a failure of governance, and it would flourish in the absence of a strong and adequately equipped state. The national integrity system concept could provide a framework in which individual countries could look at themselves and determine where the fault lines lay. The study, published as the TI 'source book', was hugely successful and was translated into some 25 languages, including Arabic, Bosnian, Chinese, French, Hungarian, Korean, Portuguese, Romanian, Russian and Spanish.

Expanding TI's mandate

At TI's first annual general meeting in Ecuador in 1994, a young Ecuadorian activist, Valeria Merino Dirani, had an immediate and profound impact. Backed by Kamal Hossein (Bangladesh), she asserted that TI would have no credibility in the developing world if it confined itself to countering corruption in international business transactions. Important as this was, she said, to the ordinary citizen this was a non-issue compared with the daily menace posed by corrupt police, customs officers and politicians. She insisted that the mandate of the organisation be widened to cover all types of corruption—whether international or domestic, whether 'grand' or 'petty'.

Some of the founding group were rattled by her suggestion, but the implications were worked through. If domestic corruption were to be on the agenda, chapters in developing countries felt that they would need a code of conduct that protected them (and the organisation) from reprisals. They proposed that TI should position itself as a positive influence, not naming names and exposing individual cases (which would be the role of journalists), but monitoring the aftermath and examining the reforms needed to prevent reoccurrences. They also proposed that TI chapters specifically declare themselves to be non-party political. Both proposals won immediate acceptance. The change was profound. Henceforth, corruption of any sort was to be regarded as a threat to human rights, the environment and sustainable development that could no longer be ignored.

Transparency International itself, however, was far from being immune to the political virus. Alberto Dahik, the chair of its advisory council and Vice-President of Ecuador, fled his country in 1995 and went into exile to avoid facing allegations of embezzlement, bribery and illicit enrichment. This event forced TI to examine itself as an organisation. Henceforth, those active in conventional politics were to be considered ineligible for membership in TI—even though this meant excluding former Zimbabwean Chief Justice Enoch Dumbutshena, who had left office to campaign against Robert Mugabe on a platform of anti-corruption. Former political figures who could throw their weight and standing behind our efforts were still most welcome. Some retained their influence, such as one former senior official with the European Commission who was instrumental in encouraging the commission to issue a directive attacking trans-border corruption.

Creating a high profile: the Corruption Perceptions Index (CPI)

Despite our best efforts, we essentially remained an insignificant organisation, but one to which a small number of journalists would refer when wanting information. Repeatedly, they asked us about the relative standing of countries: which was the 'cleanest' country? Which the most corrupt? They wanted a league table. So, one of our interns in Berlin, Johann Graf Lambsdorff, beavered away with Fredrik Galtung and in 1995 eventually produced an approach that drew on the periodic assessments of several risk-management companies whose business it was to advise exporters of the risks generally in dealing with other countries. A first experimental list was drawn up, which was fortunately leaked to *Der Spiegel* to answer a specific question, and the Corruption Perceptions Index (CPI) was born.

The genie was out of the bottle and we waited for the consequences. Our press release seemed to have fallen on deaf ears before it appeared at length, on consecutive Saturdays, in *The New York Times*. News agencies in New York picked the story up from there and suddenly corruption was on the front pages of newspapers throughout the developing world. Editors who felt constrained about publishing reports of corruption in their own countries were now able to highlight international rankings. This then generated remarkable internal debates, with some political leaders decrying the findings and their opponents latching onto them as evidence of some kind. The issue was now out in the open in countries where hitherto it had been one that journalists and editors dare not mention.

Suddenly, too, the image of TI was being projected by journalists as being a huge organisation with tentacles around the world, gathering and assessing information about corrupt activities wherever these might be taking place. The impression continues to this day, with the CPI being referred to daily by the press in various parts of the world. It showed its power when Bolivia's rating slumped sharply on the eve of national elections, and the outgoing government threatened to sue us. Little did anyone know that the CPI was the result of only a few days' work by an intern.

Building a coalition: the search for allies

Pursuing an agenda in which coalition building was at the core, we continued our quest for allies—specifically, the following.

Civil society

Within civil society, we created our own set of national chapters. Most of those involved in starting TI had little previous experience of working with civil society and had to learn the hard way that no-one could go into someone else's country and anoint chosen individuals as leaders. Any new organisation would have to be built from the ground up. A watershed for chapter building came when an existing high-profile Argentinean action group, Poder Ciudadano (People's Power), became the first existing NGO to align itself with TI, and its charismatic leader, Luis Moreno Ocampo (now the Prosecutor at the International Criminal Court in The Hague) joined our advisory council. Over time, a number of effective activist organisations added support. These included Global Witness (a small group that succeeded in tackling 'blood diamonds' and introduced the Kimberley Process to authenticate sources of diamonds and the Extractive Industries Transparency Initiative [EITI]). As well there were The Corner House, the International Rivers Network, Article 19 and Odious Debts.

In addition, a number of initiatives were funded by George Soros's Open Society Foundation, tackling issues such as budget monitoring and conflict of interest in a number of countries, and establishing the Africa Governance Monitoring and Advocacy Project (AfriMAP) to name but a few.

Private sector

Within the private sector, connections could be exploited to win allies, such as Shell International. The International Chamber of Commerce in Paris was quite another story, appearing to be concerned that it might alienate its membership—and imperil its funding base—if it were to support too enthusiastically what we were trying to achieve.

Private bankers

Major private bankers—key players in managing 'private wealth' (much of it explicable only by its being the proceeds of corruption)—could be slowly won over by working through the 'prisoner's dilemma' and agreeing to what eventually became the Wolfsberg Principles.

Development aid agency

Institutionally, a major early breakthrough came when the US development aid agency, USAID, decided to make an institution-building grant to TI for some US$2 million. Later, four European ministers for development (all of them women and all personally supportive of our initiative) met in Utstein, Norway, and decided to pool resources in the fight against corruption. They called themselves the U4. Since then the U4 Anti-Corruption Resource Centre has assisted the ministers' staff in more effectively addressing corruption challenges through development support. Today the four has grown, and the U4 now serves eight development agencies in Norway, the United Kingdom, Canada, Germany, the Netherlands, Sweden, Belgium and Australia. A help desk was set up in TI's London office (later transferred to Berlin) that continues to provide answers to queries from development agency staff in the field.

The World Bank

From the outset, we struggled to bring the World Bank into the fold. Corruption did not belong in the bank's lexicon. Its legal department insisted that corruption was 'political', and that this meant it was off limits in terms of the bank's charter. Specifically, according to Article IV, Section 10, 'neither the institution nor its officers may interfere in the political affairs of any member, nor shall they be influenced in their decisions by the political character of the member...Only economic considerations shall be relevant to their decisions, and these considerations shall be weighed impartially'. To this, we argued in vain that corruption was in fact and in law an 'economic consideration'—contributing, as it did, to distorted decision making, waste and inefficiencies, and impacting negatively on the World Bank's objectives. We argued in vain until for the first time a non-American was appointed President: the Australian James Wolfensohn.

Through Robert McNamara, we had been able to brief the new appointee, and Wolfensohn immediately set out to reverse his institution's approach. Wolfensohn promptly called a day-long meeting of his most senior staff, inviting three of us to brief them about corruption from the TI perspective. At its conclusion, Wolfensohn stated that the lawyers said the bank could not fund TI but they could not stop him supporting the organisation generously through his own private office budget. Our consultations with senior bank staff—somewhat ironically—continued with a breakfast meeting at the Watergate Hotel.

At the annual meetings of the World Bank and the International Monetary Fund (IMF) in 1996, Wolfensohn characterised corruption as a 'cancer' on the global economy and emphasised that it was time to 'put teeth' into the World Bank's efforts to address it. Two years later, at the World Bank's 1998 annual meeting in Hong Kong, Wolfensohn, ignoring the legal advice he had been given, denounced corruption and declared that the bank would do what it could to combat it. To the surprise of many close to the organisation, not a voice was raised to question him. The Managing Director of the IMF, Michel Camdessus, was equally blunt, noting that IMF officials would henceforth regard it as their duty to press for anti-corruption reforms in countries seeking to borrow money. In the wake of the annual meetings, a working group was established under the Development Economics Vice-Presidency of the World Bank to develop an integrated anti-corruption strategy.

Consultations with senior bank staff concluded with the establishment of 'blacklisting' procedures, which we were later able to invoke successfully—albeit not without opposition—when a cluster of Canadian, British and German companies was caught bribing a procurement official in the poverty-stricken, landlocked African state of Lesotho in connection with a project partly funded by the World Bank. Hence, we could include as one of our achievements changing the attitudes and policies of the World Bank. We had thought it might take a decade, but it took less than five years.

Global professional bodies

Alone among the global professional bodies showing concern over corruption was the International Federation of Consulting Engineers (FIDIC). Their members were knowingly signing off on and certifying defective work as being fit for payment. And they knew, too, that buildings devoid of the necessary steel, or fashioned from concrete that lacked the required quantities of cement, were catastrophes waiting to happen. The other professional bodies whose members were facilitating the nefarious processes that made grand corruption so profitable—the lawyers and accountants—were, in the initial stages, conspicuously silent.

Further reform achievements

I have space to mention only a relatively small number of reform exercises that TI has been involved in, and I restrict myself to describing four.

Success with international conventions

It is fair to say that TI remains inherently suspicious of the efficacy of conventions. After all, law libraries are littered with UN conventions that have never come into force. Notwithstanding, in 1994 the first major success for TI was scored when, at the request of TI's growing band of Latin American chapters, corruption was placed on the agenda of the Summit of the Americas. This was the product of an alliance between nascent chapters in Latin America and fostered in the North by the chapter in the United States, TI-USA. The Summit of the Americas initiative quickly led to the signing of a major regional convention in 1996 providing for greatly enhanced cooperation in the fight against corruption, and including a strengthening of extradition arrangements. The convention enabled TI to intervene publicly when Peru sought to extradite former President Alberto Fujimori's partner in crime, Vladimiro Montesinos Torres, from Venezuela. It was also the first effort within the TI family to foster close cooperation and relationships on a regional basis—now a feature of the movement.

The following year the United States began moves to achieve a UN convention against corruption by floating a 'Declaration Against Bribery and Corruption in International Commercial Transactions'. We were alarmed by the thought that the international effort might founder on the rock of a universal and toothless convention that would enable states to adopt the position that the matter had been dealt with—albeit by a convention devoid of reporting and monitoring requirements.

TI was more impressed by a suggestion from US officials that we support an effort within the Organisation for Economic Cooperation and Development (OECD) to achieve a convention on international commercial transactions, and agreed to do this on the basis that any convention: i) be concluded within a limited time frame (negotiations could linger for years); ii) include a fixed date by which a requisite number of countries had adopted it; and iii) provide for meaningful and effective monitoring. Securing agreement on the Convention on Combating Bribery of Foreign Public Officials in International Business Transactions was far from easy. Fortunately, a Swiss law professor, Mark Pieth, chaired the working party and emerged as one of the most significant global figures in the struggle to contain corruption, subsequently establishing the influential Basel Institute on Governance.

The OECD proposal was seen by the Europeans as an attempt by the United States to internationalise the *Foreign Corrupt Practices Act* (*FCPA*). This had been enacted at the instance of President Jimmy Carter in 1977 after investigations in the mid 1970s during which more than 400 US companies admitted making questionable or illegal payments in excess of US$300 million to foreign government officials, politicians and political parties. The anti-bribery provisions of the *FCPA* made it an offence under US law for US citizens and corporations to make payments to foreign officials for the purpose of obtaining or retaining business. The measure was so obviously one of global leadership that Carter expected other responsible Western governments to follow suit. They did not, preferring to regard the United States as having shot its exporters in one foot and given a comparative advantage to European exporters.

To say that the legislation was—and is—unpopular with corporate America is an understatement. After Carter, successive administrations were lobbied in a strenuous effort to have the *FCPA* repealed, but each president in turn recognised the negative signal that repeal of such a 'motherhood' provision would send to the rest of the world. It was President Bill Clinton who determined that if the Act could not be repealed then major competitors around the world should have to sign up to similar measures.

On taking office in 1993, he charged his officials to start to work on the issue through the OECD in Paris. In time, US officials approached TI looking for our support for their initiative. We agreed—not on the basis of providing corporate America with a level playing field for export competition, but in the interests of the victims of corrupt practices, most notably the poor in the developing world. We insisted that the exercise be time bound and with robust monitoring of compliance.

From the outset, it was clear that progress was never going to be easy. European governments were enamoured with the US *FCPA* as it created impediments for US business in the international market. Most notably, it increased risks for US exporters caught bribing—risks that none of the European corporations faced. For our part, we campaigned strenuously across Western Europe, highlighting the fact that bribes paid abroad were treated as legitimate business expenses, so were tax deductible. European taxpayers were thereby indirectly subsidising the corrupt conduct of their nationals in foreign countries and undermining the efforts of their own aid agencies in trying to foster good governance there. As corrupt transactions seldom resulted in the provision of receipts, tax inspectors simply turned a blind eye; the French even devised a schedule of allowable bribe payments calculated on a country-by-country basis.

Initially, it was the British Government (led by the Department of Trade and Industry: DTI) that led the resistance to the proposed OECD convention. By way of response, TI's UK chapter lobbied the DTI to no avail and finally turned to the minister responsible for overseas development aid, Baroness Linda Chalker. She was shocked to learn that another of her UK Government's ministries was actively undermining her efforts to improve governance in the developing world and was quick to have the British Government's position reversed from opposition to active support.

Attention then switched to the German representative. He suggested that his government would be only too happy to support a convention on the topic but, alas, it was politically impossible for it to do so. The German private sector was, he suggested, implacably opposed to any such measures. Once again, a TI national chapter (the German) switched up a gear. A small group of leading industrialists was urged to write a joint letter to the relevant ministry stating that corruption in foreign business transactions was not only bad per se, but was also bad for German business. For these reasons, they supported the preparation of a convention. TI circulated the letter to delegates on the eve of the next session working on the draft convention, and German resistance evaporated.

That left the French, who fought a rearguard battle, trying to insert an outrageous 'grandfather clause' that would allow established illicit arrangements to continue and prohibit only new ones from being entered into. Transparency International's small French chapter lobbied hard and the attempt to frustrate the whole exercise fell away.

In the event, an OECD convention was signed on 17 December 1997—the first and still the only international convention that addresses the supply side of corruption. To come into effect, however, it had to be ratified no later than 31 December 1998 by at least five of the 10 countries that had the largest export shares of global trade, and that represented by themselves at least 60 per cent of the combined total exports of those 10 countries. By the beginning of December 1998, we were still short of the required numbers. Canada alone could save the exercise from foundering. With the Christmas break approaching, TI Canada stepped in and lobbied both its government and the opposition to enable the necessary legislation to go through all its stages in a single day on the eve of the parliamentary recess. One vote against the measure in either house would have frustrated the enterprise. It was our belief that only a politically neutral actor, such as the national chapter, could have achieved such an outcome.

The OECD convention came into force in 1999 in what *The New York Times* and *Washington Post* editorial writers described as a 'triumph for Transparency International'. To date, all 31 OECD member countries and seven non-member countries—Argentina, Brazil, Bulgaria, Estonia, Israel, Slovenia and South Africa—have adopted the convention. The deadlines served their purpose; the ratification process had taken less than 14 months—something of a record for a multilateral convention with such serious domestic implications. The exercise illustrates a number of ways in which civil-society activists can contribute to reform. They can lobby; they can carry information from one part of government to another where channels of communication are failing; they can inform politicians and civil servants where they have made unjustified assumptions about the views of stakeholders; and, above all, they can work across the divides of political parties in a non-partisan manner.

What, then, of the follow-up monitoring? The convention itself establishes what the OECD describes as being 'an open-ended, peer-driven monitoring mechanism to ensure the thorough implementation of the international obligations that countries have taken on under the convention' (OECD 2009). The monitoring is carried out by the OECD Working Group on Bribery, composed of members of all state parties and chaired by Professor Mark Pieth. Its life has not been easy. Under the process, countries prepare self-assessments of their performance. These are then followed by mutual evaluations in which experts from other state parties visit and report on a country's performance—a process that includes inputs from local civil society. The Working Group then meets with representatives of the country concerned and discusses what emerged.

Generally, international dialogue is masked by a veneer of diplomacy, but the hostility of the British Government towards findings that it had failed to implement the convention by relying on existing, but inadequate, laws became so fractious that that government went so far as to try to have Pieth removed from chairing the working party. To make matters even more embarrassing for the British, a small UK NGO, The Corner House, took the Government to court on judicial review when the Serious Fraud Office (SFO) discontinued a corruption investigation into a major arms deal after Saudi Arabia threatened to withdraw cooperation on security matters should the SFO not do so. The United Kingdom did this despite a clear prohibition in the OECD convention that state parties 'shall not be influenced by considerations of national economic interest, [or] the potential effect upon relations with another State'.

The Corner House won in the lower courts but lost on a final appeal by the SFO to the House of Lords. There the Law Lords ruled that it was not for the UK courts to determine whether the decision was compatible or not with Article 5 of the OECD Anti-Bribery Convention, or to interpret and construe the meaning of Article 5, but for the OECD's Working Group on Bribery to do so as the dispute mechanism provided for in the convention. The House of Lords judgment made it quite clear that the United Kingdom had failed to incorporate Article 5 of the Anti-Bribery Convention into its domestic legislation, and that the Article's provisions (and even those of the whole convention) were unenforceable in the United Kingdom. In the absence of legislation to that effect, the courts were not able to enforce them.

All along, the British chapter of TI had been arguing publicly and privately for more explicit legislation. Their efforts were supported by other non-governmental organisations, among them the BOND Governance Group (a network of 35 organisations that focuses on governance within international development, both at a policy and a practice level). These endeavours came to fruition with the passage of the far-reaching UK *Bribery Act* in April 2010, just four days before Parliament was dissolved for the holding of the general election. Significantly, this was during the so-called 'wash-up' period after the date for the election had been announced, when all party whips individually held vetos over each outstanding bill. The passage of this Act was fortuitous, as one of the first actions of the new Conservative-led government was to delay implementation of the new Act by at least six months to April 2011. *The Financial Times* reported (20 July 2010) that

> the imminent change has induced panic among many leading companies, which are worried that a failure to comply could damage reputations and cut profits, particularly in emerging markets. As a result, [the government] has agreed to run another consultation about how companies should make sure they do not fall foul of the new law.

The head of TI's UK chapter was quoted as saying that the delay was 'extremely disappointing…The danger is that under the guise of consultation, attempts may be made by those who want to pursue business as usual to water down the Act'. The coalition government was 'in danger of undermining' its own corruption policy.

The British example illustrates that it is not enough to work for and win an international convention. This marks only the beginning of a continuing process in which the performance of the state parties has to be assessed, and reports fed into the OECD Working Group on Bribery. Transparency International chapters in OECD countries are now engaged in monitoring the extent to which their governments are complying with their obligations and in ensuring that their own private sector is fully cognisant of the risks now posed should they be caught bribing abroad. The work for civil society is likely to be unending.

The Wolfsberg anti-money-laundering principles

Money laundering and hidden deposits are major components in the grand corruption equation, and include processes facilitated by law firms, accountancy firms and, most importantly, bankers. A success came when 11 of the world's largest private banks were brought together and each participant was persuaded that it would be in its own best interests to disclose its 'Know Your Customer' rules provided the others did the same. Efforts began in 2000, and it was three years before agreement was finally reached at Wolfsberg Castle, in north-eastern Switzerland.

One of the elements in the international financial system that actively facilitates the laundering of the proceeds of corruption is the high level of competition for deposits between major banks offering private wealth management. Thus, they kept their 'Know Your Customer' rules close to their individual chests, concerned not to reveal any chink that might be exploited by a competitor. We were anxious to do what we could to close the door, at least partially, on competition for illicit wealth between the major players, and to find a solution to what on the face of it was a classic example of the prisoner's dilemma.

For a time this seemed incapable of resolution. The sums of money involved are significant and there was considerable reluctance, fostered by suspicion, on the part of each bank for it to make the first move. Finally, agreement was reached whereby each of them would provide a copy of their 'Know Your Customer' rules to a New York firm of attorneys. The lawyers would hold the disclosures in confidence and not share them until every participant had complied with the group undertaking. In this way none of the banks had to trust any of the others. It is widely agreed that the consensus would never have been achieved in the absence of a trusted civil-society group that could act as a catalyst and facilitate the brokering of an agreement. This proved to be only a beginning. The group has gone on to develop fresh approaches to deal with monitoring money movements and the security of electronic transfers.

Business principles for countering bribery

Transparency International needed to address the supply side of international grand corruption in preventive as well as prosecutorial ways. More modest in its beginnings—but perhaps even more ambitious than Wolfsberg—was the concept of bringing together a small group of major corporations and some trade union representatives to examine whether there might be scope for developing generally applicable business principles for the containment of corruption. We believed that if we could facilitate a committed group of leading businesses, it might be possible to produce a set of agreed actions that melded into a single set of principles.

This has been so successful that it has been taken up by the World Economic Forum. In 2004, the forum launched the Partnering Against Corruption Initiative (PACI), whose objective is to commit companies to a set of procedures based on TI's Business Principles. PACI is described as a business-driven global initiative with commitment from the top. Just as with Wolfsberg, this demonstrates how change can be brought about when a civil-society group builds a coalition for change around a particular issue and interests major actors in adopting the resulting new concepts.

Strengthening judicial integrity

A judiciary of undisputed integrity is the bedrock institution essential for ensuring compliance with democracy and the rule of law. Even when all other protections fail, it should provide a bulwark for the public against any encroachments on their rights and freedoms under the law. Alas, in many countries this is not the case, but in the view of TI it is an essential starting point for the creation of a fully functioning modern state. So it was that the Judicial Group on Strengthening Judicial Integrity was established, with Justice Michael Kirby as its rapporteur. At a meeting in Bangalore, India, in 2001, an informal group of chief justices and superior court judges from around the world combined their experience and skill with a sense of dedication to the task they were invited to address. Since then, the group's work and achievements have grown to a point where they have made a significant impact on the global judicial scene.

The Bangalore Principles of Judicial Conduct have since been developed progressively, receiving increasing acceptance over the past few years from the different sectors of the global judiciary and from international agencies interested in the integrity of the judicial process. The Bangalore Principles are increasingly seen as a document that all judiciaries and legal systems can unreservedly accept. In short, these principles give expression to the highest traditions relating to the judicial function as visualised in all the world's cultures and legal systems. Values defined in the principles, and given reality in practical examples, include independence, impartiality, integrity, propriety, equality, competence and diligence. The task of reaching agreement on the detail of these core principles was a challenging one but the Judicial Integrity Group—through unwavering commitment to achieving a result that would command universal acceptance—surmounted every barrier that appeared to be in the way of a universal draft.

Not only have some states adopted the Bangalore Principles verbatim, others have modelled their own Principles of Judicial Conduct on them. Additionally, international organisations have given Bangalore their own endorsements.

The UN Social and Economic Council, for example, has invited member states to encourage their judiciaries to take account of the principles when developing rules for the professional and ethical conduct of the members of the judiciary. Further, the UN Office on Drugs and Crime has actively supported the work of the Judicial Integrity Group, as have such bodies as the American Bar Association and the International Commission of Jurists. More recently, the group has operated independently from TI, and with a separate facilitator.

Conclusion

Today in TI, the locus of effective action has largely moved from its Berlin centre to the grassroots. Although international breakthroughs have been made, the task remains to have corruption prevention worked into the Millennium Development Goals. The emphasis has now moved towards monitoring, whereas it was once on being creative. Internationally, TI has national chapters in about 100 countries, great and small. Some are large and effective; others struggle to make their voices heard. Some are well funded; some grapple with little. All are addressing what they see as being key areas of their own national integrity systems that need to be addressed as a priority. Where there are commonalities, national chapters are pooling their experience. It has certainly come a long way from being the tiny ginger group of 15 or so years ago.

If we were asked what drove TI as a civil-society movement into the campaign against corruption in the first place, our collective motivation is best captured by the Nobel Peace Laureate Oscar Arias Sanchez, who did much to help establish TI. About the time that he was writing an eloquent foreword to the TI 'source book', he was asked by journalists what single point he would make if addressing all the young people of the world. His reply captures what it is that drives the thousands involved in the TI anti-corruption movement:

> I think the most important thing for the future generations is to understand that it is necessary to have ideals, to dream, to live a life of principles. It is necessary to understand that the brotherhood is more important than the self. It is necessary to comprehend that the problems of a neighbour in some way affect us too. It is necessary to live in a transparent, crystal-like world where everyone practices what they preach, to end hypocrisy and to have the courage to fight for what you believe in. I would say don't give in to the naysayers, not to give up one's dreams of bettering the world. Understand that by fighting for the impossible, one begins to make it possible. In that way, no matter how difficult the task is, one will never give up. And it doesn't matter if they

call us dreamers, idealists. I always said I would rather be Don Quixote than to be Pancho. Understand that the idealists of today will be the leaders of tomorrow. And we can't stop dreaming.

References

Klitgaard, Robert, Ronald Maclean-Abaroa and H. Lindsey Parris, 2000, 'Corrupt Cities: A Practical Guide to Cure and Prevention'. Oakland: ICS Press and World Bank Institute.

Obasanjo, O. 1995. 'Keynote Address' in A. Aderinwale (ed.), 'Corruption, Democracy and Human Rights in West Africa', Nigeria: Africa Leadership Forum.

OECD, 2009, 'OECD Convention on Combating Bribery of Foreign Public Officials in International Business Transactions: Implementing the Convention, country by country'.http://www.oecd.org/document/56/0,334 3,en_2649_34859_2017813_1_1_1_37447,00.html

Rose-Ackerman, Susan, 2004, 'The Challenge of Poor Governance and Corruption', Copenhagen Consensus Challenge Paper, p.2.

14. Sustaining water reform in Australia

Ken Matthews

Australia is the driest inhabited continent in the world, so effective water management is of critical importance. In this chapter, I will analyse the reform process of Australian water management. I will first explore the role of the National Water Commission (NWC)—a somewhat misunderstood body—in the process. I will next discuss the specific needs for reform in this field as identified by the commission, and address how best to approach, build and sustain water-management reform. I will finally present the National Water Commission's recommendations to the Council of Australian Governments (COAG) on water reform, and our appraisal of the reform process to date.

The National Water Commission: a watchdog for water reform

In 2006 the Commonwealth, states and territories signed the National Water Initiative (NWI), an intergovernmental agreement first tabled in 2004, which called for a change in the way water is managed in Australia. The NWI consisted of 40 pages detailing the specific needs and ways this should be done. As water management is essentially a state responsibility, the NWC was created to monitor the progress of water reform as pledged by each tier of Australian government in the NWI. The commission is perhaps unique for an Australian public administration body as it was established primarily to criticise and with a clear remit to advocate publicly for change. We are also a program manager in a conventional sense, much like a ministry. We provide policy advice, we audit and assess, and we play on the field by being actively involved in improving water management. The NWC's tagline is 'driving national water reform'. I am not aware of a parallel organisation in public administration terms. The commission can initiate its own actions and even do some spending without reference to others—a power related to our critical advocacy role. We are not constrained to avoid policy judgments as some of the family of assessment and audit agencies are, so we can and do make specific recommendations about what needs to be done and specific criticisms about what should not have been done.

The commission is headed by seven commissioners, each independent and appointed for their expertise. Despite the fact three of the commissioners are nominated jointly by the states and four (including the chair) are nominated by the Commonwealth, we are all required under the commission's governing legislation to act in the best interest of the organisation. Indeed, my observation is that from the first occasion the commissioners met, we quickly forgot who nominated whom. The NWC has thus been an effective exercise in federal cooperation, and, unlike most national organisations, we have a remit to report to COAG regularly and when we see a need.

Every two years the commission conducts a major national assessment of the progress of water reform (see below). We also produce transparency products aimed at casting light on poorly understood areas of water management; examples include a definitive report on Australian water markets and a detailed assessment of the performance of every water utility in Australia, both urban and rural. For the latter project, we compare the performance of each utility against scores of different performance parameters. Both projects help cast light on areas of water management that would otherwise remain opaque.

Another role of the NWC is to produce position statements to help advocate change and propose practical solutions to actually achieve such change. In other words, where we can identify a problem in Australia concerning water management, we will try to articulate the problem and produce something to fix it. The public administration processes to achieve this involve first the NWC, in our capacity as assessor and auditor, diagnosing problems needing to be addressed. If governments accept this advice, the relevant ministers and departmental advisors are then responsible for any responses to our diagnosis. We may also suggest some of that prescription ourselves, but ultimately, this is the role of ministers and government departments.

Policy is next implemented, after which we return to the role of assessing it. Often the diagnosis of a problem is the most difficult part of the process; it can take time to gain popular acceptance, meaning the commission, having established its position on a particular reform, might need to 'incubate' the issue for some time. An example of this occurred early in the commission's existence when we diagnosed that the system of water data in Australia was inadequate for quality policy formulation. We were required to argue this point for a significant period before $450 million was finally allocated to the Bureau of Meteorology (BOM) in 2008 to rectify this problem. As a consequence, BOM is no longer simply the foremost source for Australian meteorological data; it is quickly becoming the go-to place for Australian hydrological data.

Areas for reform in Australian water management

Let us focus on five major deficiencies identified in our water-management system as examples of the diagnosis process we undertake. First, we have no 'water science' strategy. We found there is no system dedicated to the critical decisions that need to be made about water science. Over the past few years the commission has consistently recommended to COAG the need for a national water-science strategy. In our opinion—developed after consultations with some of Australia's leading water scientists and science users—the lack of such a system hampers priority-setting processes. The existing ways choices are made about where we focus our water science are obscure and, as a consequence, budget-setting processes are non-existent.

Another ramification of having no water-science strategy is that the links between science and policy are currently weak, diminishing the rightful influence scientists should exercise on policy formulation. This has led to some policy makers discounting the value of scientific input in the policy-formulation process. Instead, the NWC would like to see a system in which the water managers and the water policy makers are profoundly embedded with the relevant scientists. For the moment though, in Australia, these linkages are weak, and consequently, there are many unmet research needs. What, for example, is the ecological response when you flush a particular wetland with scarce environmental water?

The second deficiency to highlight is the undefined role of environmental water managers in this country. Australia's environmental managers have traditionally been slightly technical, second-tier, public-sector people with no specific sense of self-identity. Further, they have operated under very confused governance. For example, a state government official might be taking decisions about allocation or how best to use such environmental water (that means water for environmental services), and on the same day they might be advising the minister about the allocation and use of consumptive water. In this way, their accountabilities are confounded, conflated and confused.

Third, there is a considerable lack of agreement in environmental water management about which environmental assets are to be protected and the standard to which they should be protected. For instance, not only do we typically not know which are the most important environmental assets to be protected, we also do not know how big or how green a wetland should be, how resilient the ecological system should be, or how often waterings should accommodate a nesting or hatching event. These threshold decisions, when left unmade, give the environmental water manager little chance of success.

Fourth, environmental water managers lack the necessary scientific input to know what the ecological responses might be if, for example, there is a flush of a wetland. There are different ecological responses that can be observed and we need good science to know whether the water is being used effectively— let alone efficiently. Additionally, at a strategic level there are still issues to be resolved concerning triple bottom-line objectives: is the environmental water manager responsible only for environmental outcomes, or are there social and economic imperatives to be delivered as well?

Finally, there is a stark lack of cross-jurisdictional integration in the field of Australian water management to the point that the Commonwealth and the states have made very little progress in better aligning their efforts.

Before the NWC cast light on these five deficiencies (among many other examples), they were entrenched as the status quo of Australian water management. Although far from being successfully addressed, the fact these problems have been diagnosed is a positive start. We must now strive for broader acceptance of the need for reform in these areas, which in turn will lead to the process of change. For now, however, we are at the initial stage of diagnosis.

Federalism and water management

One of the biggest political issues in the area of water management is the division of responsibilities among governments. Water management is essentially a state responsibility, but there exist strong public and media perceptions that due to continual mismanagement by this level of government, a Commonwealth takeover is necessary. This view is not necessarily shared by the NWC, but there is no doubt it is widespread. The problem with such a takeover is that it would not be achieved as easily as some media commentators might suggest. This is not only because the necessary changes to the current constitutional arrangements would lead to legal problems; practically, too, the Commonwealth could not take over, because the states hold all the levers. And, most pertinently, the Commonwealth lacks the necessary expertise.

Complicated by such problems, responsibility has instead regressed to management by intergovernmental agreements and intergovernmental machinery. This in turn precipitates the following implications: negotiated outcomes, lowest common denominator outcomes, management by committee, slow agreements, reduced scope for Commonwealth policy leadership and national outcomes that generally become compromised. Because the states have the resources, the capacity and the constitutional responsibility, delivery of water management will have to continue via this tier of government. Yet with intergovernmental machinery complicating this process, it appears likely the cycle of public and media dissatisfaction with the current division of responsibility will continue.

Approaching water reform

Once water management deficiencies have been diagnosed and accepted, how then should subsequent reforms be approached to ensure they become embedded? First, at the NWC, we believe it is fundamental to think strategically during the diagnosis process about what needs to be reformed, so the necessary research can be commissioned and we can position ourselves at the 'fall of the ball'. One of the biggest challenges for the reformer is compiling the necessary evidence and data to support their case once the public debate so demands it. In the instance of Australian water reform, this can be done with the contribution of such organisations as the Productivity Commission, the Australian Bureau of Agricultural and Resource Economics (ABARE), or the NWC itself. What we at the commission espouse is, however, not a research-led reform agenda, but a *research-equipped* reform agenda. To achieve this, we need to commission research that becomes available at exactly the right time. As any water scientist will say, there is nothing more frustrating than working in an area for years, finally getting the call from the policy maker requesting advice in that area within a fortnight, only to have to tell them that it takes two years to produce the necessary scientific advice. Timing is therefore critical to approach water management reform.

Second, a national framework that allows for local solutions is necessary to approach water reform. The previously mentioned National Water Initiative fits this description. The NWI is strategic in terms of the overall shared national outcomes to which all levels of government have committed, but at the same time it provides flexibility for jurisdictions to legislate in their own way to reflect their own unique conditions. This of course leads to the age-old argument that Commonwealth and state people have about uniformity versus consistency, which is simplistic and unhelpful. Rather, in the majority of water management reform cases, some provision for local solutions is critical to success.

It is also important to distinguish between a national reform agenda and a Commonwealth reform agenda. A national initiative—free from the resentment often attached to a Commonwealth equivalent—can improve buy-in and ownership. As the term implies, it should have a truly *national* character, defined by trans-jurisdictional cooperation, as we find with the NWI. Indeed, the NWI attempts to combine strategic policy—that is, directions—with some practical ways to achieve them. Time lines are used to establish the broad objectives for future water management each signatory shares, with a specific set of commitments to be met by each party by specified deadlines. Despite the fact that, because of some slippage, many of these commitments are yet to be met, the NWC believes the driving effect of having these time lines, coupled with annual or two-yearly assessments made by us, seems to work.

Additionally, for national water-reform initiatives to succeed there needs to be enough in the package for all parties, delivered at a balanced rate. The NWI is unusual in that it has had to carry not just the Commonwealth and state governments, but also the wide range of interest groups involved in water. Despite the fact these range from the reactionary (for example, some irrigators) to the idealistic (for example, some environmentalists), no interest group (or government) has yet walked away from the NWI. Now four years since it was tabled, the initiative could easily have failed, yet it continues to be an agreement that sticks, partly because there is enough in the package for everyone. For example, both irrigators and environmentalists find enormous value in getting property rights to water because one of the principles of the NWI is that there should be statutory equality for environmental and consumptive water. Such an arrangement is quite a far-reaching strategic change in the way water is managed in Australia. There are many other such examples of shared interests in the NWI, but this one alone has kept stakeholders committed to the package.

Providing clear and effective information to affected communities is also critical to approaching water reform, when communities in the Murray–Darling Basin are completely unaware of what their future holds for them. Indeed, the NWC has argued that there are better ways to produce the Murray–Darling Basin Plan. Had better community consultation occurred—such as, for example, progressive and interim exposure of ideas and objectives—people could have had a clearer idea of reform directions. Under the current process for developing the plan, the basin's communities, irrigators, stakeholders and environmental groups have little or no idea of what is in store for them and a negative reaction is almost certain. Surely this is not the best way to proceed. Clarity about burden-sharing arrangements—or what is called 'risk assignment' in the NWI—is especially crucial. Both this and the accompanying sense of fairness must be made transparent to people who are involved.

In thinking of stakeholder consultation, we should seek to address what issues are at 'stake', or what could be obtained for the stakeholder from the reform process. Trying to align a set of interests rather than just mindlessly dealing with a stakeholder is a much more productive and honest way of approaching consultation. I encourage my stakeholder management teams to be focused and sharp about how and why they are engaging with stakeholders.

Consultation needs to be genuine and serious at both the peak body and the grassroots level. For the former, we have a stakeholder reference group at the NWC that meets several times a year. The aim is to gather all the relevant players and their differing perspectives: the National Farmers Federation, the Business Council, the Australian Conservation Foundation and so on. At these meetings, we attempt to respectfully listen to each party and then share some of our perspectives as well—a markedly different approach to the common mistake made by bureaucrats of simply talking at stakeholders. We are conscious to dedicate a few hours at the beginning of each of these meetings to letting stakeholders talk to each other—an experience they find positive. Through this interaction, the stakeholders leave knowing not only what we are thinking and doing, but what each other is thinking and doing as well. Overwhelmingly positive feedback from various peak-body stakeholders indicates this model of consultation has been successful.

At the grassroots level, an altogether different approach is required. In order to gain respect from local actors, it is wise to travel to meetings alone, regardless of whether the news you have for the stakeholders is good or bad. There is no doubt it is not easy to deliver bad news to a group of angry irrigators. But by engaging in the discussion as personally as you can, the best possible outcome is usually achieved. This local approach is an important complement to the more formal style of peak-body consultation.

Finally, water-policy reform should be approached through a wider environmental context; it should be nested in natural-resource management, rather than being seen as a discrete, disconnected natural resource.

Building support for water reform

To build sophisticated support for water management reform, we at the commission have found the COAG imprimatur invaluable. The NWI is not just another agreement; it is a COAG-level water agreement that carries the signature of premiers, chief ministers and the Prime Minister. Consequently, it can be a persuasive tool for both governments and stakeholders. With such high-profile signatories comes a certain degree of momentum that we are using to our advantage.

To date, we have enlisted national advocates for the NWI and for wider water reform in general, including the Committee for Economic Development of Australia (CEDA), the Business Council of Australia, and peak-level irrigation and environmental groups. All are non-governmental actors; all are championing the cause of water reform. Additionally, the NWC is attempting to align the commentaries on water management of various respected national agencies, including the Australian National Audit Office (ANAO), the Productivity Commission, the Australian Competition and Consumer Commission (ACCC) and others. In this we have had some modest success; there is a general consensus among these agencies about what should be the future direction of Australian water management. This shared belief, together with third-party endorsements (for example, from CEDA), has helped build a strong wave of public support.

Second, to maximise the chances of successfully building public support for a reform, government reformers must time their run according to the election cycle. In the life of a government, the worst time to launch a reform campaign is probably just before an election. Conversely, the right time is in the early stages of a government. Canny, reform-minded officials are sensitive to their ministers' aspirations to leave their own legacy and pursue their own big issues during their ministership—including policy reform. Far from being manipulative, hitching your reform star to a minister's interests and aspirations is mutually supportive and entirely pragmatic. It also requires, however, the nous to sense what the minister is searching for and how your reform agenda can be compatible.

Third, policy makers looking to build support for their reform are advantaged by the fact that while Australia is a large country, it is a small nation. By this I mean that compared with the United States or Europe, for example, it is relatively easy to deal personally with decision makers. In each of the different portfolios I have worked in over my career, if there was an issue to be solved, I simply picked up the phone, called my counterpart CEO and said: 'we have a problem, how are we going to deal with this?' Such an approach would not be possible for my counterpart in the United States and certainly not in Europe. Consequently, Australia possesses a more governable and therefore potentially more reformable economy and polity than many countries—an advantage that provides the opportunity to forge a group of like-minded reformists among the Commonwealth and state governments. Depending on where you sit, successful dealings with one's counterparts can lead to a small but powerful group of reform advocates. In this way, Australia's small network of policy professionals can be a powerful institutional force for change—albeit an informal one.

Successfully entrenching water reform

The most important stage of any reform process is introducing automatic processes to embed and sustain the original reform—something the NWC is currently trying to achieve. The best example is markets, whose introduction will lead to further developments occurring autonomously. When we finally established water markets, there was no going back. Even the conservative irrigators who said 'markets over my dead body' are now actively using those markets and are gracious to admit they were wrong. Further, not only are such developments usually irreversible, but the self-managing nature of the process means government interference is no longer necessary. Australian water markets are now recognised as the most developed and sophisticated of their kind anywhere, such that we frequently receive international visitors coming to study the model instituted here.

Water markets cannot exist, however, without property rights. This is why under the NWI property rights were secured for irrigators—something that affirmed their commitment to the scheme. Environmentalists, too, championed the attainment of property rights as part of the NWI, because this opened the prospect of securing perpetual allocations of water for the environment. This example shows how by incorporating incentives and disincentives into a reform, relevant parties will act according to their own self-interests—a better outcome than enforcement through regulation.

Markets are one example of a self-sustaining process for change—critical to the successful entrenchment of reform. Another way of achieving such automaticity is to create, or modify, an institution. Once created, institutions will carry forward their responsibilities, particularly if they are of a statutory nature. An institution bound by legal obligations—particularly new or modified laws—can become an effective agent for autonomously entrenching a policy reform. This prevents the need for continually reworking the original reform year after year.

Adaptive-management obligations are another effective way to entrench policy reform. Adaptive management is a common term in water, referring to the idea that if some wetland were to be irrigated with environmental water, a scientific observation of the ecological response would be needed to advise on any modifications needed to the wetting regime. While this adaptive-management cycle is a generic concept that could apply to any sector, it is of particular relevance to water management, where it can act as a powerful means of entrenching self-sustaining reform. Adjustment assistance is obviously an important part of this process of changing management practices. This can come in many forms: it might be through buy-outs, or it can be a continuing process of delivering economic resources to stakeholders so as to ensure they continue to get part of the yield from the reforms, thus ensuring their interests continue to align with those of the reform process.

Governments will be required to devote more resources to achieving the goal of sustainable water management reform. Although water is fundamentally a state responsibility in Australia, too often the state water agencies are under-resourced and lacking capacity, hampering their ability to effectively manage water. And, despite having trumpeted the benefits of having a small, cohesive circle of reform-oriented professionals able to share expertise, it does not mean they would not benefit from more expertise in the field. Typically, there is only a handful of people in each state who deal with water reform, meaning their capacity to do more or to change direction is limited. There has been a recent reluctance by some governments to allocate resources for more officials in this area, but at the NWC it is our belief that the best way to make sustainable reform happen is to build capacity.

Regular public reporting is yet another prerequisite to entrenching policy reform. Indeed this is one of the principal reasons the NWC was established; we have a mandate to produce public reports on various aspects of water management, thus ensuring progress on the promises governments make on managing water is stringently monitored. In fact, we are required to publish reports at least every two years—an arrangement that has so far proved quite effective in helping sustain the reform process. In order to cast light on issues that are not otherwise well understood, all our reports are published and we try to make decision making transparent. For example, we have recommended that where a minister needs to take a decision not to deliver environmental water as promised, the reasoning behind that decision needs to be made public so that people can make their own judgments about the wisdom of making such a move.

Nurturing local champions is another strategy to maximise the chances of sustainable reform. In the NWC two of our commissioners are irrigators, and they are extremely effective in talking to their community counterparts through shared experiences and in a language they understand. The problem with the local-champion approach in rural and regional issues is that often capacity is so thin in regional communities there is a real risk of reform fatigue, because the same people have to carry the load the whole time.

Finally, for a reform to endure it must be able to stay fresh and relevant in the face of ever-changing contemporary challenges. While the NWI dates from 2004, it would be foolish for us at the commission to insist on nothing short of strict adherence to its original conditions. Rather than expecting governments to maintain the exact promises their predecessors made six years ago, we have accepted that circumstances have since changed, and consequently allow for a degree of give on particular commitments within the original NWI. Sound judgment is needed by those involved in order to achieve this successful adaptation, and thus maximise a reform's chances of enduring into the future.

The NWC's perspective: some recommendations for COAG

In order to best manage Australia's water resources into the future, the NWC has prepared several recommendations for COAG to consider, two of which I will discuss. First, we would like to see an annual program of COAG-endorsed reforms for the year ahead that responds to our assessments of how water reform is going and what is emerging. Our last report to COAG, for instance, contained 68 recommendations and more than 100 different findings. These included recommendations about how to evolve the NWI, building on the general concepts that it originally contained. Adjusting reform priorities according to progress makes sense.

Second, we have recommended COAG creates a complementary, voluntary reform process alongside the National Partnership Payments (NPPs). While we believe the NPPs have largely been successful, they have the significant disadvantage of typically being negotiated between the Commonwealth and the states, creating the real possibility of reform ambitions and aspirations being rounded down. As an alternative to negotiated reforms, the NWC would like to see the Commonwealth Government putting its money on the stump, specifying the exact reform it would like to see. Under this approach, the specific reform would be defined in an ambitious, non-negotiated way, with the states having the choice of taking the money or not. Alongside the current NPPs, such a complementary arrangement could further strengthen the water-reform process.

An assessment of the water-reform process

Four years after the NWI was first tabled, how is the NWI's reform agenda progressing in the eyes of the NWC? The NWI is unique in Australian policy-reform sectors for several reasons. First, the concept of an agreed agenda containing detailed time lines about what needs to be reformed is unprecedented. Further, compared with other sectors, here, there is reasonable stakeholder consensus; no-one has yet walked away from the NWI. There is also an independent national assessor in the form of the NWC, created by governments to criticise governments. This, especially, is a rare mechanism in public administration.

So, what aspects of water reform are we getting right? First, we have a water-reform framework in the guise of the NWI, and, despite tough conditions, that reform process is going better than it would without such a framework. In short, if we did not have an agreed agenda, there would be much that would not be happening. Second, there is currently an unprecedented amount of money devoted to water management in Australia; today we talk in billions of dollars, whereas 10 years ago we were lucky to get millions. Third, Australia has recently emerged as a world leader in opening up water markets—a development that has proved to be invaluable during the recent drought. In fact, our modelling shows Australians would have been much worse off dealing with the drought without water trading.

We have also had success in urban water supply diversification. Every metropolitan city in Australia and many inland cities have now diversified their supply from dams, ensuring a more secure portfolio of different sources of supply. And while such sources of diversification—desalination, recycled water, urban purchases of rural water, and stormwater capture—have differing costs, the fact is that people are prepared to pay for water security as opposed to simply relying on water from the hills, which has previously proven to be insecure.

Finally, we have achieved some truly historic governance reforms in the Murray–Darling Basin. Obviously, water management is a national issue and much more than the Murray–Darling Basin, but the basin is undeniably a major part of our system. Significant changes to the way the Murray–Darling Basin is managed are currently developing, and for the first time water is now being recovered for the environment, with both major political parties recently committing to a continuation of that process.

And yet, there are many aspects of water reform that are still failing. First, 15 years after the commitment to fix it was first made, the problem of over-allocation is still to be addressed. Over-allocation refers to the assignment of rights to water beyond the sustainable capacity of the water system to deliver it. This problem could be combated by creating sophisticated water management plans for each Australian river valley. Despite the promise of this, 40 per cent of such proposed plans have still not been developed, and other plans that commit to providing water security, stability, certainty and predictability have been suspended because of the drought.

Moreover, environmental aims remain unclear and some of the environmental flows that were initially agreed to have been cut. There is still a lack of clarity about environmental aims, which poses both a significant scientific and a reform challenge. What needs to be added is the reduction of some environmental flows. Obviously, such an approach is contrary to the property-rights concept of equal statutory status for the environment and for consumptive uses.

Next, there are still barriers to water trading in this country. For example, irrigation communities are yet to gain the necessary clarity and confidence about the future to effectively address the challenge of climate change. The fact that irrigators—or indeed regional communities—who are heavily reliant on environmental assets cannot plan more than three months ahead because they are not aware of what exactly the reform process entails is a serious problem. In such an ambiguous policy climate, how can these communities, businesses, individuals and families expect to make long-term investments and decisions?

Turning to urban water, another problem is the widespread presence of water restrictions—and the widespread belief they are a positive force. Water restrictions are arbitrary, inequitable, and take the pressure off urban water suppliers to do their job correctly. Unfair and overly costly, water restrictions should be regarded as a last resort to curbing water use. Their rightful role is that of a buffer, and they thus should be removed as soon as water supply improves. If we overuse this tool, we will not have a reserve capacity for when the spike really dives.

Yet another impediment to successful water reform is the often disappointing performance of the various governments involved. Intergovernmental decisions remain slow, the states continue to be hampered by resource constraints, and there is still much bickering between the Commonwealth and the states and between various states (most notably between South Australia and Victoria and Victoria and New South Wales). Such conflicts are both regrettable and embarrassing for all parties involved. The opinion of the commission is that renewed momentum for reform is needed to address this last problem, and we have therefore recommended a substantial package to COAG to deal with it. That said, the increasing role of the Commonwealth as a significant player in Australian water management is a positive development. Five or six years ago, the Commonwealth was not a significant actor in the field of water management, but that is certainly no longer the case. As a consequence, we are witnessing many institutional adjustments as the Commonwealth moves into this space.

Concluding remarks

Although the remaining problems illustrate the magnitude of existing water-reform challenges, the NWC firmly believes the current prescriptions of the NWI (for example, property rights and equal status for the environment) are the right ones to achieve such a systemic overhaul. There are some tangible examples of successful reforms due to such prescriptions; water trading is still the most significant, but the pace of reform has slowed. We are convinced of the virtues of the current prescriptions, but we must strive to convince an often-sceptical public (especially in the regions) to stay on board.

As a final observation, my experience with reforms in different portfolios has been that there is no shortage of strategic policy thinkers at the senior executive level. In fact, as I would sit around the board table in large organisations, I would be surrounded by strategic thinkers. And yet, what I would be looking for would be the practical, concrete, 'doing' people who had been weeded out because the smart strategic thinkers were promoted up the line! It is not sufficient to have a table surrounded with only strategic reformers; we need always to assemble a team that includes those tactical, concrete people with an interest in deadlines and getting jobs done. Strategic thinkers are of course vital, but it takes more than strategic thinkers to effectively entrench reform.

15. Up in smoke: combating tobacco through legislative reform

Rob Moodie

This chapter focuses on tobacco control and the reform of tobacco use in Australia—policy areas I have been involved in now for about 12 years. Combating the harm caused by tobacco has been a long battle, involving a series of difficult policy reforms. To comprehend how much progress has been made to date, think back to the famous 1946 Camel cigarettes advertisement, 'more doctors smoke Camel than any other cigarette', which resulted from a survey of 113 000 US doctors. Ronald Reagan sent packets of Chesterfields to people for Christmas. General practitioners would even prescribe cigarettes to their patients; 'Take up smoking,' they would say, 'it will be good for you'! And remember that in the 1950s three out of every four Australian men smoked!

Today, this is no longer the case. Health professionals do not endorse cigarette brands and very few actually smoke. Less than 20 per cent of Australian males now smoke. There have been huge changes in the prevalence of smoking. It became popular initially from the beginning of the twentieth century, followed by a steady increase in consumption during the world wars and the 1950s. There was a subsequent explosion in per capita consumption in the 1970s with saturation advertising, followed by a dramatic decline in popularity since that decade. Health concerns are now predominant in the minds of many. And yet, while Doll and Peto discovered a definitive link between tobacco and lung cancer in 1954, it took another 30 years for per capita consumption to significantly drop. If we measure progress by the decline in usage then there is a long lead time between when society finds something out and when we start to change our ways. There might be a change of policy, but it can take a while for a change in actual outcome.

Elements of a successful tobacco-control reform agenda

The progress made in reducing smoking's harmful impacts results from an enormous amount of sustained work, both inside and outside government. When we examine the changes in smoking legislation enacted across time, it is remarkable to think that even quite recently the situation was so different. For example, smoking on domestic airlines was banned in Australia only in 1987. It seems inconceivable that anyone would even attempt to smoke on an airline nowadays—they would be stabbed to death with a plastic knife!

Most anti-tobacco reforms have been entrenched and gradually extended, but they have not always been easy to bring about. The Victorian *Tobacco Act* of 1987, for instance, was a groundbreaking piece of state legislation, which created a tax on tobacco, allowing the government to gain revenue from tobacco sales in order to buy out tobacco sponsorship in sports and the arts, and use it for health promotion and research. It had taken Nigel Gray, then head of the Anti-Cancer Council of Victoria, decades of lobbying. In fact it took him eight health ministers until he found one, David White, who shared his interest. Gray had long been plotting such legislation, and in Minister White he found someone who was receptive—fundamentally because his father was dying of emphysema. In addition, it took a series of skilful negotiations by Gray to raise awareness of the need for such legislation, including winning the support of the churches and both major media organisations. The success of this bill also relied on some clever politicking, particularly in the Victorian Upper House, between White and his opposite number, Mark Birrel.

After the initial slog to get this bill into law, it has since proved a tremendous success. Moreover, many other countries have copied this approach. Thailand has even superseded this model, with the Thai Health Program introducing a surcharge on tobacco and alcohol. They are doing a highly effective job at health promotion, and we can now learn from their example.

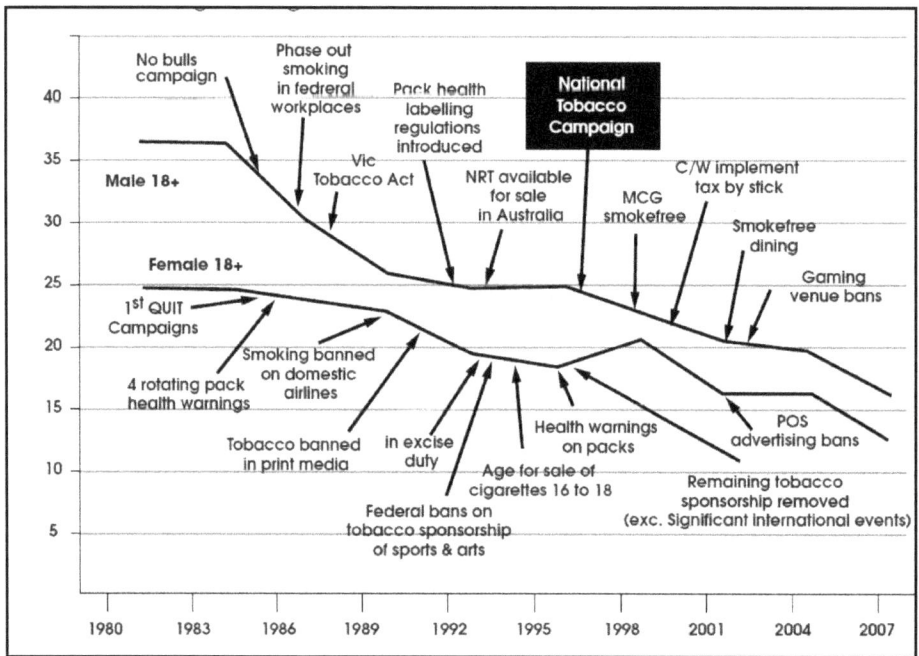

Figure 15.1 Milestones in reducing smoking in Australia, 1980–2007

Source: The Cancer Council of Victoria 2009

The key characteristics of successful tobacco reform are that it is progressive, determined, comprehensive and sustained. Often we are looking for quick policy fixes, but these rarely exist as we are dealing with substances that are highly addictive, the manufacture, promotion and the sale of which are backed by enormously powerful multinational tobacco firms. Thus, we need to build sustainable regulation and reinforcing messages that can enhance the overall approach. For instance, where we have an effective, scaled-up national anti-smoking communication campaign, this not only helps people understand why they might want to give up smoking, it will also help change community attitudes to the policies themselves.

To change attitudes, we were particularly interested to ensure that a constant flow of health communications, counter-advertising and the banning of advertising for tobacco would occur. We had to actively combat the acceptance of tobacco to see attitudes change. This is no mean feat, as the original tobacco advertising was extremely effective, and most people like me could remember all the popular jingles for a host of cigarette companies.

Evidence gathering is also critical for bringing about successful tobacco reforms. Close monitoring, annual surveys, annual evaluations and major project evaluations all ensure a constant flow of information is fed to policy makers who often have to make some very tough decisions, both within the bureaucracy and within the political part of government.

Legislation regulating cigarette advertising, promotion and sponsorship has been critical to success. There was a major shift against smoking when sponsorship was taken out of sport and the arts. I was always amused that the arts should be sponsored by tobacco, particularly the Australian Opera (after all, it is surely difficult to sing without a voice-box lost to tobacco-related cancer!). The ban put an end to this unholy partnership. And, more than anything else, smoke-free legislation applying to premises and public spaces has been instrumental in changing public attitudes towards tobacco use.

Pricing and taxation have a highly significant role in a successful tobacco-control reform agenda. But to increase taxes and enact legislation require community mobilisation—meaning community understanding *and* support for particular approaches. It is vital that we understand what these mean, and that there is good social marketing and counter-advertising against the cigarette manufacturers. One of the earliest forms of such counter-advertising in Victoria successfully utilised humour, with the popular television character Alf Garnett helping to spread the anti-smoking message.

Pushing for tobacco reform against industry resistance

The contemporary challenges associated with tobacco reform are still formidable. In 2008 I was lucky enough to be asked to chair the National Preventative Health Taskforce, where Health Minister, Nicola Roxon, asked us to look at obesity, tobacco, and the harmful use of alcohol. Regarding tobacco, we reported to the Federal Government that they should do two things: first, they should increase the price of tobacco; and second, they should improve communications on the dangers of smoking.

In May 2010, the Government acted by increasing the tobacco excise by 25 per cent, meaning the price of a packet of 30 cigarettes increased by about $2.16. This move was greatly welcomed, but remember there are now countries that have considerably higher levels of cost per pack of 30 and Australia has dropped to seventeenth among the Organisation for Economic Cooperation and Development (OECD) countries with regard to the cost of tobacco. So, relatively speaking, a packet of cigarettes in Australia remains cheap. The research behind this price hike predicts approximately 25 000 young people will not take up cigarettes as a result, and about 100 000 people will quit. In addition—perhaps counter-intuitively—this will have a bigger effect on those from lower socioeconomic strata than those at the higher end. Critics labelled this a regressive tax that will not work. But the evidence coming from the Centre of Behavioural Research in Cancer and the Centre of Tobacco Control at QUIT certainly suggests otherwise.

The big social marketing campaigns are principally aimed at the general population, but they also target high-risk groups including pregnant women, prisoners and people with mental illness. The Government is also allocating a significant amount of money to an Indigenous tobacco-control program. When I worked in an Aboriginal medical centre in Alice Springs during the mid 1980s, there was absolutely no interest in tobacco control, both in town and in remote Indigenous communities. Now that is no longer the case, and there is real potential for Aboriginal communities to take this issue on, and achieve some tangible gains. I am very hopeful they will succeed.

It is important to note here in designing these campaigns that tobacco reforms should never vilify the smoker. We target the companies because we know that if they stop producing and promoting as much as they currently do, the population will be much better off health-wise and economically. One of the few social problems with the smoke-free laws is that people end up smoking outside, which can lead to smoker vilification and ostracism. In this way, the vilification does not necessarily come from the policy makers; it comes from other individuals who do not necessarily want someone else's smoke close by or in their nostrils. Yet, it is not a particularly good idea to vilify the smoker, or the person who is overweight, or the person who is drinking too much. We must focus on the behaviour, not on the person, and we are largely succeeding in this endeavour.

In April 2010, the Rudd Government announced that, from 2012, Australia would become the first country to introduce mandatory plain packaging. This is a historic event in Australia's anti-tobacco history, as we will become the world's pioneer in introducing such tough measures. Consequently, the campaign to combat this is coming straight from New York and London—from the tobacco giants intent on preventing this law being followed by other countries. These firms have been vehemently challenging plain packaging, and they have an absolute right to do this. But paradoxically, they are saying on one hand there is no evidence that plain packaging will work, yet on the other hand they are doing everything they can to stop it. The fact they are so concerned is a fine example of what is called the 'screen test': you know a particular reform is likely to hit the tobacco companies hard when it provokes a heated response.

Yet the principal opponents of tobacco reform have painted themselves into a corner. The tobacco companies stated their position early in the debate and have largely stuck to this line for decades. In effect, for years the tobacco industry told us that tobacco did not cause cancer and was not addictive. They persisted with this position for a long time, even though it was later proven that their own internal information showed they were aware that the contrary was in fact true. This became transparent after the 'Minnesota Agreement' of 1998 under which tobacco companies were required to release millions of pages of their own internal documents to show what positions they were taking. These documents prompted many people to ask whether such companies were really working in the public interest.

Obviously, the tobacco companies remain enormously powerful and wealthy, making them ruthless in chasing down people who oppose them. An example has been British American Tobacco's attempts to sue Peter Gordon, a prominent Melbourne lawyer who has previously tackled the tobacco industry. The tobacco industry is utterly relentless in their willingness and capacity to obstruct, deny, and delay, and work without any ethical standards or moral compass.

And yet, even though the tobacco companies have great wealth and power, the tobacco industry is consistently voted as the least reputable industry in the world, thus reducing their ability to sway policy makers. By virtue of what they have done for such a long period, and denying the acknowledged dangers that tobacco is both addictive and causes cancer, most sensible politicians do not worry about them—a situation very different to 30 years ago, when these companies had much more political sway. But since then they have continually damaged their reputation to the point where they are marginal to the policy process. For instance, the National Preventative Health Taskforce wanted to consult with the alcohol and food industries about the problems related to the harmful use of alcohol and obesity, but when it came to smoking there was absolutely no obligation to consult with the tobacco companies, because they have done such a horrendous job, and have proven themselves to be unethical in so many ways, over such a long period.

Mobilising for change: framing the community debate

I wish now to highlight the features that have influenced the decision making in tobacco-control policy over time, and in particular examine how the debate was successfully framed. We must first understand that community opinion has been vital to supporting policy makers in the decisions they have had to make. So, the framing of the debate was crucial. In addition, the concerted efforts of the Australian jurisdictions are a great example of how competitive federalism works, and a testament to citizen advocacy and changing community attitudes.

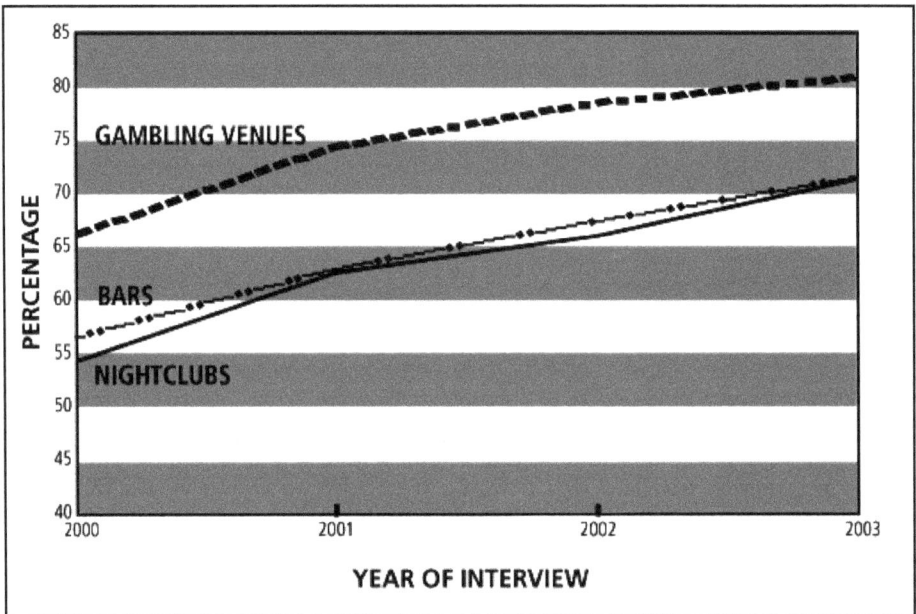

Figure 15.2 Approval for smoking legislation among Victorians

Community opinion underscored policy success. When QUIT Victoria actively began campaigning for smoke-free laws in hotel bars in 2000, public support for such measures was about 55 per cent, yet it had risen quickly to more than 70 per cent by 2003; and in gambling venues from 65 per cent to 81 per cent over the same time. Such a dramatic endorsement from the public gave legislators an enormous amount of confidence to push ahead with the reforms. We also know, however, from the obesity and alcohol debates, that such a level of public support for a particular reform does not necessarily mean it will become law, but it is encouraging nonetheless.

What is interesting from our research, however, is such endorsement is also high amongst smokers. In fact, surveys found that over three years, support from smokers for banning smoking in gambling venues went from a mere 20 per cent to a majority. It is intriguing that the majority of smokers would want to support bans on them smoking whilst they are gambling. In all likelihood, such support can be explained by the fact that about 75 per cent of people who smoke actually want to give up. Consequently, even smokers understand that tobacco reform is in their best interests.

We also found that support from smokers for anti-tobacco legislation is actually greater once it has been implemented. For example, when I was working at Vic Health, we worked with the Moonee Valley Racing Club trying to make some of their areas smoke free. Initially, the punters were opposed to such measures, but largely changed their view after the reforms were introduced. Essentially, this occurred because patrons were initially fearful such measures would be detrimental to them, but soon realised they would actually help them smoke a little less. Again, this trend is reassuring for both politicians and policy makers looking to craft anti-tobacco reforms.

A similar pattern of smoker approval was witnessed in South Australia when smoking in cars where a child was present was banned in 2007. Surveys conducted pre and post the introduction of this legislation suggested that far from a backlash against such a move, public approval had increased from both smokers and non-smokers. Such data only serve to strengthen the reform mandate.

Furthermore, over the past decade there has been an increase in support for taxing tobacco products to pay for health promotion. The winning of public support is the result of a careful campaign to inform the public that revenue from this tax is going into health education, thus differentiating it from a simple price hike. In this way, if the public can be shown that a tax has a particular worthy purpose, they are more likely to give it support. Again, such success encourages governments to intervene in this area.

So, how has the community debate been so successfully framed? There are three specific aspects to mention: redefining the problem, urging competitive federalism in policy responses, and empowering citizens. The first concern was to focus on the issue of 'second-hand smoke', because once it emerged that people have a significantly greater risk of developing health problems if they are around passive smoke—especially people living with smokers or people who are in an industry where they are exposed to a significant amount of tobacco smoke—public perceptions began to change. This development moved the problem from being one for just 'the smokers' to being one for the wider community. It also added an element of self-interest to the debate; previously non-smokers wanted smokers to quit simply for these people to improve their health, but now non-smokers realised they themselves were being impacted by smoking. This fundamentally changed how the issue was understood.

The same is also true of alcohol, where the public debate is changing from being concerned about individual drinkers doing themselves damage to being concerned about the effects their drinking has on them and on their family, through physical and sexual assaults, car fatalities and a host of other secondary effects. In this way, the issue of passive drinking has begun to gain importance in much the same way as has passive smoking.

Second, competitive federalism emerged as an important element in bringing about tobacco reform. Take the 'Dirty Ashtray Award'—an annual 'prize' presented by the Australian Medical Association (AMA) and Action on Smoking and Health (ASH) to the state deemed to have shown the least progress in efforts to combat tobacco usage. When I worked at Vic Health, I distinctly remember one health minister who was particularly keen on not winning this award. This friendly, parochial competition actually works. Overall, there is a high level of competence at the state level in bringing about tobacco reforms, and when the Commonwealth reinforces this competence, and convenes these groups together, I have witnessed how federalism can actually work for the better.

So, while it is good to have states trying to outperform each other, it is equally important that the states work well together—something illustrated in the national tobacco campaign. Such inter-jurisdictional cooperation could be used as a role model for successful federalism in many other areas.

Empowering citizens and encouraging citizen advocacy were the third aspect of the way the debate was reframed to bring about tobacco reform. A few decades ago there were many cases of graffiti targeting billboards advertising unhealthy products and unhealthy promotions by a group called BUGA UP (Billboard Utilising Graffitists Against Unhealthy Promotions). Often these were people involved in the health industry expressing their views in a very visible—if illegal—fashion. These grassroots campaigns helped drive community interest in a novel way, and there is currently a renaissance of such graffiti, most famously seen in August 2010 on a Tattersall's advertisement outside the Royal Children's Hospital in Melbourne.

We can also reflect on the following quote from Simon Chapman, a well-known public health advocate based at Sydney University, who is anxious to control the tobacco industry. For Chapman, 'tobacco advocates in Australia have successfully reframed the debate to show that tobacco advertising is a highly researched, beguiling, and deadly tune whistled to the nation's children by faceless trans-national corporations interested only in profit maximization' (Chapman and Wakefield 2001:279). It is an interesting view, and itself uses the language of advertising to convey a message.

Such grassroots advocacy against the tobacco industry can be hugely effective. We know from research undertaken by the Centre for Behavioural Research in Cancer that vilification of tobacco companies actually tends to help people give up smoking. One explanation is that people do not want to be hoodwinked into smoking.

But the companies will often attempt to strike back to encourage new demographics to take up the habit. In 1990, for instance, Marlboro launched an aggressive campaign to attract young smokers. In that year, they noted '23 percent of the population was 15 years of age and under, and 17 percent between 16 and 24 years of age—a significant market opportunity indeed' (Jones 2002:3433). Marlboro's approach was to portray their product as a cult brand. They knew that tobacco was addictive, and that it caused cancer, but they banked on Marlboro's reputation as trumping any concerns over health effects. And some young smokers will often take up the habit knowing full well the harm it can cause them.

Nowadays, however, tobacco companies prefer to target developing countries— the countries with the least regulation. In Indonesia, for example, Marlboro has bought Kretek, which makes clove cigarettes. Marlboro is now putting these clove cigarettes into Marlboro packets as a way of eventually attracting Kretek smokers to Marlboro cigarettes. Market research has shown such a ploy has an amazing capacity to deliver commercial results very quickly.

The cultivation of tobacco is also now conducted largely in the developing world. Following the political strife in Zimbabwe of the early 2000s, for example, much of that country's production moved to Mozambique, where they now have a highly effective agricultural extension-worker system. Tobacco companies are now established in Mozambique, where they are paying taxes and employing local people, meaning it will be extremely difficult to move them on.

Back in Australia, tobacco companies set up and financed the Australian Retailers Association to help oppose the government's plain-packaging legislation. We are beginning to see how these corporations function—raising doubts about even the most indisputable scientific evidence, adopting a strategy of information laundering, promoting scientific spokespeople who misrepresent peer-reviewed scientific findings, attempting to shift the focus away from meaningful action, and creating other organisations to do the bidding. In August 2010, Coles and other big retailers distanced themselves from this campaign, and it is likely others will follow.

Concluding thoughts: appraising Australian tobacco reform

Essentially, the success of Australian tobacco reform can be measured by the fact that since the adoption of anti-smoking measures, smoking rates have dropped and are forecast to drop even further. In other words, hundreds of thousands of Australians have already been spared a premature death as a result of these reforms. Similar results apply to reforms in road safety, where as a result of a comprehensive approach including legislative action and enforcement, social marketing, community mobilisation, political will and adequate funding, an estimated 45 000 people in Australia have not been killed, and 600 000 people have escaped serious injuries since 1970. Many of us can thus be grateful that someone in our family has not died much earlier because of public-policy reforms made in the areas of both tobacco and road safety.

Ultimately, as a result of the anti-smoking reforms, we hope to see the smoking rate in Australia drop below 10 per cent by 2020. If this scenario eventuates, there would then be one million fewer smokers in Australia, and of the remaining smokers, many would be smoking significantly less. It would be one of the most profound impacts on our public's health in Australian history.

We are already seeing medical evidence of the success of these reforms. Lung cancer rates per thousand in Australia are today as low as they were in 1963. This represents almost 50 years of data, so is a convincing indication that progress is being made. In women, the figure is only now starting to flatten out, but in men especially it is impressive. Moreover, death rates for chronic obstructive pulmonary disease have now dropped to levels seen in the 1950s. A similar pattern can be observed in rates of coronary heart disease, which are now as low as they were immediately after World War II. While tobacco control has been a major factor in such improvements, exercise and nutritional changes are also part of the explanation for the decline.

So, to conclude, Australia's tobacco reforms consist of a comprehensive package of measures enacted over a significant amount of time. They are the result of many tough decisions made by policy makers that were not always popular, but subsequently became so. For the most part, a tougher regulatory approach to the promotion of tobacco has been adopted in conjunction with attempts to engender community mobilisation against smoking. We might wish to contrast this proactive approach with that followed thus far in relation to alcohol reform, which has remained highly liberalised in terms of availability and new licences for provision. We do not advocate alcohol prohibition, but there are certainly problems with our country's health as a result of such proliferation. To tackle the social problems of alcohol abuse, valuable lessons could be learned from the successes of past tobacco reforms.

References

Chapman, Simon and Melanie Wakefield, 2001, 'Tobacco Control Advocacy in Australia: Reflections on 30 Years of Progress'. *Health Education & Behavior*, Vol. 28 (3) (June 2001).

Jones, S. C. 2002, 'Marlboro's marketing in Western Europe: Is it Ethical?' In R. Shaw, S. Adam and H. McDonald (eds.), *Proceedings of the Australian and New Zealand Marketing Academy Conference*, 2-4 December 2002, Melbourne: Deakin University.

16. Improving road safety: perspectives from Victoria's Transport Accident Commission

Janet Dore

Victoria became the first jurisdiction in the world to introduce compulsory seatbelts in 1970. Since then the state has become a pioneer in making progress on road trauma and reducing the death rate on the state's roads. This chapter will outline the challenges involved in getting to this stage, the progress made, and the reforms that are still to be achieved.

The role of the Transport Accident Commission

In the 1960s the road toll in Victoria was more than 1000 deaths per year, and by the 1970s it was still more than 800 deaths. To address this, the Transport Accident Commission (TAC) was established in 1986 and launched a series of hard-hitting advertising campaigns, which saw the death toll begin to decline. We have become well known for these campaigns, including the iconic television advertisements with 'Katie' in the rehabilitation unit, and the slogans 'Drink, drive, bloody idiot' and 'Don't fool yourself, speed kills'.

But no matter how notorious these campaigns have become, the TAC realised that further policy reform was required to save more lives. Working with our road-safety partners at Victoria Police, the Department of Justice and Vic Roads, we created a state government policy strategy called 'Arrive Alive'. This is a 10-year government strategy in conjunction with our road-safety partners based on evidence that shows improving road safety boils down to three main factors: safer cars, safer roads and safer road users.

Let me put it another way: if everyone was a five-star driver, in a five-star car, on a five-star road, the TAC would not need to exist because the levels of accidents and injury would fall dramatically, if not be eliminated. Further, the technology in new cars these days will make it possible that in another generation's time the cars themselves could be too intelligent to have accidents.

Why then did we at the TAC initially focus on the 'safer car' issue part of this system, and apply that to the lessons of policy reform and making them stick? The safer car part of the equation was always the one with a lag, so that is why we decided to focus on it. We know we can treat intersections, build safer roads, and can achieve much through the police with trying to get better road users, but the TAC has always tried to be bold and creative in its approach to road safety.

To date, the Victorian fleet has some emphasis on environmental issues, but perhaps not so much commitment to the five-star safety rating, and that should concern us as a community. That finding should make all of us stop and think about which car we are currently driving. So, from a public-policy perspective, how do we get Victorians into safer cars? It was more than a decade ago now that the evidence started to emerge that vehicle safety features could have a powerful impact on road-safety figures. And the Monash University Accident Research Centre (MUARC) found that if we all could drive the safest car in our class, road trauma levels would drop by one-third. In practical terms, that would result in saving about 100 lives per year, and reducing injuries by their thousands, because we have 46 serious injuries on our roads every single day in addition to the number of road fatalities. So road trauma includes the figures behind the road toll, and if we could reduce the magnitude of road accidents it would save thousands of people every year the impact of road trauma.

Before I highlight a particular case study from our experience, I must first explain that the Victorian TAC is unique in Australia. We are a no-fault insurer on behalf of the government, whereas other states have fault-based insurance systems that are either government owned, or operate within a competitive market, as in New South Wales and Queensland. I believe our reputation will eventually lead other governments to adopt the Victorian model. We are pushing the Victorian model and its success in the discussions on the National Disability Insurance Scheme, to show that this kind of no-fault scheme can work effectively provided we get a good source of revenue. There is some access to common law in Victoria, and that is always the pressure point. In other states they have full access to common law and that is where things start unravelling.

Reforming road safety: lessons from experience

To reform road safety, it is extremely important we get good research, and the MUARC certainly does that for us. And when people stop and think about the enormous economic, physical, and emotional costs of road trauma, they realise these permeate through the entire community. Our latest campaign, for example, 'The Ripple Effect', shows how up to 200 people can be affected by one single accident, and it is not just the immediate family. We hope to get that message through to people.

Consequently, we decided to tackle road-safety reform primarily through the technology area of vehicles. We narrowed our focus to two technologies with the ability to create safer vehicles: electronic stability control (ESC) and curtain airbags. Of all the technology available, these two safety features were identified by MUARC as having the highest impact on reducing transport accidents. ESC is now standard technology and cuts in when vehicles wiggle to indicate drivers are going too fast. Tests have proved that such technology potentially leads to a 30 per cent reduction in single-vehicle crashes and a 40 per cent reduction in risk of death. And if we translate this to our star-rating system, there is potential for a 12 per cent increase in protection for every star attached to your vehicle. And that is a standard rating system.

So how did we go about this reform? We had a choice. We could have gone to Canberra and sought a national approach; we could have lobbied the government to change the law and mandate that people buy safer cars. But that would have taken considerable time, and probably would not have been high on their list of priorities. Alternatively, we could have gone down a regulatory path—but again, we could still be arguing over the terms of reference of any committee that was set up to tackle that issue.

To avoid these pitfalls, we turned to a more innovative approach. And I acknowledge that as a government enterprise we can be significantly nimbler, within the terms of legislation, than perhaps a department can. So I give credit to the Victorian Government for setting up the TAC to be able to facilitate these approaches.

The TAC Board took a deliberate policy decision to engage with the community and to have them demand safer cars. Essentially, the policy approach aimed to get the public leading the policy reform, rather than the other way around. We called it a market-demand model, and the goal was to encourage consumers to demand safety features, therefore pressuring the manufacturers to respond.

Our web site and media coverage were an important part of this strategy, as the more times safety features can be publicised, the more people will demand them when buying new vehicles. And the more people demand them when buying, the more likely manufacturers are to tailor their products to suit the market. The intent was for people to walk into showrooms and say 'if it doesn't have electronic stability control, I'm not interested'.

While we succeeded in eventually attaining a five-star safety system, it is important to understand, however, that at the time the strategy was not without its critics. Many argued that jobs would be put at risk if the public started to demand these features and that local production in particular would suffer. It was also called a 'pie in the sky' idea devised by road-safety boffins, even though it was actually evidence based.

This is an important point, because however simple or good a reform is, not everybody gets onboard immediately. Consequently, when we are speaking about long-term reform—and this is a 10-year journey—we must be prepared to stick the course and fight for change. I am extremely proud to head an organisation that was able to achieve that, and did not waiver and say after a couple of years 'oh, well, that's not being taken up, we should abandon it'.

We were fortunate to be able to use the mass media to do these things, and we also established a web site to try to infiltrate the consciousness of buyers. But we recognised it was important to use different tools. The web site was created to provide the information about the safety features on cars, and the TAC had to promote it everywhere we went, because it is not the sort of web site that would just pop up on somebody's *Facebook* page.

Because we know information is power, this web site has played an important role in raising the issue of safety in influencing vehicle-purchase decisions. The duel themes of education and emotion have been present throughout TAC campaigns, and have been key ways in which we have influenced people's thinking and actions. We knew we were starting to have success when we saw headlines in motor journals along the lines of 'stability control for every Camry soon'. But one or two headlines does not equal success.

As car manufacturers will tell you, the only problem with ESC is that not many people know what it is. Even describing it is difficult, but as a technology it saves lives. And if it saves lives, it is a good thing to have. By increasing the exposure of ESC, TAC was thus influencing not simply consumers, but also manufacturers. And although they were struggling to define what it was, they knew that it was a good point. In time, the safety features started moving into standard features rather than optional extras.

At that point the manufacturers themselves started using the star ratings to promote their own cars. That is when we knew we really had some grip and successes were achieved. For instance, we should recall that in 2006 less than one-fifth of Victorians had ESC in their cars. By 2008 that percentage was more than 40 per cent and today the figure stands at just more than 67 per cent. Thus, much has been achieved in just five years. The benefits will also be felt in the longer term as people sell their cars, and these vehicles start to go through the second-hand car market, meaning the whole fleet will gradually be populated with safer vehicles.

We also worked with trucking companies and other car fleets to help understand buyers' decisions. And we keep trying to get the message out there that safety is more important than anything else. We are now combining this safety message with the environmental message—pushing eco-driving—because if we push eco-driving it is going to result in safer driving. And that will have the next tranche of advocates for safety.

Education was a vital part of our strategy, and educating the key intermediaries—the salespeople in the car yard—was vital when spreading the message of car safety. We supplemented this through education in schools, and through sponsorship of the TAC Cup, Victoria's premier under-18 Australian football competition. Again, we were focusing on the consumer to challenge the salespeople. To encourage this, we urged consumers to look at the Australasian New Car Assessment Program (ANCAP) web site and the star-rating system, so they could challenge the salespeople on the subject of safety features. We thought we had a better chance of success in an informed market.

Of particular concern to us was the well-publicised over-representation of adolescents in road accidents. We needed to influence the purchasing decisions of younger or new car drivers. For the most part, young people's buying decisions are going to be influenced by two principal factors: price, and their parents. Consequently, we had to educate parents of the importance of safe vehicles for their children, and wait for the new safer cars to go through the system. The supply of safer second-hand cars was a key indicator. We knew we could not change everything overnight. First and foremost though, we wanted young people to drive safely, so they did not need the safety features. Second, we had to wait for a time when those cars would start to flow through the system, and unfortunately, that might be up to 20 years away.

To ensure young drivers got off to the best possible start, we also had the 'L120' campaign, whereby L-plate drivers must experience 120 hours in different driving conditions before getting their licence. As earlier stated, our sponsorship of the TAC Cup was also instrumental in improving the driving habits of young people.

Having the desired impact

While road safety does not have a simple, single solution, the principal lesson we have learned is that it can be improved through years of work, sticking to the message, building momentum and influencing behaviour. For the results, one need only look at the fact that Australia is a world leader in this field—something of which we should be proud. Many Australian lives have been saved simply by installing ESC in cars. Further, thanks to this technology, many accidents that have occurred have resulted in people being injured rather than killed. That is the real benefit of this reform.

As a consequence, thousands of people have not had to endure the devastation of road trauma. Some of our advertisements give a small insight into the impact that road trauma can have on people's lives. And if you put yourself in those people's shoes, you cannot put a cost on the change in people's lives. It is a very sobering thought.

And though we are pleased to have influenced consumer behaviour, we cannot become complacent. We need to also focus on the uptake of side-curtain airbags, and that will have a huge difference on the number of people who finish up with a brain injury, because of the cushioning of people's heads when they do have accidents. And once again Victoria is leading the nation in the take-up of the standard fitment of curtain airbags. In effect, in 2001 only 3 per cent of new cars sold had this feature; the figure currently stands at more than 50 per cent. This is another tremendous result, and a great example of real public-policy reform.

To avoid complacency, we also diligently track the impact of our campaigns. For example, if we are getting no traction with our campaigns then we know we must take a different approach. We are thorough in monitoring our progress, and one of the most depressing parts of my job is getting the daily road-toll bulletin delivered to my desk each morning. Such monitoring, combined with consumer sentiment, discipline, rigour and the advice of our expert board, prevents complacency at the TAC.

The TAC has deliberately tried to pursue a market-demand model, and history shows this has been a wise choice. This does not mean, however, that we do not work through government or industry players; it is a multi-pronged strategy working through road-safety partners and with successive governments. We are fortunate in this regard to have always had bipartisan support.

By giving good advice to governments and influencing the road-safety debate in a positive way, the TAC is testament to the fact that legislative change is not the only way to achieve reforms, and that government bodies can lead and influence behaviour in the marketplace. I have used road safety as an example, but the anti-smoking and the QUIT campaigns have worked similarly as educational policy instruments.

Entrenching road-safety reforms

In the case of implementing road-safety reforms, if the government had taken a solely regulatory route, we might still be arguing about the terms of reference. Instead though, due largely to the efforts of the TAC, as of December 2010, all new cars sold in Australia will be required by law to have ESC, with head protection becoming mandatory one year later.

Once again, it was Victoria that was the first jurisdiction in Australia to announce that ESC would be mandatory. For a period, there was some doubt at the national level about whether the nation would join us, but it has now come onboard. We acknowledge, however, that the TAC did not do this on its own. We worked with Victoria Police, Vic Roads and the Justice Department to ensure a complete package was created.

But it is really the momentum in the community that has made this reform work—the awareness, the web site, the technology and the availability of the information. We have encouraged a situation where people now demand safety features; it is no longer an 'option'. One need only consider the fact that car manufacturers actively use the five-star safety-rating system as a point of competitive advantage—an outcome nobody would have predicted 20 years ago. The TAC is a good example of making policy reform stick, because vehicle safety is now embedded into policy, and saving countless lives in the process.

The aspects of the TAC I have discussed in this chapter are only part of our broader plans for improving transport safety. At the same time as we are informing the public through advertising, for example, we are funding $30 million a year in road safety on intersection treatments and other parts of our road infrastructure. Moreover, we fund extra police campaigns, such as cracking down on people driving without seatbelts—a crime that seems unfathomable nowadays, but which is sadly still a problem. It would be wrong to assume the TAC is focused solely on improving car safety, because we are dedicating tens of millions of dollars to addressing transport accidents in other areas, with the ultimate aim of building up tangible exponential benefits over time.

In conclusion, has the campaign for road-safety reform been run and won? We still have about 300 people killed on our roads every year, and although that was a record low last year (305), it is 305 too many. As with occupational health and safety, here, the only acceptable figure is zero, and we will not rest until that is achieved. If there is one thing we have learned in the years of this campaign it is that we have to continue to innovate and push the boundaries. We cannot simply congratulate ourselves for winning the latest advertising award; we must stick to the task at hand. Because we operate from the premise that no-one should be killed on the road, our vision is a future in which every journey is a safe one. In order to achieve this, we need to continue to challenge ourselves and the community, to engage the public in debate and continue the reform process.

17. Epilogue: rules for reformers

Paul 't Hart

From imperatives to lessons

There is a widespread need for adaptation, change and even 'paradigm shifts' in the way societies are governed and how their governments organise themselves. Many contributions to this volume highlight this need. Let us look at some of the main drivers.

Citizens, companies and governments everywhere are, first of all, trying to come to terms with the true implications of the information age. The boardroom and street-level consequences of life in the information society are challenging the system-level architecture of governance. Technologically driven possibilities and culturally embedded expectations now demand that governments follow corporations and engage in mass customisation—responsive, real-time and holistic service delivery. An example in Australia is the 'Government 2.0 Taskforce' focused specifically on the implications of the digital revolution for government. Its clarion call for reform is loud and clear: 'Leadership and policy and governance changes are needed to: shift public sector culture and practice to make government information more accessible and usable; make government more consultative, participatory and transparent; build a culture of online innovation within Government; and promote collaboration across agencies' (<http://gov2.net.au/report/>). The drivers of this development are not going to go away, and governments that lag behind in adapting to them effectively diminish their country's or region's international competitiveness and quality of life.

In addition, governments are called on to adapt to an age in which their public authority has become more dependent than ever upon their capacity to 'deliver'. As predicted a century ago by German sociologist Max Weber (1978), contemporary society is one in which tradition, mysticism and even charisma simply do not cut it as foundational principles for state power and legitimacy. Democratic mandates today are more conditional and fleeting than ever before. We live in the age of value for money. In a value-for-money environment, citizens take the rule of law and the democratic authenticity of the state largely for granted (ignoring their fundamental value and precariousness). Instead, they judge their rulers on their perceived contribution to their own prosperity and wellbeing. Public leadership in such a world becomes entirely transactional.

Citizens pay taxes, vote in legislatures, and, mostly, obey the law. They are perfectly willing to do all that, as long as they feel their efforts are met by governments keeping their part of the bargain: providing safety, prosperity, care, sustainability and all the many other things they say they will. In a value-for-money society, we judge government first and foremost by its results. In a world of unprecedented technological change, fierce global economic competition, demographic shifts, ecosystem imbalances and socio-cultural transformation, governments can 'deliver' such results only if they manage to achieve ongoing institutional reforms and societal learning processes.

A third major driver of reform I want to single out is the inexorable rise of resilience considerations in public policy and administration. The end of the Cold War has not heralded the kind of benign, Western-led, democratic new world order that former US President George H. W. Bush foresaw. Instead, we have a geopolitical disequilibrium, small wars, refugee flows and mass-casualty terrorism. This new reality has combined with the growing awareness of climate change and the occurrence of a series of natural and human-made catastrophes to teach Western governments that the ever-growing complexity and transnational interconnectedness of the economic and infrastructural systems that sustain our way of life constitute a two-edged sword. They make us richer but not necessarily safer. If risk is a product of the impact and the probability of harmful events then the news is not great on both fronts. Relatively small mishaps in vital systems can cascade quickly and widely throughout and across societies; at the same time, a changing climate as well as a more conflict-ridden world are more likely to throw up significant disruptions. The changing risk matrix they face requires contemporary societies to be agile and resilient in the face of rude surprises. In many cases, this requires deep reforms that far transcend technical tinkering with emergency plans.

This volume has brought together insightful accounts of past and ongoing public-policy reform efforts designed to meet some of these adaptive challenges. These accounts have been written by some of Australia's and New Zealand's most respected reform architects, advocates and observers, as well as by the American policy scholar Eric Patashnik. It was his landmark study *Reforms at Risk* (Patashnik 2008) that provided the main intellectual impetus for organising the conference on which this volume is based. With so much expertise and analysis bundled in the one volume, I felt it would be worth trying to distil the common lessons that can be drawn from what effectively are decades of recent and ongoing reform experiences across a range of policy sectors in three countries. Rather than doing so in the form of a typical academic piece full of complexity, contingency and provisos, I will throw the usual academic caution to the wind and jump into prescription.

What follows is unabashed advice and exhortation addressed to a hypothetical 'leader' within or outside government who finds him or herself in the middle of a policy sector in which 'reform' is on the agenda. What, on the basis of this volume, should they 'need to know' about the challenges involved in developing and entrenching reform in the public sector? What, in other words, are the 'rules of reform' that reform proponents (and indeed opponents) can ignore only at their peril?

Rules for reading the context of reform

No pain, no reform

Do not expect to gain traction on reforms when most people feel the status quo is not so bad at all. When you do, the perceived costs of reform—uncertainty, adjustment, enforcement—can all too easily be construed by your opponents as not being worth the potential gains. Tackling complacency comes before everything else. Raise the public salience of change by demonstrating how intolerable present arrangements and practices really are. Give ample voice to those who feel the pain of the present and to those who can communicate authoritatively what future pain will result in the absence of reforms.

Do not let a 'good' crisis go to waste

Avoid the temptation to switch to reactive, defensive, firefighting mode when a major, unexpected 'shock to the system'—a major incident, a damning set of numbers, a media feeding frenzy, a geopolitical surprise—presents itself on your watch. History rewards those who have the capability to understand and interpret the crisis of the day to underpin hitherto infeasible attitude and policy changes. Be prepared to err on the risk of exaggeration in (re)framing crises if the strategic opportunities for breaking existing policy deadlocks they present are worth it. 'Turning up the heat' is a *sine qua non* of reformist leadership, and unscheduled adversity provides a rare opportunity to do so without overspending your political capital.

Have your bottom drawer well stocked

When a sense of crisis takes hold and discredits the legitimacy of the status quo, the public is ripe for new ideas that hold the promise of moving them towards a better future. But the pressure-cooker of crisis management is hardly the time to start thinking up such ideas—that needs to have been done beforehand. You need to invest in an ongoing brains trust doing regular 'what-if' exercises, scenario development and strategic contingency planning. This helps you provide the intellectual leadership when the time is ripe. And having a few concrete, symbolically significant and readily implementable designs for programs and projects does not hurt either. Crises concentrate the mind, free up money and reduce procedural barriers—and you had better be ready for them when they occur.

Rules for making reforms happen

Use the 'R' word judiciously

History tends to look most kindly on reforming leaders—those who are credited with the transformation of old orders into new ones. The growing awareness of this reality has led to every government and every minister compulsively talking up their reformist credentials. Reform has become, in other words, a political must for leaders. No self-respecting new CEO can afford not to announce grand plans for reorganisation; no self-respecting government can avoid employing the rhetoric of reform. The risk is that even the most timid, technical and trivial policy changes are talked up as 'reforms'. This gives reform a bad name.

The term 'reform' ought to be reserved for methodical attempts to achieve far-reaching changes in key beliefs and behaviours within a community and the governance structures underpinning them. Marginal adjustment of existing practices—however defensible—is not reform; it is public policy as usual. To oversell it as reform sets you up as an emperor who has no clothes.

When you feel that the time for needed reform is simply not ripe in your sector or organisation (for example, because the power of the status-quo players arguing that things 'ain't broken' is momentarily too entrenched), content yourself with trying to create that ripeness by trying to rub people's noses in the reality of the problems they (ought to) face rather than prematurely selling them ready-made 'reforms' as solutions for those problems. Whatever you do, concentrate your rhetoric of reform on a limited number of areas where you feel not just the need but also the sense of urgency for significant change are most palpable.

Prepare to be unloved

Reforms that have only winners all of the time are few and far between. If things were that beneficial, they would already have been adopted a long time ago. True reforms have redistributive effects. They shake up the status quo. They will therefore be opposed by those who benefit from that status quo, as well as by people who are fooled into thinking they benefit from it. You do not have to go as far as to fully embrace Machiavelli's assertion that it is better for a ruler to be feared than loved. But you still need to be prepared for pushback—anticipate it, wear it gracefully but resolutely, and most of all find ways to keep talking meaningfully to reform opponents.

Reform zeal without analysis is bound to end in tears

Never forget that the burden of proof is always on the reformer; you need to be able and willing to articulate the implicit theory of behavioural change that underpins your reform vision (and encourage it to be tested as much as possible before it is put into wholesale practice). If you do not have the killing arguments, do not expect to be able to persuade anyone. And if you do not have the power to persuade, do not expect to make reform happen by brutal imposition in any except the direst circumstances (for example, war and violent conflict, acute fiscal crisis, systemic breakdowns, popular revolts). Kevin Rudd learned this the hard way; he failed to persuade on climate change and he failed even to try to persuade on the resource super profits tax. Crucial to the power to persuade are impeccable analysis and compelling narratives. Let us look at each of them in turn.

Holistic analysis rather than expert monopolies

Too often reformers focus their mental energy on bolstering their preferred interventions in one particular area instead of methodically working through how they stem from and will impact upon the larger system in which they are embedded. This gets you nowhere.

Developing truly 'killing' reform arguments requires an investment in holistic analysis—in particular, in systems thinking. You need to know the system that you propose to reform inside and out—all of it, not just a particular part of it. Water reform cannot succeed without a systemic analysis of natural-resources management. Traffic congestion cannot be tackled without a systemic analysis of urbanisation. Hospital reform cannot succeed without a systemic analysis of public health.

And you should never forget that key knowledge of the intricacies of any system does not reside exclusively at the top or within government. The task of underpinning reforms cannot be left to government economists, lawyers and technical specialists just because the Public Service happens to be full of them. Your role is to make sure that the expertise of multiple professions, government insiders and outsiders, and strategic thinkers is brought to bear in a rigorous fashion.

Every reform needs a compelling narrative

Killing arguments require more than just sound analysis. They also require an investment in public communication: your language, your timing and your performances. A compelling narrative is essential in 'selling' the reform to the mainstream of uncommitted 'wait-and-see' public servants and stakeholders out there to have a guiding narrative to help them literally 'make sense' of what is going on. This is not about spin; it is about building a public case designed to make people face the need for major change.

Too often reformers get caught up in arcane policy detail and forget that the ultimate source of authority and momentum lies with the populace, not the community of technocratic sectoral insiders. In the absence of a compelling narrative, a reform effort misses the chance of making a significant discursive impact; it will not change the language in which we think and talk about ourselves and the challenges we face. That is a missed opportunity, as discursive interventions cost little yet can have great effects.

Most importantly, a coherent narrative delivered in a compelling fashion can give people reasons to *believe* in the process and the changes they are expected to make in their thinking, rules and practices. Bob Hawke and Paul Keating won most of their reform battles because, between them, they covered a wide spectrum of persuasive skills and target audiences, and experimented with a range of persuasive formats (including well-orchestrated stakeholder 'summits'). Rudd and Penny Wong failed to get traction on the carbon pollution reduction scheme (CPRS) not just because of the machinations within the Liberal Party but first and foremost because they could sing only one, fairly incomprehensible ('CPRS') reform tune, which a large part of the Australian public simply did not 'get'.

Leading from the front is not your only option

The Lange–Douglas reform episode in New Zealand is a classic example of a 'heroic' reform style (Goldfinch 2000). They went out there, argued the case, got the numbers, and took the plunge. Though appealing to romantic ideals of 'true leadership', this style works only when the number of decisional forums and the number of veto players in each of them are comparatively small. When that number is larger—as tends to be the case in the post-mixed-member proportional representation world of coalition bargaining in New Zealand politics, the COAG world of federal–state relations, and the hyper-complex world of global trade and climate governance—barging in through the front door just does not work. Patient coalition building does.

Though both Hawke and Keating entertained *über*-romantic visions of themselves as strong leaders, they were smart enough to realise that the kind of economic transformation of Australia they envisaged would not work without coopting organised labour and, to some extent, the big end of town into co-determining the pace and shape of the reform process. Backstage diplomacy is as vital—and often even more vital—in building support for reforms as front-stage dramaturgy. To use a military analogy: the wars to reduce smoking and make Victoria's roads the safest in the country described in this volume were not won by public-sector equivalents of the charismatic general of the Montgomery and Patton kind; they were won by persistent coalition building in the Eisenhower and Marshall mould.

Grand plans are not the only way to package reform

Grand ambitions do not necessarily require a 'crash, or crash through' approach to achieve all targets in one fell swoop. In fact, the big-bang approach can create such levels of uncertainty, fear and resistance that it can be its own undoing—as Gough Whitlam found out at fatal cost. Even Roger Douglas—hardly a patsy when it came to taking political risks in the service of reform—sometimes used salami tactics and patience to work through sticky points during lengthy deliberations. Grand designs are always high on lofty but abstract promises yet low on specifics and therefore prone to peter out in implementation. Those grand reforms that are more concrete—such as Jeff Kennett's privatisation agenda in Victoria in the early 1990s, or the Al Gore-led 'reinventing government' operations in the US federal bureaucracy under Bill Clinton—also invite big opposition. Kennett fought his way through, but more often than not, political sponsors are jittery when it comes to spending political capital on grand reforms that run into headwinds. They need it more badly on the big-ticket substantive policy struggles of the day. Or they simply lose interest when they realise that there are no votes in the reforms that are on the table.

When political backing is sporadic and inconsistent, a piecemeal, seemingly technical reform approach is not such a bad choice. It allows for proceeding much more unobtrusively and therefore less controversially. Charles Lindblom— cited by various of our experts in this volume—was fundamentally right that small, mutually reinforcing changes when maintained and accumulated over a period can get you a long way away from the status quo. His ploy—smuggling in successive incremental change—fits the reality of public policy making in democratic systems a lot better than the raw energy of Whitlamesque 'programs' and 'duumvirates', which inevitably entice reformers to try too much too soon.

Engage widely early on

Reformers always face the temptation to keep the circle of those in the know as small as possible. This temptation should be resisted. Do not succumb to the 'groupthink' that results from talking only to fellow reform proponents (or opponents, as the case might be). It sets you up for unpleasant surprises: badly vetted ideas, unexpected opposition, and implementation problems. Widening the circle and broadening the substance of the conversation are generally good ideas; in case of doubt, err on the side of inclusiveness. It is simply foolish not to bring to the design table the groups whose position and behaviour are to change as a result of the reform.

It is equally foolish not to benefit from the practical experience of those who will be implementing the reforms, both inside and outside the public service. You should, moreover, bring those actors to the table at a time and in a manner that they can still have a significant impact on the framing of key reform parameters. Expecting them to turn up to essentially swallow proposals precooked by a tightly held inner circle is naive and most likely counterproductive.

Yes, engaging widely even at the early stage of reform design will increase the transaction costs of the design process. Getting more and more diverse stakeholders to the table and nudging them towards agreement can be time consuming and energy sapping. These discussions are not love-ins. They can be tough and painful as well as creative and empowering. But more often than not the costs of collaborative design are a good price to pay for what you get: more robust proposals and the all-important buy-in from those whose collaboration is essential in making reforms work.

Create reform packages and bandwagons

It is astounding how often reformers forget some basic principles of negotiation and bargaining. One such principle is that of enlarging the pie. Research in this area finds time and again that people will fight to the hilt over individual issues but are more often than not able to reach agreements over creatively designed broader reform packages (bundling up a range of issues and areas) or bandwagons (where short-term costs for actors are offset by the certainty of longer-term gains on subsequent reform moves in the same area). This is especially so when they have been able to take part in the very scoping and framing of those packages and bandwagons.

Whatever you might think of the European Union's policies and pitfalls, it has been an astounding saga of cascading institutional reform against all odds. In just a few decades, its architects and entrepreneurs have been able to extend its depth (the degree of delegation of state sovereignty granted to EU-level institutions), scope (the range of policy areas covered) and membership. Creating bandwagons and packages to overcome impasse and circumvent veto power has been vital to this success every step of the way. They are the best possible ways of sharing the gains as well as splitting and trading the pains of reform.

Rules for making reforms stick

A minimum winning coalition is not good enough

Few if any contemporary democracies are constitutionally wired in the way New Zealand was during its last great reform period of 1984–90. The name of most public-policy games is dispersed power, not executive dominance. Reformers who think they can simply impose big changes once they are adopted in cabinets or legislatures will find themselves forced into humiliating backdowns and u-turns. Reformers who rely on the smallest of possible coalitions and ignore the other 49 per cent set themselves up for relentless rearguard battles during implementation and quite likely for outright policy reversals once they lose the power to impose.

The long-term viability of reforms is greatly enhanced when the coalition that is carrying it is 'oversized'. If this can be achieved only at the price of some of the ideological purity of the original reform philosophy then so be it. You will need the broad support base to withstand the forces of reaction that will seek to undermine the reform process. You will need to embed the reform momentum as widely as possible within the government bureaucracy—pivotally including the central agencies—so as to make its memory, diligence and paradoxically its inertia work for rather than against the integrity and continuity of already enacted reforms.

Just because they are big achievements does not mean reforms succeed

Therefore, winning the battle to get them designed and adopted is a necessary but not a sufficient step to make reforms work and to make them last. Reforms are wars not battles. When you do not attend to their implementation and long-term maintenance, do not expect them to deliver the goods. When their implementation is ill designed and under managed, their negative unintended consequences end up dwarfing those that were aimed and planned for. Well-intended reforms can easily end up looking like 'fatal remedies' (Gillon 2000; Sieber 1981). Reform opponents seize their chance to fight back, sabotage and twist the process of putting intentions into action.

It is hard to find reforms that are reversed as soon as the political tide has turned, and there are plenty of reforms that suffer from what Patashnik in his book labels 'death by a thousand cuts': while nominally still in force, their force and integrity are undermined by lobbying from special interests, resulting in watered-down implementation or legislative emasculation. What goes for public policy in general applies even more so for high-stakes reforms; as a proponent, you cannot rest on your laurels once the bill has become the law. You have to be in it for the long haul. You need to be as equally attentive, inventive and tenacious in the implementation and consolidation phases as you are in the design and adoption processes.

Incorporate mechanisms that make reforms self-sustaining

It is important to think about why citizens and stakeholders change their behaviour as a result of the implementation of a reform. You need to understand that basic carrots and sticks buy only opportunistic compliance that is costly to keep bankrolling and policing. Sometimes there is no other way—for example, in industrial relations and health and safety, where employers will always be tempted to engage in races to the bottom given the relentless pressures on them to raise productivity (by reducing costs).

Yet the most robust reforms are truly transformative. They change people's norms and values. Once new standards of appropriateness have been internalised and disseminated widely, compliance costs tumble, and so does the risk of reform erosion or reversal. Child labour is now considered to be simply unacceptable in countries such as New Zealand and Australia. Smoking is now firmly socially stigmatised (though pivotally not made illegal). Drink-driving is getting there, though there is a way to go.

These ideational changes have not happened by accident. As Patashnik's study as well as some of the case studies in this book show, they are the product of clever reform designs that have managed to create behavioural incentives that get into people's heads and hearts. If you are serious about protecting the long-term integrity of reforms, this is the way to go. It is about cleverly combining the logic of economics (as Keating learned long ago from his political mentor Jack Lang: bet on self-interest because at least it is always trying) with the logic of behavioural research in psychology, sociology and communication studies (teaching us to bet on the subconscious and social drivers of human perception, identity, judgment and preference formation). Thaler and Sunstein's rightly best-selling book *Nudge* (2008) is a good place to start if you are serious about this ambition. Sunstein was subsequently appointed Barack Obama's regulation tsar, so do not think it is just two eggheads talking.

Afterword

This 'memo' has summed up what I think our current knowledge about reforms allows us to convey to reformers and stakeholders in reform processes. It is up to them to explore how they can make some or ideally all of these lessons work for them. This will no doubt include exploring the potential tensions between these various imperatives. After all, the craft of reformist leadership is an art, not a science. The rules of experience provided above do not make a cookbook, nor could such a book ever be written. In most instances, there are multiple potentially passable paths to reform. There will always remain a need for situation-specific judgments and intuitions about the what, when and how of going down one or the other road—and when to reassess that choice.

To inform those judgments as well as possible, however, it is important that institutions such as ANZSOG keep documenting the experiences and views of those who have already travelled the road of reform, and that public-policy academics in Australia and New Zealand step up their efforts to conduct the methodical, comparative and longitudinal research into reform dynamics that is essential to putting these practitioner tales into a broader perspective. To begin with, ANZSOG should make it part of its mission to hold a major 'learning from experience and research' conference on public-sector reform every five years to create a platform where both types of insights can be aired, compared and bundled up.

References

Gillon, S. M. 2000, *'That's Not What We Meant To Do': Reform and its unintended consequences in twentieth century America*, W. & W. Norton, New York.

Goldfinch, S. 2000, *Remaking New Zealand and Australian Economic Policy: Ideas, institutions and policy communities*, Victoria University Press, Wellington.

Patashnik, E. 2008, *Reforms at Risk*, Princeton University Press, Princeton, NJ.

Sieber, S. D. 1981, *Fatal Remedies: The ironies of social intervention*, Plenum Press, New York.

Thaler, R. and Sunstein, C. 2008, *Nudge: Improving decisions about health, wealth, and happiness*, Yale University Press, New Haven, Conn.

Weber, M. 1978, *Economy and Society: An outline of interpretive sociology*, University of California Press, Berkeley.

www.ingramcontent.com/pod-product-compliance
Lightning Source LLC
Chambersburg PA
CBHW040838300326
R18048200001B/R180482PG41927CBX00010B/1